The Criminal Trial in Law and Discourse

Also by Tyrone Kirchengast

THE VICTIM IN CRIMINAL LAW AND JUSTICE

The Criminal Trial in Law and Discourse

Tyrone Kirchengast
University of New South Wales, Australia

© Tyrone Kirchengast 2010

All rights reserved. No reproduction, copy or transmission of this publication may be made without written permission.

No portion of this publication may be reproduced, copied or transmitted save with written permission or in accordance with the provisions of the Copyright, Designs and Patents Act 1988, or under the terms of any licence permitting limited copying issued by the Copyright Licensing Agency, Saffron House, 6–10 Kirby Street, London EC1N 8TS.

Any person who does any unauthorized act in relation to this publication may be liable to criminal prosecution and civil claims for damages.

The author has asserted his right to be identified as the author of this work in accordance with the Copyright, Designs and Patents Act 1988.

First published 2010 by
PALGRAVE MACMILLAN

Palgrave Macmillan in the UK is an imprint of Macmillan Publishers Limited, registered in England, company number 785998, of Houndmills, Basingstoke, Hampshire RG21 6XS.

Palgrave Macmillan in the US is a division of St Martin's Press LLC, 175 Fifth Avenue, New York, NY 10010.

Palgrave Macmillan is the global academic imprint of the above companies and has companies and representatives throughout the world.

Palgrave® and Macmillan® are registered trademarks in the United States, the United Kingdom, Europe and other countries

ISBN 978-0-230-57785-5 hardback

This book is printed on paper suitable for recycling and made from fully managed and sustained forest sources. Logging, pulping and manufacturing processes are expected to conform to the environmental regulations of the country of origin.

A catalogue record for this book is available from the British Library.

Library of Congress Cataloging-in-Publication Data
  Kirchengast, Tyrone, 1978–
    The criminal trial in law and discourse / Tyrone Kirchengast.
    p. cm.
  Includes bibliographical references.
  ISBN 978-0-230-57785-5
    1. Criminal procedure–Social aspects. 2. Trials–Social aspects.
  I. Title.
  K5404.K57 2010
  345'.07–dc22   2010023829

10 9 8 7 6 5 4 3 2 1
19 18 17 16 15 14 13 12 11 10

Printed and bound in Great Britain by
CPI Antony Rowe, Chippenham and Eastbourne

Contents

Preface		viii
List of Abbreviations		x
Chapter 1	**Criminal Trials, Foucault, Discourse**	**1**
	The trial as contested territory	7
	A note on method: 'Effective history', discourse and legal hermeneutics	14
	Is the criminal trial in crisis?	17
	The adversarial criminal trial as rhetoric	19
	Local and magistrates' courts	20
	Courts of therapeutic justice	22
	The trial as hermeneutic: Terrorism, the victim and human rights	24
	Terrorism, national security and domestic order	25
	Victim rights and human rights	31
	The adversarial criminal trial in transition	32
	Examining the trial in history and discourse	34
Chapter 2	**A Genealogy of the Trial in Criminal Law**	**39**
	The criminal trial as an institution of social power	40
	The trial in customary law	42
	The trial of animals	48
	Ecclesiastical trials	48
	Secular trials	49
	The criminal trial as local governance	51
	Communal rule: Hundred court and the rise of presentment	51
	The general eyre	57
	Commission of oyer and terminer	59
	Commission of gaol delivery	59
	From inquisitorial to adversarial justice	60
Chapter 3	**Shifting Boundaries: Recent Changes to Criminal Justice Policy**	**65**
	Expedient justice	66
	Committal proceedings	67
	The rise of summary disposal	70
	Infringement and penalty notices	71

	Dispensing with the jury	72
	Charge bargaining	78
	The law and order debate	81
	Extending policing power	82
	Bail	85
	Control orders, ASBOs and domestic order	87
	Modifying the criminal trial	92
	Defences: Provocation	93
	Double jeopardy	95
	Victims' lawyers	97
	England and Wales	98
	United States	100
	Australia	108
	The International Criminal Court	109
	The rise of terrorism	110
	Control orders – A criminal charge?	110
	Non-derogating control orders and the ECHR	113
Chapter 4	**The Transformative Criminal Trial Emerges**	**119**
	Rethinking the public/private dichotomy	121
	Emerging human rights discourse: Victims' rights, human rights and due process	125
	Human rights under the ECHR	126
	Human rights and statutory reform	133
	Criminal procedure in European civil law	137
	The International Criminal Court	138
	Auxiliary prosecution in adversarial criminal trials	139
	Adhesion proceedings	142
	Therapeutic jurisprudence and problem-solving courts	143
	Origins of problem-solving courts	144
	The principles of problem-solving courts	145
	Case study: The community court	147
	Sentencing and punishment	151
	Intervention programs, forum and circle sentencing	153
	Victim impact statements	156
	Victim's compensation, proportionality and the sentencing process	160

Chapter 5	**The Criminal Trial as Social Discourse**	**165**
	Discourse defined	167
	Power, knowledge and the adversarial criminal trial	171
	R v Camberwell Green Youth Court [2005] 1 All ER 999	174
	Gately v The Queen (2007) 232 CLR 208	175
	Crawford v Washington (2004) 541 US 36	179
	The criminal trial, disciplinary power and the periphery of justice	183
	Decentralised justice	186
Chapter 6	**The Trial as Hermeneutic: A Critical Review**	**189**
	Adversarial, inquisitorial and integrative approaches	192
	Discursive tensions: Re-asserting the adversarial model	194
	History, discourse and genealogy: Displacing truth claims	200
	A note on normative thinking	205
	Law and social systems	207
Chapter 7	**Implications for Criminal Justice Policy**	**211**
	Substantive and procedural justice	212
	On discourse and power	217
	Revolutionising criminal law and justice	220
Notes		226
References		232
Index		240

Preface

The Criminal Trial in Law and Discourse brings together various materials from law, history and policy to demonstrate how the modern criminal trial is a transformative institution of justice. The modern criminal trial is thus more than the popularly conceived notion of the adversarial trial before judge and jury. This does not simply mean that the trial is increasingly circumvented for alternative pathways to justice, such as summary justice. Rather, the criminal trial is transformative because it functions as a decentralised site of sociological engagement. This book explores the notion that the criminal trial is a discursive institution of social power that, consistent with its genealogy and history, transforms to meet new social needs. This book follows the argument that the criminal trial is now open to discourses that, before the advent of victim rights, human rights and the critique of state power, were more narrowly conceived around the locus of the criminal.

The modern criminal trial has responded to the rise of an international human rights movement, a law and order politics, terrorism, the rise of victims' rights, and a movement toward therapeutic and problem-solving justice. As such, the debate has shifted toward the extent to which the criminal trial is transgressive, as evidenced through the debate on the classification of control orders and other forms of preventative law as an exercise of criminal or civil law. A large number of cases canvassed herein suggest that the scope of the criminal trial is negotiated with regard to competing discourses of justice, each of which present ideas as to the form and scope the trial ought to take. As these discourses are competing, there is no generally agreed model as to the criminal trial, and this is being increasingly realised through the jurisprudence of various common law jurisdictions. Arguably, this realisation has spawned a counter movement for the concerted re-assertion of the bounds of adversarial justice, mainly through the rejection of principles of inquisitorial justice. Such a counter argument remains problematic, given that the adversarial trial never took a specific form, and that comparative law tells of the significant overlap between adversarial and inquisitorial models. The point remains, however, that the criminal trial is neither normative nor prescriptive but discursive and decentralised, and its genealogy suggests that this has always been the case.

In part, this book adopts a text and commentaries approach to the organisation of a diverse set of materials relevant to the parameters of the criminal trial. Case law and policy documents are thus extracted to illustrate the formation of discourses, a method significant to Foucault's approach, to demonstrate the use of statements and the archive from which they draw their reference and power. This book draws upon substantially unpublished materials but does include short extracts previously published across two articles: Kirchengast, T. (2009) 'Criminal Injuries Compensation, Victim Assistance and Restoration in Australian Sentencing Law', *International Journal of Punishment and Sentencing*, 5, 3, 96–119; and Kirchengast, T. (2010) 'Recent Reforms to Victim Rights and the Emerging "Normative Theory of the Criminal Trial"', *Criminal Law Quarterly*, 56, 1 & 2, 82–115.

Tyrone Kirchengast
Sydney

List of Abbreviations

AC	Appeals Cases
A Crim R	Australian Criminal Reports
All ER	All England Law Reports
ALJR	Australian Law Journal Reports
B & Ald	Barnewall and Alderson's English King's Bench Reports
ASBO	Anti-Social Behaviour Order
BHRC	Butterworth's Human Rights Cases
BOCSAR	Bureau of Crime Statistics and Research
CCP	Code for Crown Prosecutors
CDA	Crime and Disorder Act
CJ at CL	Chief Judge at Common Law
CLR	Commonwealth Law Reports
CPS	Crown Prosecution Service
Cth	Commonwealth
Cr App R	Criminal Appeal Reports
CVRA	Crime Victims' Rights Act
ECHR	European Convention on Human Rights
ECJ	European Court of Justice
ECtHR	European Court of Human Rights
EU	European Union
EHRR	European Human Rights Reports
EWCA	Court of Appeal of England and Wales
EWHC	High Court of England and Wales
F 2d	Federal Reporter (United States Court of Appeals)
F 3d	Federal Reporter (United States Court of Appeals)
FLR	Federal Law Reports
F Supp	Federal Supplement
F Supp 2d	Federal Supplement
ICC	International Criminal Court
ICJ	International Court of Justice
ICTR	International Criminal Tribunal for Rwanda
ICTY	International Criminal Tribunal for the former Yugoslavia
LCEW	Law Commission of England and Wales
LEPRA	Law Enforcement Powers and Responsibilities Responsibilities Act

LEXIS	LexisNexis
NSW	New South Wales
NSWCCA	New South Wales Court of Criminal Appeal
NSWLR	New South Wales Law Reports
NSWLRC	New South Wales Law Reform Commission
NSWSC	New South Wales Supreme Court
NZ	New Zealand
NZLC	New Zealand Law Commission
NZLR	New Zealand Law Reports
ODPP	Office of the Director of Public Prosecutions
PACE	Police and Criminal Evidence Act
Qld	Queensland
QB	Queen's Bench
QWN	Queensland Weekly Notes
RPE	Rules of Procedure and Evidence (ICC)
SA	South Australia
SASC	South Australian Supreme Court
SSCA	Secretary of State for Constitutional Affairs
SCR	Supreme Court Reports (Canada)
Tas	Tasmania
TEU	Treaty on European Union
US	United States Reports
USC	United States Code
Vic	Victoria
VIS	Victim Impact Statement
VLRC	Victorian Law Reform Commission
VPS	Victim Personal Statement
VR	Victorian Reports
WA	Western Australia
WL	Westlaw
WLR	Weekly Law Reports

1
Criminal Trials, Foucault, Discourse

> We must question those ready-made syntheses, those groupings that we normally accept before any examination, those links whose validity is recognized from the outset; we must oust those forms and obscure forces by which we usually link the discourse of one man with that of another; they must be driven out from the darkness in which they reign. And instead of according them unqualified, spontaneous value, we must accept, in the name of methodological rigour, that, in the first instance, they concern only a population of dispersed events.
> Michel Foucault (1969) *The Archaeology of Knowledge and the Discourse on Language*, p. 22

> Archaeology still isolates and indicates the arbitrariness of the hermeneutic horizon of meaning. It shows that what seems like the continuous development of a meaning is crossed with discontinuous discursive formations. The continuities, he reminds us, reveal no finalities, no underlying significations, no metaphysical certainties.
> Hubert L. Dreyfus and Paul Rabinow (1982) *Michel Foucault: Beyond Structuralism and Hermeneutics*, p. 106

The adversarial criminal trial is held out as the model by which accusations of wrongdoing are heard and determined in common law jurisdictions. Debate abounds, however, as to the form that the modern criminal trial ought to take. This debate is characterised by diverse opinions which range from the safeguarding of the adversarial trial as the only means by which defendant rights will be successfully protected against abuses of state power, such as charges brought on the weakest of evidence, police misconduct, false accusations or political imperative. Others suggest that the scope of the adversarial trial, as an exclusive contest between police, prosecution and defendant, and as presided over by an independent magistrate or judge, represents a model of justice that is in decline, or at least requires rethinking (see Schwikkard, 2008; Summers, 2007; Nonet and Selznick, 1978; Simon, 1978). Such perspectives suggest that the trial and adversarial model more generally ought to be construed in terms of those procedures significant to the functions of justice – the requirement of a 'fair trial' that seeks to balance the competing needs of witnesses, victims, defendants, the community, and state. Various common law jurisdictions have now moved away from the strict requirements of the adversarial trial to other innovative or nuanced modes of determining liability for wrongdoing, or in meting out punishment following conviction.

A movement toward therapeutic courts such as community courts, or modes of sentencing that include the victim and community, such as circle or forum sentencing, provide new ways of doing justice that significantly modify traditional adversarial processes. The broader inclusion of victims in trials, by way of human rights decisions that protect the rights of vulnerable rape or child victims, or in sentencing, by way of victim impact or personal statements, has attracted criticism from those advocating an orthodox approach to the way criminal liability and appropriate punishments ought to be determined (see Sebba, 2009: 65). Those advocating such approaches suggest that the traditional scope of the adversarial trial is under attack from a punitive law and order ideology, such that the key functions of the trial ought to be reaffirmed to countenance the new or innovative developments of law and justice that are manifestly identified as detracting from the rights of the accused (see Wolhunter, Olley and Denham, 2009: 173; Duff, Farmer, Marshall and Tadros, 2007). Alternatively, such perspectives also realise the potential for change, principally within the confines of the adversarial tradition, which may be extended to include inquisitorial or other approaches without unacceptably detracting from the core functions of adversarialism. The rise of victim lawyers as an adjunct to the rights of victims in the criminal justice system may be one such inclusion.

This book moves away from the examination of the criminal trial as an institution constituted by the rules of adversarial justice, for an examination of the transformation of the criminal trial as an institution of social justice and discourse. By examining the history of the trial as a means to justice that sought to include, rather than exclude, the key stakeholders of justice, this book asserts that victims, defendants, police and communities each have a vested and valid interest in justice, characterising the current transformations of law and justice seen across the common law world. Through the consideration of the genealogy of the dominant mode of trial that emerged in the eighteenth century, the adversarial criminal trial, this book suggests the decline in the hegemony of adversarialism is consistent with the history and genealogy of the trial from antiquity. Rather than be seen as an attack on law and justice, changes to the criminal trial in the modern era are consistent with the history and development of the trial as a transgressive institution of social power.[1]

Langbein (2003: 253) notes the emergence of adversarialism with the rise of a professional class of lawyers representing Crown interests, and perhaps most importantly, the interests of the accused:

> Across the half century or so from the 1730s into the last quarter of eighteenth century, the altercation trial gave way to a radically different style of proceeding, the adversarial criminal trial. Lawyers for the prosecution and especially the defence assumed commanding roles at trial. In this prototype of the fully lawyerized trial, solicitors gathered and prepared evidence in advance of trial; counsel then conducted the fact-adducing work at trial, examining and cross-examining witnesses and raising matters of law... In place of the 'accused speaks' trial there had developed a new mode of trial, adversary trial, which largely silenced the accused. With it came a new theory and purpose of the trial, which endures into our day, that trial is primarily an opportunity for defence counsel to probe the prosecution case.

This being so, changes to the dominant mode of eighteenth century adversarialism that include persons relevant to justice are only possible because the trial, as an institution of social justice, is flexible enough to adapt to new and innovative social conditions. The trial, in this way, is a sociological institution of power. This view of the transformation of the trial is consistent with important new movements toward the recognition of rights in the context of fundamental human rights; to the inclusion and protection of victims; to the emergence of expedient means to justice in the form of infringements and summary disposal; to the emergence of new forms of trial that seek to protect the community from serious, recidivist offenders; to changes to the law of evidence that allow vulnerable witnesses including children to be protected from potentially harsh trial processes; and to the modification of rights long taken to be constitutive of the 'fair trial', including the modification of the rule against double jeopardy and the right of self-representation. No doubt many of the changes that comprise this non-exhaustive list are controversial in the way they negotiate the extent to which certain defendants may be afforded protection under the law. Alternatively, arguments have emerged for the need to consider other perspectives alongside those of the defendant. What is clear is that this list brings together competing voices and perspectives that comprise the polemic of the modern criminal trial, and a strict adherence to the tenets of adversarial justice may only seeks to complicate, rather than resolve the tensions. What is needed is a different perspective than that offered amongst normative theorists. Rather, the trial needs to be conceived as an institution of power contested between relevant agents or stakeholders of justice.

Drawing from Foucault's (1969, 1982, 1984, 1994; also see Dean, 1994: 15–16) use of hermeneutics as challenging the certainty of truth of language and doctrine, the history of the adversarial trial is displaced for an institution understood as multidimensional, as an institution founded on people, conflict, change and social inclusion. Thus, the history of the trial is not interpreted narrowly in terms of the requirements of adversarial justice that focus on the needs of defendants as against the state. As Goodrich (1992: 44–45) articulates, through the realisation of the power of discourse, the historical function of law as self-referential and exclusive of the interests of society may be displaced:

> In genealogical terms the above historical fiction combines two questions of extreme interest to the inhabitants of an era and discourse that has challenged the veridical language, the truths, and the certainties of doctrinal transmission.... The genealogical reconstruction of doctrine, however, interestingly implicates legal doctrine in a series of other discourses. It will be argued in historical detail that far from being a technical and internal development the new jurisprudence responded to and was molded by a series of discourses external to law. Jurisprudence was marked by external discourses and desires, and its subsequent reformulations still carry those marks even though the historians of law prefer to recycle the juridical fiction of a true discourse and its authoritative judgments.

In this genealogical perspective, the trial is more than the repository of legal power that holds wrongdoers to account for their conduct in particular ways. Trials provide for a sociological process that influences the development of the criminal law by affirming principles of liability, rules of evidence and standards of proof that, in the modern adversarial context, indicate who is 'heard' and who is 'silenced'. This is particularly so in the adversarial tradition, which is said to currently characterise the whole of the criminal law in common law jurisdictions, including both pre and post trial phases of inquiry (see Summers, 2007: 3–20). This being said, the criminal trial is not without some structural specificity. Foucault (1969) could not be said to be a pure hermeneuticist in that he is not seeking to engage in what Dean (1994: 16) describes as 'inexhaustible decipherment' of things past and present. Rather, Dean (1994: 16) suggests:

> [i]t is no longer the task of history to memorise monuments of the past and thus to transform them into 'documents' of a reality and a consciousness of which they are but traces. Rather, history has become, he suggests, that which transforms documents into monuments, into a mass of elements to be described and organised.

The history of the criminal trial is fundamental to any interpretation of the modern criminal trial as an inclusive and flexible institution of justice. It is not that the trial comes to be whatever we hold it out to be. Rather, the modern criminal trial is characterised as an institution of adversarial justice only because the characteristics of adversarialism developed out of conditions that were palpably unfair to key stakeholders of justice, namely defendants and those accused of crime. Langbein's (2003) account of the rise of the adversarial criminal trial attests to conditions in which the accused was denied rights we now see as wholly constitutive of the trial process: access to counsel; the right to remain silent; to proceed before an independent magistrate or judge; to discover the accusation and evidence against the accused; and, where available, to confront the accuser in court. Foucault's (1969) method, therefore, is not to completely revise the past only to produce an interpretation of events entirely disconnected from anything previously imagined. Rather, hermeneutics assists us in our awareness that history makes the adversarial trial what it is today. The lack of defendant rights and an overly powerful state render the modern lawyer with a certain appreciation for the rights which defendants enjoy today. Most lawyers spend their entire careers defending access to those rights as a result. The point is that this mode of operation is a product of the history of the trial. However, other aspects overshadowed or silenced by our need to protect the vulnerable accused from abuses of power and process are also present. Foucault's (1969, 1984) method thus brings to the fore those discourses that may not present in a contemporary retelling of the rise of adversarial justice. The dynamic perspective of the criminal trial adopted here thus recognises, rather than challenges, the hallmarks of adversarialism. What is challenged is the notion that this is the only 'correct' or 'true' form that the criminal trial may take.[2]

Gaudron J in *Dietrich v The Queen* (1992) 177 CLR 292, a case concerning the accused's right to counsel for serious offences, indicates how the principles that constitute the modern adversarial trial are inextricably linked to the notion of what may be fair in an individual case (at 364):

> The notion of a fair trial and the inherent powers which exist to serve that end do not permit of 'idiosyncratic notions of what is fair and just' any more than do other general concepts which carry broad powers or remedies in their train. But what is fair very often depends on the circumstances of the particular case. Moreover, notions of fairness are inevitably bound up with prevailing social values. It is because of these matters that the inherent powers of a court to prevent injustice are not confined within closed categories. And it is because of those same matters that, save where clear categories have emerged, the enquiry as to what is fair must be particular and individual. And, just as what might be fair in one case might be unfair in another, so too what is considered fair at one time may, quite properly, be adjudged unfair at another.

This view of the criminal trial, informed by Foucault's (1969, 1982, 1984) effective history and hermeneutics of the subject, is one that is, arguably, consistent with the trial as an artefact of history and society. Furthermore, this perspective explains why the trial continues to change its form and function, as an institution of significant governmental power, to meet new social needs and conditions over time. On this view, the modern criminal trial ought to be conceptualised as an institution of social justice that is open to, and influenced by, varying and competing discourses. The modern criminal trial thus emerges as a transformative criminal trial by virtue of the fact that it forged of competing discourses of justice that do not adhere to any particular model of justice. By focussing on emergent issues in legal discourse identified through an international literature, this book will demonstrate how the modern criminal trial ought to be conceptualised as a significant institution of social justice that is open to, and influenced by, a range of discourses.

The trial as contested territory

Historically, the trial, as the means by which accusations of wrongdoing are tested against an accused, have taken on many and varied forms. Even in the English tradition, the criminal trial has been subject to influence and change over the numerous centuries since conquest. If one delves deeper into the antiquity of the trial, the process that stands as the 'centrepiece' of criminal law is shown to have intermingled roots. Much of what we identify as the hallmarks of the modern criminal trial at common law – presentment of an accusation, an impartial adjudicator or judge, a test of proof involving ordeal or jury – derive from customary practices for the resolution of disputes and conflicts within a village or group. Historically at least, the criminal trial cannot be reduced to an isolated process disconnected from the content of the criminal law, its institutions and custom. The trial was the criminal law, at least in terms of a customary bringing together of individuals for the hearing of accusations of wrongdoing, to which particular punishments were applied.

Deane J in *Dietrich v The Queen* (1992) 177 CLR 292, identifies the modern criminal trial as one that is characterised as an adversarial, accusatorial tribunal, before an independent magistrate or judge (at 334–335):

> A criminal trial in this country is essentially an adversarial process. Where the charge is of a serious crime, the prosecution will ordinarily be in the hands of counsel with knowledge and experience of the criminal law and its administration. The substantive criminal law and the rules of procedure and evidence governing the conduct of a criminal trial are, from the viewpoint of an ordinary accused, complicated and obscure. While the prosecution has a duty to act fairly and part of the function of a presiding judge is to seek to ensure that a criminal trial is fair, neither prosecutor nor judge can or should provide the advice, guidance and representation which an accused must ordinarily have if his case is to be properly presented. Thus, it is no part of the function of a prosecutor or trial judge to advise an accused before the commencement of a trial about the legal issues which might arise on the trial, about what evidence will or will not be admissible in relation to them, about what inquiries

should be made to ascertain what evidence is available, about what available evidence should be called, about possible defences, about the possible consequences of cross-examination, about the desirability or otherwise of giving sworn evidence or about any of a multitude of other questions which counsel appearing for an accused must consider and in respect of which such counsel must advise in the course of the preparation of a criminal trial. Nor is it consistent with the function of prosecutor or trial judge to conduct, or advise on the conduct of, the case for the defence at the trial. Nor, in the ordinary case, is an accused capable of presenting his own case to the jury as effectively as can a trained lawyer.

As Deane J indicates in *Dietrich*, the criminal trial is held as a separate part of the criminal process through which accusation is made, counsel appointed, and guilt determined, usually by jury, as instructed by independent magistrate, or judge sitting alone. The trial is therefore seen to be separate from the various other pre and post trial processes that constitute the means by which defendants are held to account for their wrongdoing. While the policing of the initial incident, arrest, charge, committal, arraignment, and then sentencing and punishment of the prisoner are indeed separate from the trial in a procedural sense, they are closely connected to the trial in a discursive sense. While the separation of the trial is supported by doctrinal approaches that constitute the trial as a discrete mode of inquiry concerned with establishing guilt beyond reasonable doubt, the discourses that comes to bear on the trial, both its substantive character and the form it takes, are very much common to the broader content of the criminal law, and society more generally. It is thus not possible, in a discursive sense, to isolate the trial from the issues that constitute it.

Trials are arguably constituted as social processes that connect people and institutions in specific ways. This approach challenges the assumption that trials are nothing more than a discrete, forensic process, solely concerned with establishing the truth of a criminal accusation. For instance, the focus on the trial as a 'truth finding' institution has long been criticised given the way evidence is adduced strategically to accord with a particular version of events, and distorted in terms of the case counsel make for their client. This is what Langbein (2003: 103–105) terms the 'combat effect' of the adversarial criminal trial. This criticism notwithstanding, the trial remains an important means by which we determine criminal liability for acts of wrongdoing. What is less clear is whether the trial can be identified as an institution set in form, as manifestly concerned with a function and purpose limited to certain agents of justice over others.

It is arguable that trials, as a means by which defendants are held to account for their conduct, are a result of a complex array of discourses that seek to satisfy various social and political ends. These discourses identify those individuals relevant to justice, which also suggests the extent to which each individual may contribute to, or benefit from, the justice system. Certain discourses speak to the status of the defendant. Others suggest that victims and witnesses, those deemed peripheral to or outside the relevant boundary of the trial, require further integration. In this discursive sense of the criminal trial, the issue is whether we adopt an interpretation of the trial that acknowledges its genealogy as a dynamic institution of sociological power, an institution not rigidly bound by doctrine but as hermeneutic, which, in a Foucauldian (1969, 1982, 1984) sense, is one that is capable of change over time. The form trials take thus facilitates debate as to the means by which we, as a society, hold people to account for their conduct. As an institution significant to the social fabric of society, the trial should not be confined to a narrow interpretation or purpose, but be identified as an institution of criminal law and justice that is inclusive, discursive and communicative. The trial, in this way, becomes a reflection of the content of the criminal law and society more generally. It is not possible to argue that the trial ought to take a prescribed form, or function according to a particular narrative, as it is a product of the intersection of varying needs, debates, issues and conflicts, over time. The trial is not normative; it is discursive.

Such perspectives are increasingly realised by parliaments and courts across various common law jurisdictions. Over the last decade or so we have seen the proliferation of new and innovative courts and tribunals and suggestions for further reform, each of which significantly depart from the adversarial model. The rise of problem-solving courts, such as the sex offence or domestic violence courts of the State of New York (see Berman and Feinblatt, 2005), or drug courts as found within various jurisdictions including those across the United States and Australia, ably demonstrate departures from the traditional adversarial paradigm by realising the importance of meeting the needs of various agents of justice, including those the defendant, victim and community.[3] Alternative processes have also been established to hold wrongdoers to account in new, at times contentious ways. The rise of special powers for the further detention of serious sex offenders, or even members of organised motorcycle clubs or 'bikies', on the basis of consorting or suspected violent behaviour, demonstrates a significant departure from the adversarial model.[4] The attempt to depart from conventional adversarial models for statutory schemes which give courts the power to continue the detention of a prisoner despite them having reached their head sentence, or issue control orders against suspected individuals to limit their freedom of movement or association, characterises the latest attempts to depart from the nominal adversarial trial process. Such departures are indeed highly controversial.

The High Court of Australia, however, determined in *Fardon v Attorney-General (Qld)* (2004) 223 CLR 575 that such departures are indeed possible. This case questioned the constitutionality of the *Dangerous Prisoners (Sexual Offenders) Act 2003* (Qld) to order the supervised release or further and potential indefinite detention of a sex offender deemed a high risk of recidivist behaviour. Gleeson CJ held, dismissing the appeal and affirming the validity of the legislation (at 592):

> The Act is a general law authorising the preventive detention of a prisoner in the interests of community protection. It authorises and empowers the Supreme Court to act in a manner which is consistent with its judicial character. It does not confer functions which are incompatible with the proper discharge of judicial responsibilities or with the exercise of judicial power. It confers a substantial discretion as to whether an order should be made, and if so, the type of order. If an order is made, it might involve either detention or release under supervision. The onus of proof is on the Attorney-General. The rules of evidence apply. The discretion is to be exercised by reference to the criterion of serious danger to the community. The Court is obliged, by s13(4) of the Act, to have regard to a list of matters that are all relevant to that criterion. There is a right of appeal. Hearings are conducted in public, and in accordance with the ordinary judicial process. There is nothing to suggest that the Supreme Court is to act as a mere instrument of government policy. The outcome of each case is to be determined on its merits.

McHugh J also dismissed the appeal albeit in the context of a lack of an Australian Bill of Rights providing for particular rights to justice and a guaranteed trial experience (at 600–601):

> The bare fact that particular State legislation invests a State court with powers that are or jurisdiction that is repugnant to the tradi-

tional judicial process will seldom, if ever, compromise the institutional integrity of that court to the extent that it affects that court's capacity to exercise federal jurisdiction impartially and according to federal law. State legislation may alter the burden of proof and the rules of evidence and procedure in civil and criminal courts in ways that are repugnant to the traditional judicial process without compromising the institutional integrity of the courts that must administer that legislation. State legislation may require State courts to exercise powers and take away substantive rights on grounds that judges think are foolish, unwise or even patently unjust. Nevertheless, it does not follow that, because State legislation requires State courts to make orders that could not be countenanced in a society with a Bill of Rights, the institutional integrity of those courts is compromised.

Clearly McHugh J is signalling some disapproval with the proposed legislative framework but also signals that such departures may be valid to the extent that they do not pre-empt a court's decision to order the continued detention of a prisoner. Discretion is retained.

Other notable examples of the departure from the adversarial model arise under the Framework Decision on the Standing of Victims in Criminal Proceedings (2001/220/JHA) of the Council of Europe, binding on member states. Certain sates, including Italy, adopt adversarial principles within their inquisitorial approach (Lorenzmeier, 2006: 583). Such Framework Decisions, then, have the capacity to challenge such adversarial approaches where no formal role is actually provided for the victim. Framework Decisions do not have a direct effect on the domestic laws of member state, however, but form part of community law which, under the principle of harmonious interpretation, obliges national courts to interpret domestic law in conformity with community law. Such decisions do not have a direct effect but may give direction to the overall result to be achieved, rather than the processes for achieving such results. The interpretation of such laws, moreover, must be consistent with the defendant's right to a fair trial. The Framework Decision of 2001 provides victims with several important rights. These include the right *inter alia* to: respect and recognition in each of the member states' legal system (art. 1); the right to be heard and to supply evidence (art. 3); receive information relevant to their protection (art. 4); protection, safety and privacy including the right to be shielded from the negative effects of giving evidence in court (art. 8); and the right to compensation (art. 9).

These rights are enforceable within member states, however, to the extent recognised by the European Court of Justice (ECJ)[5] in *Criminal Proceedings Against Pupino* [2005] 3 WLR 1102. *Pupino* concerns a series of charges brought against a nursery school teacher in Italy for allegedly committing several offences involving the misuse of discipline against students aged less than five years of age. The offences were punishable under the Italian Code of Criminal Procedure, which under art. 392 also provided measures for the use of evidence gathered at the preliminary enquiry for use at trial, in order to protect vulnerable victims aged less than 16 years. Article 392, however, was limited to strictly enumerated sexual offences. Article 398 additionally allowed for the taking of evidence by special arrangement so as to protect the dignity and character of vulnerable witnesses. Pupino opposed the application, arguing that such provisions were not contained in art. 392. In *Pupino*, the ECJ ruled that art. 35 of the Treaty on European Union (TEU) gives the ECJ the power to give preliminary rulings on Framework Decisions, including the measures used to implement them. *Pupino* rules that individuals may apply the Framework Decision of 2001 to seek a conforming opinion of national law. The duel effect of harmonious interpretation and the rights of individuals to invoke the Framework Decision in national courts allows for the enforcement of victim rights on a domestic basis. Victims may rely on the Framework Decision to the extent, however, that a member state or national court is willing to give it indirect effect in their interpretation of domestic law.

Although not confined to common law jurisdictions, *Pupino* demonstrates how trial processes that are adversarial in nature, particularly those procedures that seek to challenge the prosecution evidence, may be modified to allow for the protection of vulnerable parties. Similar approaches are adopted throughout the common law world, with regard to special provisions for the examination and cross-examination of rape victims, or other vulnerable classes of victim, such as children.

The Convention for the Protection of Human Rights and Fundamental Freedoms, otherwise known as the European Convention on Human Rights (ECHR), also presents a challenge to nominal adversarial processes. The ECHR has been used to challenge domestic processes for the protection of vulnerable victims, such as child victims or witnesses or victims of sexual assault or rape. Under the ECHR, such victims deserve certain protections and rights to privacy during the course of the trial. It is well known that vulnerable victims will often endure additional trauma by being called as a witness to testify in court in order to secure a conviction against their alleged offender. Articles 6 and 8 of the ECHR provide rights to a fair trial and rights to privacy respectively. Both articles have been interpreted by the European Court of Human Rights (ECtHR)[6] in the context of the extent to which each article provides certain protections for victims of crime called to participate in the trial process. The ECtHR takes the view that, when a victim or witness may be too afraid to testify, that their rights and interests may legitimate the use of anonymous evidence, hearsay evidence, or special measures, including using pre-recorded interviews.[7] *Demski v Poland* (2008) 22695/03 (4 November 2008), for example, stands as an example of the extent to which the ECtHR will go towards balancing the interests of the victim against those of the defendant:

> The Court reiterates its case-law regarding rape cases in that there exist requirements inherent in the States' positive obligations to establish and apply effectively a criminal-law system punishing all forms of rape and sexual abuse (M.C., cited above, s185). The Court acknowledges that the special features of criminal proceedings concerning rape might require balancing the needs of the defence against those of witnesses or victims called upon to testify. Such proceedings are often conceived of as an ordeal by the victim, in particular as they entail being confronted again with the defendant. However, in the light of the findings above, in the present case it cannot be said that the witness's whereabouts were unknown or that she sought ways to avoid a confrontation with the defendants (see *Scheper v the Netherlands* (dec), 39209/02, 5 April 2005). Had the domestic court made more effort to summon the witness to the proceedings and had she demonstrated that her participation would have had an adverse effect on her mental state, the applicant's complaint that his defence rights had not been respected would have been put in a different perspective. The Court further observes that arrangements could in any event have been made to allow M.H. to give evidence in a manner which spared her the ordeal of an adversarial procedure while respecting the rights of the defence (see *W.S. v. Poland*, no. 21508/02, s57, 19 June 2007 and S.N., cited above, s47).

The varying perspectives on the scope and form of the criminal trial considered in this section suggests that the combination of parliament, the courts, and human rights frameworks, allows for the dynamic modification of the adversarial trial process. As such, the criminal trial may be best understood as an instrument of society, to be applied variably and even perhaps inconsistently in order to achieve its goals of dispute resolution. On this point Dworkin (1986) reminds us that, on a principled basis, that law should not merely advocate consensus or be seen as a vehicle of politics. For Dworkin (1986), law should act to restrain politics to ensure that the political community acts in an ordered, coherent and principled way, with regard to all members of society. It is not a simple matter of arguing, then, that the trial is to take whatever form expedient to a given moment of people, politics or community expectation. Rather, in order to be true to the essential characteristics of the trial as it has emerged over the centuries, we must be critical of those normative perspectives that proscribes the form and function of the trial as an *a priori* product of adversarialism to the exclusion of alternative ways of doing justice (as to the range of normative assumptions in the work of the ECtHR, see Summers, 2007: 3–10). By examining the character of the trial as a vehicle of inclusion, the trial can be developed in a principled way that is consistent with its genealogy and history as an institution of social power, as an institution that holds wrongdoers to account against the varying needs and contexts of law and legal practice. This approach provides that the criminal trial is not prescribed by law, but rather acts as a hermeneutic of social issues and agents. Furthermore, it means that voices and perspectives are not necessarily silenced out of the need to maintain a normative, prescribed perspective.

A note on method: 'Effective history', discourse and legal hermeneutics

Various authors have traced the development of the criminal trial from the common law tradition (Holdsworth, 1903–38; Kiralfry, 1958; Tobias, 1979; Hyams, 1981; Emsley, 1983, 1987; Damaška, 1986; Hay, 1975; Pollock and Maitland, 1968; Shapiro, 1991; Kirchengast, 2006; Langbein, 2003). These authors agree that while the victim may have been central during the early formation of the trail (pre-1250), the Crown and state soon came to monopolise the right to bring offenders to justice. This history indicates, however, that the trial was never constituted as a mere reaction to state power, but was informed through a combination of victim, Crown and state interests as they have emerged over centuries. The growth of the institutional capacity of the Crown and the control of prosecution in the name of the Crown and then state increasingly exposed defendants to abuses of power out of the paucity of rights afforded to defendants compared to the might and power of the state.

Not only were the interests of defendants directly prejudiced through a lack of representation and due process, where defendants were refused a copy of the accusation bringing them to court in the first instance, but they were increasingly exposed to a prosecution armed with the endless resources of the state. As I have explained elsewhere (Kirchengast, 2006: 75–78), this can be seen as the point at which defendant rights became a growing concern in the criminal law, and would be the advent of what Langbein (2003) identifies as the origins of the adversarial criminal trial. As a result of the lack of defendant rights compared to those of the state, the law of evidence, legal representation, modes of proof, the availability of the grand and petty jury, and a more rigorous trial process separating the role of prosecution from judge and defence, developed to provide defendants with substantive and procedural rights. Such reforms are now largely taken as constitutive of pre-trial and trial processes.

For Foucault (1969: 26), knowledge, when linked to power, not only assumes the authority of 'the truth' but, as he argues, it provides the basis upon which one may assert particular truths as essential fact. The problem with these truths is that in a given context, including doctrinal perspectives on the criminal trial process, these truths become largely incontestable. They are taken as a given. Those who critique such truths are said to be wrong. Foucault (1971, 1982, 1984) eschews such perspectives of the essential nature of truth, favouring a more informed perspective whereby knowledge may be disciplined and interpreted to suit those in positions of power. The rise of doctrinal approaches in criminal law that attest to the trial in a prescribed and given form indicate how knowledge may be disciplined to give effect to a particular 'correct' or 'truthful' rhetoric that may not be easily contested or challenged (see Norrie, 2001: 7–8, 15–31; also see Horwitz, 1981). The adversarial criminal trial as the centrepiece of modern criminal law and justice is considered such a construction.[8] It is not that the criminal trial does not play a significant function in the justice system. Foucault's (1969, 1984) method of discipline and discourse realises that we are not bound by normative or fixed interpretation of what the trial, or the criminal law for that matter, ought to be (see Foucault, 1971: 26; see Chapter 5). Doctrinal approaches within criminal law, most readily found in a criminal trial textbook, all too often impart the impression that the criminal trial and justice process is largely determinative. Law students spend whole semesters learning about the scope of the trial in terms of bodies of rules and procedures that are not taught as transcendental but rather as established and immovable rigidities of a self-referential system of rules, precedents and procedures (see, for example, Haydock and

Sonsteng, 1991). The criminal trial has emerged as something larger than the sum of its parts, as Hay (1975: 33) suggests:

> The punctilious attention to forms, the dispassionate and legalistic exchanges between counsel and the judge, argued that those administering and using the law submitted to its rules. The law thereby became something more than the creature of a ruling class – it became a power with its own claims, higher than those of prosecutor, lawyers, and even the great scarlet-robed assize judge himself.

To this end legal hermeneutics questions the extent to which the law is bound by a self-referential method of interpretation based on a rigid system of rules and processes. Teubner (1993: 13–19) articulates a method of legal interpretation as based on self-referentiality, whereby law may only be propagated or challenged by reference to the internal modalities of the law itself. External change or challenge is limited by virtue of the self-referentiality of the 'hypercycle' of law and legal processes. On the other hand, various perspectives defend a hermeneutics of law by providing for the interpretative basis of legal texts and processes. It is not that the hermeneutics of law is a theory that guides interpretation in any normative sense. The method provided is one that aims to free the legal scholar, lawyer or jurist, rather than shackle them. Hoy (1992: 180) examines the possibilities of a legal hermeneutics when revising the classical or original interpretation of legal texts:

> Hermeneutics tries to describe the conditions for the practice of interpreting the law rather than legislating a 'method' or 'theory' that will stand outside the practice of legal interpretation, grounding and guiding it.... What hermeneutics would say is that the original intention can be taken into account as one possible interpretation. The original intention is not the most privileged interpretation, however, and is not necessarily the correct or best interpretation of the entire text.

In a similar way, Leyh (1992: 248) situates hermeneutics in terms of an opportunity to place law in context:

> One educational objective of the hermeneutical approach would be to undermine the tendency to view law as a discrete activity

by situating legal issues in a broader intellectual and social context.

Reflecting on the example provided above, that of the criminal trial textbook as an artefact of normative practice, Leyh (1992) reminds us that law is historically and interpretively constituted around a set of interests that may empower some over others. Further, Leyh (1992) suggests that we ought to be suspicious of those who interpret legal doctrine as fixed or given, or even stable or incontestable. Legal hermeneutics then, combined with Foucault's (1971) disciplining of knowledge as 'truth', provides a significant methodological basis upon which the doctrine of the adversarial criminal trial may be questioned as excluding people, perspectives and agents quite relevant to determinations of offence liability and seriousness. Further, such an approach is bound to open our minds to future possibilities and innovative reforms to bring the stakeholders of justice together in ways that may well overcome Langbein's (2003) 'combat effect' that defies the very capacity for the adversarial trial to arrive at an agreed version of events. We must be critical of the constitutive contexts of the taken for granted or assumed approaches of the criminal law that provide that there is only one acceptable means by which justice ought to be done.

Is the criminal trial in crisis?

There have been numerous modifications to victim and defendant rights that have changed the very nature of the criminal trial. Historically, the criminal trial was widely acknowledged as protecting defendants from an abuse of state power. This view of the criminal trial, the adversarial criminal trial as Langbein (2003) has put it, is constituted as the means through which defendant's rights and interests are protected against state power. Such procedure also protects defendants from other interests deemed outside the adversarial criminal trial, such as those of the victim or other rights based groups, said to be peripheral to the interests of justice, at least in a common law sense. Common law 'justice' is this defined narrowly in terms of a due process that identifies the defendant as the relevant subject of proceedings, whose liberty is protected by a swathe of rights constitutive of the trial itself: right to be heard and represented by defence counsel; to confront their accuser; to an independent magistrate or judge; a right to the indictment and the prosecution case; and now, a right of appeal on issues of law, and usually with leave, on issues of fact and for sentencing.

Duff et al. (2007) accept that this view of the trial needs to be supported through a 'normative theory of the trial' given the numerous interests now weighing on the substantive and procedural character of the criminal trial. For Duff et al. (2007), the accepted function of the criminal trial involves the determination of the guilt of the accused through the testing of evidence by application of objective rules, standards and procedures that would otherwise protect the innocent. Out of the need to accede to the demands of victims and the state, in terms of a law and order politics and out of the fear of terrorism, for example, the hallmarks of due process are being wound back for a modified trial form that jeopardises the adversarial trial as we have come to know it. Duff et al. (2007: 5) remark:

> Trials are thus of purely instrumental value: they serve the more fundamental interest that the state has in establishing whom we can justly punish for their crimes. Let us call this the standard account. Even on this account, other values serve at least to restrain the main aim of the trial. Defendants have various rights which must be protected, partly in order to ensure that ... accurate verdicts are sought with a proper degree of respect for the defendant as citizen.

The issue with this normative model is that victims and others have been excluded in order to maintain the characterisation of the criminal trial as fair, independent and free from undue influence. Any modification of these standards for the consideration of alternative views, such as those of the victim or state, may erode such principles, exposing defendants to an unacceptable risk of conviction, or chance of being sentenced to heavier, excessive punishments. Blackstone's (1783, 4: 352) precept 'that it is better that ten guilty persons escape, than that one innocent suffer', supports the need to restrain state power through an independent, objective and fair trial procedure.

There is room for the inclusion of alternative perspectives within the trial but these are limited to a communicative process in the 'public interest'. Duff et al. (2007) argues that the adversarial criminal trial is able to include perspectives that would ordinarily sit outside the parameters of the trial, such as those of the victim. However, these perspectives are represented in the context of the public prosecutor, who, as a matter of course, is concerned with the harms and injuries occasioned to the victim. This, in itself, is a well-founded observation. Prosecutors are indeed concerned with the interests of victims. However, as most prosecution guidelines explicate, prosecutors are manifestly concerned with the public interest and therefore will only represent the interests of victims to the extent to which this public interest will allow. In criminal law, the victim is only provided a role as witness for the prosecution, who will only be called should their testimony be needed to secure a conviction. If a conviction can be secured without the testimony of the victim, the prosecution will generally not call them. Doak (2005a) indicates the limited extent to which victims are included in prosecutorial decision-making. Edwards (2004) sees this limited role as flowing from their ambiguous status in the prosecution process. Victims are material to the prosecution but are displaced by a normative framework that requires a mode of participation beyond the subjective standing of any one individual. As a result, the inclusion of alternative perspectives in the 'public interest' may be rather narrow, and will not call for direct input from individual stakeholders to any significant extent. Duff et al. (2007: 214) observe:

> We have suggested that criminal wrongs are best understood as public wrongs. We understand this not in the traditional way, was a wrong done against the body of the sovereign, but rather as a wrong with which the public are right to be concerned *qua* public. That concern itself normally flows from a concern with the wellbeing of the victim, wellbeing that has been diminished by the wrong.

Over the last decade, and as canvassed in the previous sections, defendant rights have been increasingly abrogated by the rise of a multiplicity of new interests in criminal justice. The criminal trial is now emerging as a tribunal in which various stakeholder interests are mediated and weighted. Victim interests, as well as those of the state, have made a clear impact here. The trial now attempts to represent various, competing views, which challenge established notions that the trial ought to be defined as a mechanism singularly determinative of the status of defendants.

The adversarial criminal trial as rhetoric

The jury trial is situated as the centrepiece of criminal justice despite its limited use as a tribunal of fact. The influence of discourse on the form and function of the trial evidences how the trial is responsive to change, albeit at times quite questionable change, and how this has been a characteristic of the trial since it emerged out of rituals of customary justice

(Unger, 1976). Furthermore, the modern influences on the form and function of the trial, namely those asserted by the victim of crime, defendant and the state, evidence how the criminal trial is more appropriately recognised as a repository of disciplinary power that includes voices and perspectives as a hermeneutic of social issues and agents. This section examines the rhetoric of the adversarial criminal trial from a number of perspectives, from the dynamics of justice in the local or magistrates' court, and through the emergence of therapeutic jurisprudence and problem solving justice.

Local and magistrates' courts

The rhetoric of the trial as the centrepiece of the criminal law is most ably demonstrated by the fact that today few defendants actually proceed to trial by judge and jury. In most common law jurisdictions, processes have been established to guide the defendant from trial by judge and jury for summary proceedings before a magistrate sitting alone. Certainly in New South Wales (NSW), the vast majority of charges are dealt with by the local court constituted by a magistrate sitting alone. In 2007, 241,896 matters were finalised in the local court with 3198 matters being finalised in the District and Supreme Courts, before judge and jury (BOCSAR, 2008: 22, 77). These statistics indicate that 98.68 per cent of charges were finalised before a magistrate. Similar statistics can be found throughout the common law world, where the criminal trial now sits as the 'exemplar' of justice, the rhetoric of which deems that defendants are extended the full measure of procedural fairness, including committal for trial on the basis of the review of evidence or alternatively by grand jury process, arraignment of the indictment, state funded counsel for serious offences, access to a jury of 12 laypersons, and an independent judge of senior rank. On the other hand, the local court has been characterised as an institution of technocratic justice, where defendants are offered a compromised due process in order to process defendants quickly and efficiently (McBarnet, 1981a: 143–149; as to the history of summary justice, see McBarnet, 1981b: 190). McBarnet (1981a: 143) indicates why this characterises local court justice:

> Due process was and is ruled out of the lower courts as unnecessary on two grounds: first, both the offences and the penalties are too trivial; second, the issues and processes are such that the niceties of law and lawyers are irrelevant.

Processes are in place to facilitate this rapid delivery of justice with significant discounts being available for a guilty plea at first instance.

In fact, in NSW in 2007, 200,507 of the 241,869 Local Court matters, or 82.9 per cent, were disposed of by guilty plea. These statistics indicate how the claims of the trial as the 'centrepiece' of criminal law and justice have long been displaced by expedient measures for the delivery of swift, technocratic justice. Furthermore, this indicates how the adversarial 'judge and jury' trial sits as a hallmark of criminal law and justice in a most undeserved way.

Although jurists hold that the trial sets the standard by which we measure rules of due process that, to varying extents, are available in the summary courts, the reality is that the criminal process for most defendants and other participants exist outside any notion of the criminal trial experience as it is captured in the common rhetoric of criminal law and justice. This adds to the weight of evidence suggesting that criminal law is largely shaped by doctrines of knowledge that assume the significance of the trial throughout the criminal law. Rather than shaping the whole of the criminal law, however, the trial is today only one element of a highly evolved institution of justice that includes a variety of means to justice. In the local court perspective, this includes new and innovative processes that call for the participation of agents of justice, including victims of crime and members of the community, who would otherwise be excluded if the ideological 'centrepiece' of the adversarial criminal trial was seen to be actually constitutive of the whole of the jurisdiction.[9]

The local court, for instance, despite being convened as a court of adversarial justice, has been said to be less adversarial than inquisitorial (see Carlen, 1976: 53; McBarnet, 1981b: 188–195; Duff, 2001; McConville, 1984). This is phrased perhaps in the context of the triviality of local court justice and the way the formality of adversarialism may be dispensed with for a more informal approach at the discretion of the magistrate. Local court magistrates do occupy the unique position of arbiters of law and fact, which means that they find themselves in the position of being able to enquire in to the lives of defendants in a way that may not characterise the independence of the adversarial process in the higher courts. This is especially the case given the large number of litigants in person that regularly appear before the local court. With the exception of judge alone trials in the higher courts, local court thus provide a unique tribunal through which members of the community gather in a relatively informal environment, without the processes, procedures and personnel that otherwise characterise the 'removed' justice of the higher courts.

Courts of therapeutic justice

The last decade has seen the rise of a number of courts and tribunals created to deal with specific classes of offences, criminals and victims (see King, Freiberg, Batagol and Hyams, 2009: 138–169). The problem-solving courts of the State of New York evidence the movement away from traditional common law courts that seek to deal with all matters criminal within the one adversarial model (Berman and Feinblatt, 2005; Kaye, 2004). Problem-solving criminal courts now comprise several courts that seek to deal with particular and discrete issues in criminal justice in the New York court hierarchy. These courts include the drug court, mental health court, domestic violence court, sex offences court, youth court, and a community court. Each court demonstrates a departure from the principles of adversarial justice for alternative intervention based planning and welfare support. Knipps and Berman (2000: 10) suggest:

> Unlike traditional courts, the drug treatment courts shift the focus of proceedings from adjudicating past facts to changing future behavior – specifically, to the promotion of defendant sobriety through rigorous judicial monitoring of drug treatment. Treatment court judges play an active role in defendants' recovery process, imposing sanctions when program requirements are violated, dispensing rewards when treatment goals are reached. Because of the reduced emphasis on litigation, many practitioners describe proceedings in these courts as distinctly less adversarial, with the prosecution and defense both working toward the same goal of defendant sobriety.

Alternative courts of therapeutic justice are found throughout the common law world, however, the State of New York has demonstrated a particular drive toward these alternative pathways to justice. What is so significant about these courts is the way they are designed to deal with criminal offending in a way that intentionally departs from the rigidities of the adversarial trial. While not all therapeutic courts deal with liability, such as Drug Courts, which may only deal with supervised placement following a guilty plea, others replace the nominal trial process altogether. Domestic violence and sex offence courts are two such examples. These courts are specialised in that they offer an adversarial alternative to the trial court. The New York domestic violence and sex offences courts are diversionary courts. These courts will deal with all offences of a certain character. These courts are still constituted through an adversarial prosecution process, but are alternative to the extent that offer a process that better suits the specific needs of those persons involved in domestic violence and sexualised offences. These persons include the defendant but also include others excluded form nominal adversarial justice – such as the victim of crime. Knipps and Berman (2000: 10) highlight the significance placed on the victim:

> For all of their diversity, New York's domestic violence courts all follow a common set of principles that were first developed at the Brooklyn Domestic Violence Court in 1996. Key among them is an emphasis on victim safety. Complainants are linked to an on-site victim advocate, who helps them locate needed services such as shelter and counseling. The advocate also serves as a liaison between the court and victims, assuring that complainants are aware of new court dates, court orders and case outcomes – and that the court knows immediately if any further abuse occurs.

The alternative focus on providing ongoing support to victims can be seen through the rise of sex offence courts. Originally piloted in the counties of Nassau, Westchester and Oswego in 2006, sex offence courts provide for the trial of the offender but also allow for the ongoing support of victims and monitoring of the prisoner following conviction. These courts also take an active role by increasing judicial awareness of the consequences of sexual assault by having specifically trained judges and support personnel. Herman (2006: 77) suggests that such courts work closely with local service providers to facilitate victim access to advocacy counselling and other services. These courts take a victim-centred approach, which Herman (2006) indicates has proven key to the success of the program. By focussing on the needs of victims throughout their trial, the victim is given a measure of participation, as are ongoing support agencies and advocacy groups, which are invited to participate in the training, planning and operations of the court (Herman, 2006: 77).

The adversarial criminal trial, at least in terms of the rhetoric of the trial as an exclusive institution of defendant, state, judge and jury, is thus of limited relevance for large numbers of persons accused of an offence. With the advent of problem-solving courts, this number is increasing as fewer defendants and victims are subject to traditional adversarial processes. As the local court statistics and movement towards problem-solving courts indicate, few defendants proceed before a judge and jury in the sense of the adversarial trial noted by Deane J in *Dietrich*, above. Rather than confine ourselves to the rhetoric of the primacy of adversarial justice, we must examine the various dynamic ways by which wrongdoers are called to account for their actions as based on the interplay of agency, voice and representation that, arguably, constitutes a more informed view of the dynamics of the criminal trial in modern society. Moving away from the notion that the trial is prescribed allows for the mapping of power relations that would otherwise be diminished or discounted as somehow relevant to the modification of the criminal trial.

The trial as hermeneutic: Terrorism, the victim and human rights

The criminal trial is more than a prescribed apparatus of law, borne out of adhesion to a strict body of rules that define the substance and procedural limitations of an institution separate from society. In a Foucauldian sense, the trial is hermeneutic, constituted beyond the approved texts, or familiar ways of practice, that prescribe its form. Instead, historically and today, the criminal trial has been constituted by discourse, many of which are competing as to the extent to which the various agents of justice may be given formal standing and be heard as part of a judicial inquiry into an offence. These discourses will continue to shape the form and substance of the trial into the future. Furthermore, these discourses interact in a way that is decentred to the extent that each discourse is, at least in part, independent of the other. To demonstrate that the criminal trial is discursive and decentred this section will consider the influence of an array of social and political influences on the form and content of the trial and sentencing process.

None the more significant of these influences involves the modification of common law processes to accommodate the needs of the state, defendant and victim. These needs have been challenged across a range of reforms,[10] but are ably demonstrated through the recent focus on the modification of criminal law and procedure on two significant fronts. These include, the threat of terrorism or issues of national security, and, in terms of the call to include the victim of crime in the trial and sentencing process, the rise of a human rights discourse in domestic and international law. These reforms have impacted on the scope and content of the criminal law and trial process in vast ways. Pre-trial process including police investigative powers, prosecution decision-making processes, committal proceedings, evidence in trials, and the sentencing of offenders following conviction have each been modified, arguably quite significantly, to appease needs that are deemed outside the nominal criminal prosecution process. Whether these needs are asserted by a state concerned about national security in light of international acts of terrorism, or the more discrete needs of individual victim or victim rights groups, the criminal law and trial process has been subject to reforms that have resulted in serious criticisms as to the acceptable parameters of criminal law.[11] As a result, the role of the trial as an objective, impartial tribunal through which accusations of wrongdoing are heard and determined according to a set of transparent principles that would otherwise protect the innocent has come under criticism.

A vast literature now critiques the extent to which standards of due process or procedural fairness have been modified to allow for the investigation or prosecution of terrorist incidents or for the further confinement of persons, such as serious sex offenders, deemed to be a particularly serious risk of recidivist conduct (for a summary, see Keyzer and Blay, 2006; Smallbone and Ransley, 2005; Mercado and Ogloff, 2007). Much has also been written on the emergent role of the victim, and the way the integration of victim rights at common law are seen to be ambiguous (see Edwards, 2004), or even inconsistent or incompatible (see Wolhunter et al., 2009: 181), with establish doctrine. Further still, the balancing of the rights of defendants and victims in human rights law has increasing manifested in the modification of domestic law, specifically the rights enjoyed by the defendant or victim at trial or during sentencing. This section will briefly examine the legislative response to terrorism and domestic order, victim rights and human rights, to suggest how the boundaries of the criminal trial have been challenged, shifting to accommodate interests that previously rested beyond the normative scope of the trial. Arguably, it is the dynamic status of the criminal trial against the modern influence of national security legislation, the influence of victim rights on pre-trial, trial and sentencing processes, and the articulation of a human rights discourse that seeks to maintain fundamental rights of procedural fairness for defendants and victims, that has led some to argue that the trial, as an institution that ought to be concerned with defendant rights, has now reached a point of significant, yet unacceptable transformation.[12]

Terrorism, national security and domestic order

The advent of acts of terrorism and mass destruction against Western nations, particularly since the beginning of the twenty-first century, has resulted in the promulgation of a variety of measures to better detect and investigate terrorist individuals or organisations. Inherent in this approach is the extent to which such measures have challenged or modified rights and freedoms otherwise protected by an individual's access to justice and to a fair and open trial process. Thus, alternative means by which individual liberty may be suppressed in an attempt to control or contain certain individuals identified as terrorists or as affiliated with terrorist organisations known for their use of gross violence are now able to be subject to control orders or preventative detention or other limits to freedom, outside of any sentence or custody arrangement that results from the nominal process of the criminal law. Such processes now identify various procedures otherwise unknown to criminal law and procedure, such as preventative detention, control orders and prohibited contact orders (see Fairall and Lacey, 2007). In Australian and English law, control orders have received the most judicial attention to date.[13]

Control orders were introduced by the *Anti-Terrorism Act (No. 2) 2005* (Cth), as amending the Commonwealth Criminal Code, to provide for restrictions on the movement, association and communication of persons suspected of being involved in the planning of a terrorist act. Such orders are available on the balance of probabilities and may be issued on the basis that such an order would substantially assist in the prevention of a terrorist act. Arguably, such arrangements challenge the boundary of the criminal law and trial process by providing for extra-judicial considerations not borne of the nominal adversarial trial process (as to the English provisions, see *A v Secretary of State for the Home Department* [2005] 2 AC 68; *Prevention of Terrorism Act 2005* (UK); *Secretary of State for the Home Department v MB and AF* [2008] 1 AC 440; *Secretary of State for the Home Department v AF (No. 3)* [2009] 3 WLR 74).[14] Control orders were introduced in Australian law with a raft of other legislative reforms that significantly modify the criminal trial. Such other reforms include new rules for trials involving security issues, the 'licensing' of lawyers by security clearance, and the modification of the right to discover the prosecution case against the defendant (see Fairall and Lacey, 2007: 1075). It is the blurring of the line between executive will and the role of the courts that evidences the way the traditional ambit of the criminal trial is, most controversially, subject to change and modification.

Walton (2005: 3) indicates that a control order is an order of a court that essentially limits a person's freedom of movement and association pursuant to s104.5(3) of the *Anti-Terrorism Act (No. 2) 2005* (Cth). The conditions include: restricting a person's movement within specified places; limiting a person's ability to leave the country; having a person wear a tracking device; limiting a person's capacity to talk to other people (including his or her lawyer); limiting a parsons use of a telephone or the internet; having a person contact the police regularly; or even that a person be required to participate in specified counselling or education. A court may impose various conditions on a person subject to a control order for up to twelve months for an adult, or up to three months for people between 16 and 18 years of age.

A court can make a control order if it is satisfied, on the balance of probabilities, that the order would 'substantially assist in preventing a terrorist act' or because the individual subject to the control order 'has provided training to, or received training from, a listed terrorist organisation'. Of lesser relevance is whether the suspect person is not planning, or aiding someone who is planning, an actual terrorist incident. It does not matter that the person has not been charged with, or convicted of, a terrorist offence. Nicola Roxon MP (2005: 12), the then Shadow Attorney-General, said of the legislation:

> But terrorism forces us to re-evaluate many of the norms of criminal justice, particularly its focus on the past. Criminal law is variously described as driven by punishment, deterrence, rehabilitation or prevention of re-offending. All of these react to past conduct and seek to affect future conduct. None of them have much relevance for those on a suicide mission – they see no future for themselves beyond their crime and are prepared to die in the act of killing others.

The insertion of the availability of such orders into the legal process has proven most contentious. Walton (2005: 4), however, indicates how the process may be likened to other common law processes such as bail, although the accused does not have to be charged with a criminal offence in order to be eligible for a control order to be taken out against them:

> A control order is really just bail or parole, or even in some cases home detention, for innocent people. It permits people to be punished, and their liberty restricted, for what police believe they might do, rather than what they have done or what they are planning to do. The Attorney-General has been quoted as stating that control orders are intended to reduce the need for expensive covert

surveillance by simply restricting the liberty of (innocent) persons of interest to police.

The capacity to seek a control order under the Commonwealth Criminal Code was challenged in *Thomas v Mowbray* (2007) 233 CLR 307. In this case, a declaration was sought that Division 104 of the Commonwealth Criminal Code was invalid. An interim control order had been made pursuant to s104.4 of the Code, restricting the plaintiff in the prescribed ways. The High Court of Australia, Kirby J dissenting, held that Subdivision B of Division 104, specifically those powers granting the court the capacity to make a control order, was within the power of the Commonwealth Parliament and was supported by s51(vi) of the Constitution of Australia.

Gummow and Crennan JJ, with whom Callinan and Heydon JJ generally agreed, considered various aspects of nominal adversarial justice, including modes of appearance and the standard of proof, and parliaments ability to modify traditional criminal trial processes, in order to establish an alternative means by which a person's liberty may be corralled. Their Honours agreed that *ex parte* applications were not new, although the *Anti-Terrorism Act (No. 2) 2005* (Cth) did allow for a contested hearing if the 'defendant' sought to enter an appearance. Further, it was not contrary to Chapter III of the Australian Constitution for the standard of proof to be prescribed on the balance of probabilities, as compared to the criminal standard placed on the prosecution in *Woolmington v DPP* [1935] AC 462, proof beyond reasonable doubt. Their Honours stated that it was for parliament to determine the relevant standard of proof. The scope of the criminal trial, however, is considered to the extent that orders restricting an individual's liberty need not come by way of a traditional criminal trial process. Gleeson CJ reflected generally on the scope of the trial process leading to a depravation of liberty.[15] In *Thomas v Mowbray* (2007) 233 CLR 307, Gleeson CJ cites the examples of bail and the restrictions available to a court on apprehended violence orders as indicating that such powers have never been foreign to the exercise of judicial power, citing Blackstone's (1783, 4: 248) notion of 'preventative justice' as indicating an enduring power to maintain the peace (at 328–329):

> Those observations apply to the legislation in question in this case. Two familiar examples of the judicial exercise of power to create new rights and obligations which may restrict a person's liberty are bail, and apprehended violence orders. The restraints imposed

on the plaintiff by the order made against him are similar to conditions commonly found in a bail order. Of course, there are differences between bail and a control order, but the example of bail shows that imposition of restrictions of the kind imposed on the plaintiff is not foreign to judicial power. Apprehended violence orders have many of the characteristics of control orders, including the fact they may restrain conduct that is not in itself unlawful. For example, an apprehended violence order may forbid a person to approach another person, or to attend a certain place. As a matter of history, apprehended violence orders have their origin in the ancient power of justices and judges to bind persons over to keep the peace. Blackstone, in his Commentaries, wrote of what he called 'preventive justice'. He said:

> This preventive justice consists in obliging those persons, whom there is probable ground to suspect of future misbehaviour, to stipulate with and to give full assurance to the public, that such offence as is apprehended shall not happen; by finding pledges or securities for keeping the peace, or for their good behaviour. This requisition of sureties has been several times mentioned before, as part of the penalty inflicted upon such as have been guilty of certain gross misdemeanours: but there also it must be understood rather as a caution against the repetition of the offence, than any immediate pain or punishment.

Arguably, control orders or other such measures may not be affiliated with trials at all as they sit as an adjunct to judicial proceedings that would otherwise limit the liberty of 'risky' persons. On the other hand, control orders provide a means by which an individual may be subject to constraints that are more consistent with sentencing options following a criminal trial. Such orders now apply to a range of 'risky' offenders, including recidivist sex offenders and more recently, members of organised motorcycle clubs or 'bikies'. The rise of a counter-terrorist legislative framework and control orders for members of outlaw motorcycle organisations provides, at the least, an alternative means of extrajudicial control of persons suspected of associating with other outlawed or controlled persons, involved in organisations identified as engaging in potential terrorist or other criminal activity.

The legislation providing for control orders for domestic law and order clearly indicates intent to establish a new procedure to bind persons over to restrain future offending. The notable examples include the rise of the

Anti-Social Behaviour Order (ASBO) in England and Wales, and the control order limiting the association of bikies in South Australia and NSW.[16] In South Australia, control orders are provided under the *Serious and Organised Crime (Control) Act 2008* (SA). This Act has recently been challenged in *Totani and Anor. v The State of South Australia* [2009] SASC 301. Section 14(5) of the 2008 Act proscribes that a court may make an order limiting the defendant from *inter alia* associating or communicating with specified persons or persons of a specified class, or entering or being in the vicinity of specified premises or premises of a specified class. Section 14(1) empowers the court to make the control order as follows:

> The Court must, on application by the Commissioner, make a control order against a person (the 'defendant') if the Court is satisfied that the defendant is a member of a declared organisation.

The full court of the South Australian Supreme Court in *Totani* ruled, by majority, that s14(1) of the 2008 Act was invalid to the extent that it requires a court to accede to the request of the Attorney-General to limit the movement and association of persons identified by the Attorney-General. Such persons were identified on the basis that they are a member of an outlawed motorcycle organisation, representing a risk to the public safety and order of South Australia. Bleby J takes issue with the fact that this significantly limits the discretion and thus institutional integrity of the court and on this basis rules that the section is invalid (at par 156–157):

> That fact in itself would, in my opinion, be sufficient to undermine the institutional integrity of the Court, as the most significant and essential findings of fact are made not by a judicial officer but by a Minister of the Crown. It is as though the legislation provided for the required elements to be proved on application to the Court, but that the Court was to refer the findings on the major elements to a non-judicial officer, acting without any judicial safeguards, whose decision would be final, not reviewable and binding on the Court. In a very real sense the Court is required to '[act] as an instrument of the Executive'.
>
> It is the integration of the administrative function with the judicial function to an unacceptable degree which compromises the institutional integrity of the Court.... It is not merely a question of the separation of powers, a principle which is not binding on the

States in the way that it is with respect to Commonwealth institutions. It is the unacceptable grafting of non-judicial powers onto the judicial process in such a way that the outcome is controlled to a significant and unacceptable extent, by an arm of the Executive Government which destroys the Court's integrity as a repository of Federal jurisdiction.

Bleby J raises issues fundamental to a court's character. These issues include a court's ability to act independently on its own forensic judgement of evidence put before it by counsel. Such issues, or the scope of the evidence tenable before the court, ought not be determined or prescribed by government or the state. The dissenting opinion of White J (at par 206), on the other hand, finds such discretion:

> What is plain is that there is nothing in the Control Act, and in particular, nothing in the privative provision (s41), which modifies the ordinary obligation of the Magistrates Court to satisfy itself that its jurisdiction has been properly invoked.

Special leave to appeal to the High Court of Australia has since been granted. The hearing will be held in the latter half of 2010.

Victim rights and human rights

The case of *Criminal Proceedings Against Pupino* [2005] 3 WLR 1102, discussed above, indicates how the victim of crime has been increasingly integrated into trial processes (including the adversarial aspects of inquisitorial approaches) on an international basis. Several decisions of the ECtHR are seminal in further demonstrating the impact of the victim of crime on the shaping of a modified trial process that challenges the traditional boundaries or 'exclusivities' of the adversarial criminal trial. Several aspects of traditional adversarialism have been challenged by virtue of the integration of victim rights under art. 6 and 8 of the ECHR.[17] The areas that demonstrate this challenge to conventional proceedings include the admission of anonymous witness evidence, hearsay or out of court statements, the use of pre-recorded testimony, and a victim's right to privacy both in their personal lives, and at trial. Although art. 6 does not refer to the victim, the ECtHR has nonetheless incorporated the victim in terms of the proportionality requirement of the defendant's right to a fair criminal trial. Victims have been accorded an independent right to a fair civil hearing under art. 6 as well.

The extent to which witnesses are able appear anonymously was at issue in *Doorson v The Netherlands* (1996) 22 EHRR 330. In *Doorson*, a drug trafficking case, witnesses had been granted anonymity out of fear of reprisals from the defendant. Although victims' rights are not expressly covered by art. 6, other rights that concern the victim, such as those that protect the life, liberty and security of the person (art. 5), and respect for private and family life (art. 8), are included in the ECHR. As such it is for the court to balance the interests of defendants to know their accuser and/or the individuals providing evidence against them, in appropriate cases, with the personal interests of those witnesses. Proving testimony anonymously can therefore be used to ensure that the key witnesses are protected while allowing the defence to test their evidence in a way that maintains that anonymity. It is for the court to ensure a fair process is implemented that gives the defendant access to the prosecution witnesses without compromising the anonymity of the witnesses.

As a result, anonymous witness statements may be used in relevant cases where the victim or witness is scared of testifying in open court. *PS v Germany* (2003) 36 EHRR 61, a case involving a child victim of sexual assault, held that art. 6 requires that the interests of young witnesses be sufficiently protected, albeit in this matter, as the witness statement was the only direct evidence against the accused, the court ruled that art. 6(3)(d) had still been violated. In *SN v Sweden* (2004) 39 EHRR 13 a victim of sexual assault gave evidence via video recording, forming almost the sole evidence upon which the defendant was convicted. The ECtHR held that, out of recognition of the vulnerability of sexual assault victims, and the realisation that the trial is likely to cause further trauma, a victim's right to their private life must be considered in determining whether the defendant indeed received a fair trial. However, any special arrangements adopted to help protect the victim must not stop the defendant from being able to contest the evidence. The ECtHR ruled that art. 6(3)(d) had not been violated due to the defendant's counsel consenting to the victim being interviewed by police without the defence present (see Ellison, 2002: 67, 78, 154).

The adversarial criminal trial in transition

As the preceding sections indicate, the criminal trial as discursive emerges through the modification of trial processes as a response to the changing needs of society. The form and content of the criminal law may be modified by common law or statute, as a response to various sites of discourse, including human rights, terrorism and law and order perspectives. As can be seen through the issues canvassed in this chapter, the form and scope of the criminal trial is often debated in terms of the extent to which the various agents of justice hold rights that ought to be considered relevant to the trial process. As can be seen through the various recent changes to the criminal trial, the number of agents of justice now seeking to press their rights over the form and scope of the criminal trial are increasingly beyond those traditionally recognised under a model of strict adversarialism. Each of the agents of the state, government, police, community, individual victims or victim groups, lawyers and professional associations, and individual defendants now seek to influence the nature of the trial, some being more successful than others.

The criminal trial as transgressive emerges through the modification of the trial process as a response to the changing needs of society. Almost all aspects of the criminal trial have been subject to social debate and discourse, and include recent developments, such as: control orders for suspected or released terrorists, serious sex offenders and even bikies; the creation of summary disposal for the expedient administration of justice; the removal of grand jury bills of indictment for a committal hearing before a magistrate; the creation of judge alone trials even for matters proceeding on indictment; the modification of the law against double jeopardy; majority jury verdicts or modification of the requirement that indictments proceed before a jury and the verdict of the jury be unanimous; the scope and number of the technical defences for murder, and the abolition of those that may prejudice or privilege certain members of the community, such as provocation; the rise of new police powers out of the fear of gross social disorder, and for the control of risky, deviant persons; increased involvement of the victim by the provision of personal counsel at public expense; and the creation of new and innovative courts of therapeutic justice, including sexual offences, domestic violence and drug courts and now even community courts, to name a few. Much has been written on each of these developments and many are controversial in their re-shaping of the criminal trial. The extent of each of these debates also varies significantly between jurisdictions. However, many have focussed on the transformation of the criminal trial as a response to growing social need or awareness.

Such reforms also include the modification of key 'criminal law' processes, such as bail, which is now significantly guided by statute that references easily changed criteria upon which bail will be granted or not, to meet the requirements of different offenders; displacing grand jury determination of true bills of indictment for committals determined by a magistrate sitting alone; the rise of penalty notices or infringements that usurp the trial altogether; the use of charge and plea bargaining as an alternative to trial; and perhaps most significantly in terms of the future direction of the criminal trial, the emerging influence of an international human rights discourse that centres both defendant and victim rights as significant to procedural justice.

Discourses of human rights, law and order, voice, participation and agency, may be seen to be social influences impacting on the shape and content of the trial. These changes may destabilise the notion that the criminal trial has given purpose and form. Further to these broader 'institutional' changes lies a subjective power that influences the scope and content of each individual decision to prosecute, and the hearing or trial that may follow. Trials may also be susceptible to subjective influence in terms of police discretion to charge or not, and to continue a prosecution or not. Much has been said of the need to replace police prosecutors with an independent, organised prosecutorial service like the Crown Prosecution Service (CPS) in the England and Wales. Sentencing as a discretionary process may accede to certain dominant views despite judicial resistance to the notion that judges are partial to any extent. Most common law jurisdictions now have an independent Office of the Director of Public Prosecutions (ODPP) who makes the decision to prosecute free from any interference from the Attorney-General. Whether decisions regarding individual trials are susceptible to political interference needs to be evaluated on an individual basis. Historically, evidence abounds as to the political basis of treason trials and trial before the Act of Settlement 1701 perhaps could not be said to be independent in any event, given the lack of judicial tenure and thus independence from the King.[18] Checks and balances are in place today to provide for the assertion that, save the continued role of police prosecutors in initiating charges in court, that magistrates, judges and ODPP prosecutors, and the prosecution decision-making process itself, is largely independent and free from obvious political interference albeit a subjective discretion is exercised at every step in the prosecutorial and judicial decision-making process.

Examining the trial in history and discourse

The perception that the trial seeks to guard against the abuse of state power alone will be destabilised in Chapter 2, *A Genealogy of the Trial in*

Criminal Law. This chapter focuses on the review of historical sources to show the various forms the trial has taken over the last millennia. This chapter begins with a consideration of the various notions of the trial in criminal justice: as a place of customary justice and as a site of local governance. Historically, the last vestiges of victim 'controlled' justice shifted around 1250 to increasingly reflect modes of 'public' prosecution in the name of the Crown. A detailed law of evidence followed, protecting the rights of the accused from unfair conviction by limiting what evidence could be adduced at trial. Increasingly throughout the eighteenth century, court procedure was also solidified from general custom to a more established set of rules to constitute standard processes for each court. These procedures sought to limit discretion in favour of a more prescribed trial process with defined roles for the judge, jury, prosecution, defendant, counsel, witnesses, and public (see generally, Langbein, 2003). At the same time the number of offences grew rapidly, from a few felonies designed to protect the integrity of the body and the right to personal property, to the creation of specific offences against the sovereign, the government, and peace and good order. This saw the beginning of the period in which the defendant was at risk of an abuse of power from over or unfair prosecution. Personal liberty was at stake – the Crown now possessed the institutional capacity to prosecute more offenders, and the courts were established to trial them *en masse*. This history indicates how the trial evolved in accordance with the growing needs of society and the state. As a result, various powers constitutive of the modern adversarial trial were informed by the discrete needs of defendants, and the unfair advantage of the Crown and emerging state as prosecutor. Significantly, this perspective debunks the notion that the trial was always constituted as an independent tribunal – the protector of defendant rights – as a reaction to the growth of state power. Rather, the trial evolved to meet specific social conditions, which, genealogically, represents the trial not as an institution of prescribed or positive control, than social and discursive power.

Chapter 3, *Shifting Boundaries: Recent Changes to Criminal Justice Policy*, will map the various contemporary influences dislocating the criminal trial from those characteristics that identify it as an institution of adversarial justice exclusively. As such, this chapter will consider various changes to law and policy that seek to modify various aspects of the adversarial process. This chapter will argue that criminal justice policy is operating in accordance with a number of competing discourses that challenge the adversarial model in various ways. The need for expedient justice in all its forms, in particular, the rise of summary justice, plea and charge bargaining, committals, dispensing with the jury, and the expanded use of infringement and penalty notices, shows how the adversarial trial is being sidestepped for a number of inventive measures depriving the accused a traditional 'judge and jury' trial. The law and order debate calling for extended police powers, new offences and punishments, restrictions to bail, and the rise of domestic control orders or ASBOs for the regulation of identified deviant or 'risky' groups within the community, further identifies changes to criminal justice policy that impacts on the trial by dislocating or usurping the trial for increased police power and discretion, and the genesis of a new 'civil' procedure to restrain future offending. The abolition of the defence of provocation and the reform of the rule against double jeopardy indicates the modification of the substantive character of the trial for a range of considerations that seek to incorporate new perspectives, such as those realising the gendered nature of the law of provocation, or to provide for a re-trial where the original trial was tainted. The rise of victims' lawyers as an adjunct to the criminal trial, the rise of derogative and non-derogative control orders and the ECHR, including the extent to which such reforms are constituted as 'criminal law', also suggest dynamic changes to criminal justice policy that impacts the scope and content of the modern criminal trial.

That a less adversarial and increasingly decentralised trial experience is emerging in common law jurisdictions is the focus of Chapter 4, *The Transformative Criminal Trial Emerges*. This notion of the trial, a transformative criminal trial as it might be termed, is not based on any normative or prescribed account of what the trial ought to be. It is experimental to the extent that it seeks to break some of the given rules of criminal procedure, while holding onto others. The various policies that argue for the emergence of a transformative criminal trial are canvassed in Chapter 3. This chapter will further argue that the transformative criminal trial is neither normative nor prescriptive. As such, it is impossible to delineate the exact way in which this notion of the trial seeks to operate. It is not that rules and processes of general application constitute particular aspects of the criminal trial. Trial processes and rules of evidence are of application between trials. The point is that the criminal trial is not restricted to the notion of an adversarial trial, before judge and jury. This chapter indicates that the modern era of experimental justice, where the criminal trial is influenced by a variety of sources – the shifting notion of public vs private, human rights discourse, movements in European civil law, problem-solving courts, challenges in sentencing and punishment – demonstrate how the adversarial criminal trial is being dislocated for a trial experience that transcends normative boundaries and expectations. The criminal trial as a prescribed, normative experience is being increasingly sidestepped for alternative means to justice. This, arguably, is consistent with the genealogy of the trial discussed in Chapter 2.

Chapter 5, *The Criminal Trial as Social Discourse*, draws on various literatures including sociology, jurisprudence and philosophy to establish that the criminal trial is indeed discursive and decentred. In the context of the destabilising of the singular notion of a normative adversarial trial discussed in Chapter 2, and given the discussion of current policy issues and examples of cases raised in Chapters 3 and 4; Chapter 5 will examine how the trial operates as a reflection of a competing number of discourses that seek to reposition the scope of the trial to accommodate new interests and agents of justice. The trial as an apparatus of social power will be examined leading into the discussion of the extent to which we ought to tolerate 'outside' influences on the criminal law. To this end, a comparative analysis of three approaches to accommodate 'out of court' or hearsay evidence in England and Wales, Australia and the United States, and the underlying discourses informing each approach, will demonstrate the interconnectedness of the criminal trial to particular discourses of justice, and the changing values of society more generally. This will further the argument that the modern criminal trial is discursive and decentralised to the extent that is it not normative nor prescriptive but transcendental in that it allows innovative approaches for the participation, or protection, of various agents of justice.

Chapter 6, *The Trial as Hermeneutic: A Critical Review*, examines the notion of the emergence of a transformative criminal trial to the extent that we are moving away from prescribed and normative approaches to justice for inclusive and transformative institutions that make connections between various agents relevant to the justice system. This notion, for some, is rather controversial. Some deem it offensive and dangerous to think that the institution through which we determine liability for criminal wrongdoing should be influenced by various needs that sit beyond the normative scope of a contested trial between defendant and state. They argue for a more determinate institution constituted by general principles that define the trial as autonomous from the sectarian and popular influences of the community and society. This chapter argues that the transformative criminal trial, as a hermeneutic of traditional adversarial discourse, is more than the adversarial criminal trial grappling with changes to law and policy. This chapter will argue against the notion that the transformative criminal trial as hermeneutic merely represents the adversarial trial struggling in the modern age. As underpinned by Chapter 5, this chapter examines the genesis of a new vision of the trial as one that is always discursive. As such, although the parameters of adversarial justice remain largely intact, at least as a matter of a general legal principle or model of justice available in common law jurisdictions, the criminal trial cannot be reduced to a single normative approach. In its attempt to grapple with and control legal and social change, our understanding of the trial is necessarily transforming, incrementally but substantively, leading to a rejection of the normative model for one that is more discursive and decentred. As a counter perspective, Chapter 6 examines the emergence of the anti-inquisitorial movement in the United States as evidenced in the recent jurisprudence of the Supreme Court of the United States in *Crawford v Washington* (2004) 541 US 36.

The transformative criminal trial does significantly more than sit in judgement of a normative theory of the trial. Chapter 7, *Implications for Criminal Justice Policy*, will discuss how the transformative criminal trial provides a basis for understanding, evaluating and integrating criminal justice policy, agents of justice, and the community more generally. The conceptualisation of the trial as discursive advances our understanding of the criminal trial by acknowledging how it is shaped by competing social values. By moving toward the notion of the trial as hermeneutic, the criminal trial is identified as open to a broad array of discourses once excluded as irrelevant to justice. The trial as transformative thus acknowledges how the trial is shaped through general principles constituted through competing statements and discourses as to what form the trial ought to take. Against this approach, the criminal trial is an evolving institution of social justice. Such perspectives ensure the appropriate balancing of defendant rights with those of other stakeholders, including victims and the community. The transformative criminal trial thus emerges as much more than a simple re-conceptualisation or critique of the assumed autonomy of the adversarial criminal trial. It provides a vehicle for the integration of criminal justice policy by providing a model whereby various viewpoints may be taken into account – those of the defendant, victim and state – in a way that balances the needs of these various proponents of justice. This book will conclude with a commentary on the 'modern criminal trial as hermeneutic' as a means to substantive and procedural justice. It will argue for the viability of this new way of conceptualising the criminal trial as vital to the continued development of criminal law in common law jurisdictions by arguing that the criminal trial is a vehicle for change in a way hereto unrecognised.

2
A Genealogy of the Trial in Criminal Law

> The danger lies in regarding history as something that is always already there, evolving 'down through time' in a positive direction.
> Patrick Nerhot, *Law, Writing, Meaning: An Essay in Legal Hermeneutics*, p. 54.

The history of the criminal law and trial process has been published across various works. The work of some authors, such as Sir William Holdsworth, extends far beyond the scope of criminal law and procedure, developing this history through a chronology of the development of English law across some seventeen volumes. Other historians, such as Sir James Fitzjames Stephen, focused on the history of the substantive criminal law and trial process. This chapter departs from the approach of the legal historian for Foucault's (1982) genealogical method to indicate the rise of the trial as a discursive institution of social justice. This method is adopted because it allows for an account of the criminal trial that differs markedly from previous historical accounts. Rather than focus on the trial as an institution that gradually adopted rules and procedures that made it more adversarial in character, I will examine the trial as an institution that was always 'sociological', as associated with the rights and interests of various parties and agents of justice. This analysis will consider more than traditional accounts of the emergence of adversarial justice from the eighteenth century: defendant rights, the introduction of counsel, a law of evidence, Crown or state prosecutors, and the independence of the judiciary. It is not that these developments are irrelevant to the development of the criminal trial. Instead, a different perspective on these developments will be considered that also accounts for the significant role played by victims, the community, and state. This perspective advances the argument that the criminal trial is an inclusive institution of social justice.

The assumption that the history of the criminal trial only speaks of its gradual evolution toward adversarialism will be considered in the context of Foucault's (1982, 1984) genealogical method. The dominant perspective challenged is that the criminal trial evolved from arbitrary customary and religious practice to a model of doctrinal and procedural efficiency that seeks to test the prosecution case against a defined standard of proof that, in the end, gets to the 'truth' of the accusation of wrongdoing. This chapter will examine the customary, religious and sociological bases of trials as they have manifested historically. This will inform the argument that the criminal trial is a socially productive apparatus of power. This genealogical perspective, which extends on my previous work in the area (Kirchengast, 2006: 28–43), suggests that the criminal trial is a socially inclusive and transformative institution of justice. This is significant given the tenets of adversarialism that characterise much of the contemporary debate over what form the trial ought to take. Such perspectives, arguably, mask our full realisation of the capacity of the trial as an inventive problem-solving institution.

The criminal trial as an institution of social power

The criminal trial has always existed in one form or another. This institution, which may have been as informal as unrestrained vendetta, is significant because it founded the institutional and procedural characteristics of the criminal trial as we know it today. The involvement of the victim and offender, and their kin, provided for a form of interfamilial dispute resolution that resulted in the development of an informal mode of accusation, proof and punishment. Such forms of early trial resolved the dispute by meting out further violence or the reaching of some agreed settlement. The significance of this form of trial was that once resolution was reached, however bloody, the matter was deemed to be resolved. The parties, and their kin, were then free to move on. By today's standards, the meting out of punishment following a guilty plea or conviction may not end the matter, and it is feasible to suggest that victims, the defendant, and the community may continue to live with the emotional, financial and social consequences of an offence for some time. This fact notwithstanding, the criminal trial is an institution of social significance and power that brings individuals together in specific ways to resolve the conflict, which, depending on the outcome, may appease some, but not others.

The criminal trial as an adversarial institution of justice appears significantly removed from the epoch where customary law reigned supreme. The formalised rules and processes for the management of the defendant, within a system for the presentment of the accusation, pre-trial, trial and sentencing processes, and the requirement that procedural fairness be adhered to at all times, appears removed from any customary practice for the resolution of conflict in an informal way. The original courts therefore looked less like the courts of today and more like communal gatherings for the advancement of local governance and order (Stone, 1991: 3). Findlay and Henham (2005: 319) remind us that the adversarial environment of the modern common law trial does not dislocate the notion that the trial is still a 'social construct' shaped by a 'positivist legal paradigm' that provides for a socially acceptable or official mode of accusation and punishment, thus:

> The essence of discretionary decision-making within the adversarial paradigm prevalent in common law jurisdictions can be seen through the division of the trial into the stages of pre-trial, trial, verdict, and sentence, each stage being predicated on the fundamental requirement to establish guilt. Since the trial is a legal and social construct, the social reality of decision-making within the trial is informed by its adversarial context; in other words, the ideology of the adversarialism influences both structure and norm. Decisions as social reality represent transformative outcomes; they are transformative in the sense that they attribute moral status to ideologies. This means that they (and the decision-makers) provide the structure and agency for transformation. Adversarialism provides a distorting context for establishing truth since it is designed to establish criminal liability (responsibility) – this may coincide with establishing truth. Hence, the sites for decision-making within the adversarial paradigm are essential reference points for creating the liability and accountability conventionally accorded to a strictly positivist legal paradigm which envisions the law and legal process as the means of providing accountability and justice through officially structured sanctioning and punishment.

This section demonstrates that the criminal trial is a socially significant institution of power by examining the role of the trial in customary law. Customary law, in so far as it engages victims, the accused and members of the community, remains a significant determinant of the characteristics of the modern criminal trial. This is despite the modern criminal trial's appearance as a procedural entity through which lawyers tactically engage one another in an adversarial process held out, on a doctrinal and procedural basis, as removed from the everyday practices of the community. The customary basis for accusation, contest and remedy that we known as the modern criminal trial provides for the transformative capacity of its modern form. Although the adversarial contest provides the normative framework in modern common law systems, it is the customary basis of criminal law that forges the ongoing connection between people, conflict and punishment. Adversarialism is thus reduced to the present means by which we make this context palatable. As Findlay and Henham (2005) note, adversarialism provides the structure and the norm. Adversarialism, therefore, provides the means by which 'social reality' comes to be represented in a particular way. It is thus possible to deconstruct the modern adversarial trial in terms of the very processes that held the individual to account for wrongdoing in antiquity, before the twelfth century formalising of a common trial process in English law. Direct links can be seen, arguably, between the customary processes of accusation and punishment with those of the criminal trial today.

The trial in customary law

Processes of accusation and punishment are widely recognised as part of the life of the collective under customary law. It is not possible to separate the means by which such accusations are dealt with as the process is connected to the life of the group. Customary law provides that all relevant participants including the accused, the victim, tribal elders, and members of the community, are drawn together for a process of confrontation that involves judgement and sanction. The trial is not discrete but inclusive of the community and the sanction is heavily weighted upon the type of wrongdoing and the sensibilities that have been offended, as a result. Unger (1976: 48) indicates how customary practices of tribal warfare refer to implicit standards of conduct rather than to prescribed, posited or formulated rules. Such rules are 'non-public' to the extent that they are common to a whole society or group, rather than associated with centralised government.

Such practices, for Unger (1976: 48), refer to the accepted modalities of behaviour upon which communication and exchange is practiced. Further, deviations from social rule are the very processes that mark the rules themselves. Conformity or disobedience of established social rules becomes part of the social processes through which customs are defined. These social processes, and the means by which disobedience is disciplined, is instrumental to the shaping of the connections between individuals and groups. The process of judgement and sanction is thus reparative of the needs of all parties involved, including those of the victim and their kin, and the broader needs of the group or community. It is not that one cannot draw direct connection between customary processes of punishment and the modern criminal trial. There are several connections ranging from mode of prosecution, an accusation made by a victim, the calling to answer of an accused, and a judge, which speak to some of the main characteristics of adversarial trials today. The point is that the criminal trial was an opportunity to redress and repair conflict between family members, or perhaps members of the community.

The blood feud, an informal challenge mounted between kinsmen and decided by the head of the family, indicates the constitutive purpose of early trials. Though informal by today's terms, the blood feud was the main means by which serious disputes between family members were resolved. Blood feuds involved a cycle of retaliatory violence in which the individual harmed or wronged, or their kin in cases of death, would seek to inflict a similar harm upon the culprit. Jacoby (1976: 152–153) indicates how the blood feud, as a form of restrained vendetta, sought to appease human emotions to the extent that it often led to a sense of restoration amongst family members and kinsmen:

> After the abandonment of unrestrained vendetta, the unsettled, and unsettling, mixture of vindictiveness and mercy characterised nearly every human arrangement for the domestication of revenge. However bitter the disagreement over solutions, there was a general agreement on the nature of the problem posed by the vindictive drive. It was taken for granted that human beings had a deep need – a need as sharp as hunger or sexual desire – to avenge their injuries, to restore a sense of equity when they felt their integrity had been violated. Different cultures accorded differing degrees of legitimacy to this need, but all societies took it upon themselves to regulate the vindictive impulse and, whenever possible, to bend it to some constructive purpose. The strong emotional appeal of vindictiveness was balanced by an awareness of the dangers unrestrained vengeance posed to orderly existence.

Jacoby (1976) sees the significance of restrained vengeance not only in terms of settling a desire for revenge, but also in the gradual control of unrestrained vengeance for the sake of an orderly existence. This is significant, as the customs associated with the blood feud ensured participation of the aggrieved parties in a process of settlement that provided for the meting out of human emotions that also, and perhaps most importantly, ensured the end of the feud or conflict. The customs associated with the blood feud therefore established a system of familiar regulation that provided for the first criminal 'trial' experience. This 'trial' involved direct participation by those parties involved in the dispute from accusation to punishment.

The role of blood feud and revenge is indicated by the relative longevity of the private settlement. Private settlements were a process whereby tribal clans or families agreed on appropriate retribution or restitution for the death or disablement of a member of one of the groups. This process transferred the harm or injury occasioned to the victim to the family or group, who assumed the responsibility for accruing, punishing or settling the dispute. The private settlement was an important advance on unrestrained vendetta for it removed the dispute from individuals to extend the consequences of crime outward to members of the victim's family or group. Thus, the decision to seek revenge, or to settle, not only impacted the victim themselves, but the whole group or family. The process of private settlement, therefore, was a socially significant one that brought communities together. The problem of private settlement, however, was that the meting out of revenge or the act of settlement agreed between the families may result in another killing which would then set the process of collective vendetta into motion again. Jacoby (1976: 123) explains:

> The historical meaning of 'private settlement' is an agreement between families, or tribal clans on appropriate retribution and/or restitution for the death of a member of one of the groups. A group, not an individual, therefore becomes the injured party or the offender. Private settlement was itself an advance over unrestrained vendetta; without such settlement, human beings would undoubtedly have rendered themselves extinct. The obvious deficiency of private settlement is that it does not always work; instead of a murder's being settled by restitution and a peace agreement, it is settled by yet another murder and the always unsettling resumption of collective vendetta.

Jacoby (1976) examines systems of legalised revenge, in terms of those states that prescribe retributive punishments by promulgating laws or codes by which such retributive punishments may be passed. For Jacoby (1976), revenge is still very much part of the criminal justice system of developed states even into the twentieth century. It may be that revenge comes to be codified in a set of rules governed by a penal code or sentencing law that requires a court to consider the seriousness of the offence, culpability of the offender, the justifications for punishment, and a range of punitive options, before determining the final sentence to be observed. Revenge is now reduced to a set of prescribed measurements that provide for an open or fair process that removed, as Jacoby (1976: 115) suggests, an individual's 'animus' for the even application of the rule of law. Rather than advocate a system of legalised revenge at the hands of victims or their kin, however, modern states remove the personal animus for three functions of law that seek to: punish the guilty, exonerate the innocent and deter those who might offend. An increased degree of mercy in the meting out of punishment does little to restrain revenge, though, as Jacoby (1976: 116) suggests, mercy is consistent with the process of judgement as to the deservedness of a particular punishment in given circumstances. Bloch (1961: 125–126) indicates how significant the blood feud was to familial groups:

> The Middle Ages, from beginning to end, and particularly the feudal era, lived under the sign of private vengeance. The onus, of course, lay above all on the wronged individual; vengeance was imposed on him as the most sacred of duties...
>
> The solitary individual, however, could do but little. Moreover, it was most commonly a death that had to be avenged. In this case the family group went into action and the *faide* (feud) came into being, to use the old Germanic word which spread little by little through the whole of Europe – 'the vengeance of the kinsmen which we call *faida*', as a German canonist expressed it. No moral obligation seemed more sacred than this...
>
> The whole kindred, therefore, placed as a rule under the command of a 'chieftain', took up arms to punish the murder of one of its members or merely a wrong that he had suffered.

Elias (1982a, 1988: 179–184) also sees a fundamental connection between conflict, community and the social. Elias (1982a) describes a civilising process whereby the control of violence shifted from individuals to the state such that the state comes to monopolise violence in order to control and pacify individuals. Elias (1988: 180) observes:

> The crucial point is the balance between the two functions of the monopoly of violence: the function for its controllers and for the members of the state-regulated society and, thus, the degree of

internal pacification. In former times power was distributed so unevenly that the controllers of the monopoly of violence could give absolute priority to its function for themselves over its function for those they ruled.

The civilising process, then, tells of the dislocation of the control of violence from individuals and groups to the state. Elias (1982a, 1982b) is critical of the assumption that the state ought to control violence as something alien to individuals. For Elias (1988: 178–182), violence is formative of individual social connections such that violence becomes an aspect of social structures. Violence is a part of human existence, as Elias (1988: 178) explains:

> The potential for aggressiveness can be activated by natural or social situations of a certain kind, above all by conflict.... Our habits of thought generate the expectation that everything we seek to explain about people can be explained in terms of isolated individuals. It is evidently difficult to adjust our thinking and, thus, the explanations of how people are interconnected in groups: that is, by means of social structures. Conflicts are an aspect of social structures. They are also an aspect of human life together with non-human nature: with the animals, plants, the moon and the sun. Human beings are by nature attuned to this life together with other humans, with nature, and with the conflicts all this entails.

However, feudal England did not possess a fully formed 'state', and the reach of the Crown was incomplete. Bloch (1961: 128–129) suggests that the customary practices of the blood feud outlast the Norman Conquest, and was even codified into local law into the thirteenth century. The English did seek to prohibit the more extreme instances of blood feud, directing wronged individuals or their kin to the local courts. However, the customary basis of the feud as providing the kin of the injured or murdered subject access to the body of the accused was such a significant aspect of communal rule that it was difficult to abolish. King William I did attempt to limit lawful blood feuds to the murder of a father or son. All other wrongs would need to be heard by a court in order to bring the feuding parties to reason, and to have them agree to 'treaties of armistice or reconciliation' (Bloch, 1961: 128). However, even where the King had provided direct orders limiting the blood feud, local Lords struggled to control the tendency toward such private means to justice. This was the era where crime was private, committed against one's self and one's kin, and individuals and families were reluctant to defer their historical right to the body of the accused to the local Lord or Crown:

> In short, except in England, after the Conquest, the disappearance of any legal right of vengeance was one of the aspects of the royal 'tyranny', they confined themselves to moderating the more extreme manifestations of practices which they were unable and perhaps unwilling to stop altogether. The judicial procedures themselves, when by chance the injured party preferred them to direct action, were hardly more than regularized vendettas. A significant illustration, in the case of wilful murder, is the allocation of rights and responsibilities laid down in 1232 by the municipal charter of Arques, in Artois. To the lord is assigned the property of the guilty man; to the kinsmen of his victim his person, so that they may put him to death. The right of lodging a complaint belonged almost invariably to the relatives alone; even in the thirteenth century in the best governed cities and principalities, in Flanders for example or in Normandy, the murderer could not receive his pardon from the sovereign or the judges unless he first reached agreement with the kinsmen or the victim.

The number and types of offences, which could be settled by blood, gradually decreased as the King asserted his right to regulate flagrant offences, and then all crimes as against the King's peace. Not all offences to the person were settled by the spilling of blood, with most victims extracting a pecuniary settlement, called wergild, from the offender. Where a simple wrong was involved, customary practice and habit would limit the payment required to settle the matter, which was ordinarily passed to the injured person. However, where the wrong was one of murder or mayhem, wergild would pass from the kinsmen of the offender to the kinsmen of the person wronged (Bloch, 1961: 130). This early mode of settlement, much like the blood feud, was thus communal in character and served to limit the personal resolution of disputes for judgement passed from one group, to another. Payment would only indemnify the offender when it came with an apology to the family of the victim. The group or clan thus became the basic organisational unit, which maintained its dominance as a mode of trial and dispute resolution well after England was conquered in 1066 and which may not have been substantially eroded until the Assize of Clarendon 1166 requiring itinerant justice and administration of each local county.[1]

The trial of animals

Trials are not limited to human wrongdoers. Animals were also commonly prosecuted in both ecclesiastical and secular courts. Animals were put on trial since antiquity, but the practice was common throughout the middle ages, and even throughout eighteenth century Europe. The court before which the animal was summonsed depended on the species and nature of the harm caused. Animals causing nuisance, which included acts such as destroying crops intended for human consumption, generally went before the ecclesiastical courts to be heard by a church official. The church courts also claimed jurisdiction over wild animals and even insects, such as plagues or swarms, potentially harmful to crops or feared as harbourers of disease. Where an animal caused serious injury or death to a person, the animal was tried and then punished in one of the secular courts. Domestic animals usually went on trial in the secular courts (see Girgen, 2003; Evans, 1987: xvii).

Both secular and ecclesiastical courts took proceedings against animals seriously, and there was a set trial procedure to be observed in each instance. Often animals accused of wrongdoing were afforded counsel at the expense of the community. Animals accused of an offence could be remanded in custody, at times with human prisoners. Where an animal was found guilty, they were punished. Punishment was usually death by hanging, and a professional hangman was often engaged for the purpose.

Ecclesiastical trials

Early records indicate that, as far back as the year 824, proceedings were commenced against a group of moles in Aosta, Italy, for destroying crops (Evans, 1987: 265). The moles were said to have harmed the people whose livelihood depended on the successful reaping of the crops. Other trials date back to the year 666, although such records may be informed by legendary sources and are thus unreliable (Evans, 1987: 265; see Girgen, 2003: 100). Ecclesiastical trials were first held across Europe, but Girgen (2003) indicates that records have them occurring in Switzerland, France, Germany, and Italy in particular. As church doctrine spread across Europe, the trial of animals became common in Denmark, Spain, Turkey, and even in Canada and Brazil. Like the moles of 824, animals put on trial by the church included pests, swarms and plagues, but generally not domesticated or farm animals. Such pests usually destroyed crops required for human survival. The practical advantage of putting a pest through an ecclesiastical trial was that it identified the source of the problem and possibly abated any further destruction. Unlike secular trials involving an individual domestic animal, the purpose was not to physically punish or kill the assailant. As would be expected, ecclesiastical judges almost always tried such plagues in the absence of the accused.

Ecclesiastical trials followed a fairly rigid procedure. The individual alleging the harm made their complaint to the judges of the ecclesiastical court, who would appoint a church representative to investigate the matter. The court then required public procession and prayer to satisfy God before the trial. If prayer failed, the judges would summon all offending animals to appear before the court. A procurator was appointed to represent the accused. Defence counsel applied themselves to their task, and generally took three approaches in order to seek an acquittal. If delay tactics failed, counsel would submit that the court had no jurisdiction over the accused, and failing that, would need to enter a defence that attempted to exculpate their client's actions. Bartholomew Chassenèe, a French defence lawyer, was one such animal lawyer (Evans, 1987: 18–20). By 1540 Chassenèe was appointed to the judicial assembly of the Parlement de Provence (a position corresponding to Chief Justice), but before that appointment he was called to defend the rats of Autun, in 1522 (see Girgen, 2003: 101–102). The rats were accused of destroying the province's barley crop. Defending the fact that his clients had failed to appear once summonsed, Chassenèe initially argued that his clients lived in various locations such that a single summons could not be served upon them. The court upheld the motion, and the summons was read throughout the parishes inhabited by the rats. Not surprisingly, the rats did not appear following the second summons. Chassenèe then submitted that the length and difficulty of the journey to court, and his client's fear of cats along the way, kept them from appearing. The usual result of the animal's failure to appear was a default judgment against them. The judges ruled that the animals were required to vacate the land or crop they had harmed and were given a short period of time, usually a number of days, to do so.

Secular trials

The more serious harms caused by animals, usually to humans by injury or death as a result of a direct attack, were dealt with by the secular courts. In 1457, in Savigny-sur-Etang, France, a five year old boy was killed by a sow and her six piglets, the animals found stained with blood. The sow was found guilty and was sentenced to be hanged by her hind legs. The six piglets received a pardon, on the basis of their youth and the fact that their mother had incited the offence (Evans, 1987: 153–154). These trials were common across Europe but also spread to the American colonies. In 1642, for example, in Massachusetts, a mare, a cow, and other cattle were executed along with Thomas Graunger, who stood accused of sexually assaulting the animals (Powers, 1966: 303; also see Girgen, 2003: 108).

The procedure for secular trials differed from that of ecclesiastical trials (Girgen, 2003: 99). Although ecclesiastical trials often focussed on groups of unknown animals or pests, crimes prosecuted in secular courts were often against an individual animal. The animals were also more likely to be kept domestically, which gave such animals ready access to humans, that in turn allowed for their individual identification should they cause harm or mischief. The animal accused would be generally punished by sentence of death, as opposed to the mode of punishment in ecclesiastical courts, by blessing or prayer. After an allegation of harm had been levied, the animal was apprehended and brought to court. The animal was then prosecuted by way of formal accusation before a judge, together with the assistance of defence counsel (see Girgen, 2003: 99). Once the trial commenced, witnesses were called to testify against the accused. As with charges dealt with in an ecclesiastical court, the animal defendants were most often found guilty and sentenced to death. There is evidence that some trials resulted in an acquittal, as with the 1457 case involving the sow and her piglets. Acquittals generally resulted where the animals could not be blamed for the damage occasioned, and crimes of bestiality may have resulted in a successful human prosecution, whilst the animals went free (Evans, 1987: 150).

The punishments exacted against animals were similar in many respects to those imposed on human prisoners. Evans (1987: 206–207) indicates that punishments inflicted against animals 'sought to inflict the greatest possible amount of suffering on the offender and showed a diabolical fertility of invention in devising new methods of torture even for the pettiest trespasses'. Animals were also put to the rack, in an attempt to extract a confession, although they were usually hanged. Animals were also buried or burned alive, beheaded or stoned to death. If the animal was highly valued or useful, such as a workhorse or oxen, the judge may exercise their discretion to merely confiscate the animal (Girgen, 2003: 112). What this indicates is that the prosecution of animals was symbolic to the extent that the trial was more about localising human wrongdoing, where evident, or restoring local harmony through the sacrifice of the animal accused. This was significant, given that direct parallels present between the prosecution of animals and that of humans. The trial was significant because it resolved a local dispute.

The criminal trial as local governance

The customary roots of the criminal trial remain significant even though the trial, from the end of the eleventh century onwards, became a more formal apparatus of monarchal rule. The formation of hundreds and the tything system for the management of local crime proved to be too parochial for the regulation of crime and social order as a matter significant to the Crown. A national system for the management of crime, and the trial of wrongdoers in particular, was required (as to the foundation of this system, see Baker, 1990: 26–28). This section demonstrates the significant shift in governance from the use of hundred courts to the rise of the appeal of felony and system of presentment as constituted under the reign of King Henry II by the Assize of Clarendon 1166 and Assize of Northampton 1177.

Communal rule: Hundred court and the rise of presentment

The resolution of conflict as an aspect of customary law as based on vendetta or the blood feud demonstrates how the early criminal trial sought to reconcile individuals and families by including those individuals relevant to the original harm. Although this form of trial is significant to the genealogy of the criminal trial the informality and inconsistency of customary practices did little to control violence between groups. This was especially the case where families and groups grew into larger units, villages or towns. The English devised a means by which traditional customary practices could be preserved into a more organised structure for the management and regulation of local conduct, which included dealing with offences. For the purpose of establishing a local administration and means of justice freemen were grouped into ten, called tythings, with a tything-man appointed as a representative of each. Each tything was further grouped into ten to form the hundred. Above the hundred stood the shire (see Baker, 1990: 8; Cam, 1960: 9–19, 167–187). At a time where the reach of the Crown to all England was incomplete, and where some hundreds fell on private land, a steward was appointed to connect the hundred to the local lord and manor.

In the tenth century, the laws of Athelstan noted the division of the shires or counties into hundreds for the government of local order. A hundred was defined as a parcel of land that could contain around one hundred freemen, headed by a hundred-man or hundred eolder. The hundred-man was responsible for the administration of justice between the members of the hundred, who were further divided into groups of ten called tythings. Each tythings was headed by a tything-man. Each hundred held a court for the maintenance of order and government within the hundred. By the twelfth century, the hundred court was held up to twelve times each year. Certain hundreds held their court in a given place while other hundreds moved their court with each sitting. The hundred court was charged with the resolution of local disputes and also sought to maintain the system of familial responsibility and loyalty, known as frankpledge, to local lords and eventually the King (Baker, 1990: 7–8). Frankpledge required families to share responsibility and swear an oath of fealty to the local lord or knight and required the tything-man to produce any person from within their tything that was suspected of a crime. To facilitate such a process the hundred court met monthly to transact ordinary judicial business, but also met twice yearly to ensure that every member of the hundred was 'in borh', that is, pledged good behaviour. This also provided a mechanism for the presentment of persons accused of wrongdoing, or of allegations requiring investigation (Baker, 1990: 8). The fifteenth-century saw the decline of frankpledge, as local constables were increasingly introduced reporting to the justices of the peace.

A rudimentary system of localised justice was thus created to control local crime and to assist in the production of those suspected of committing an offence to the tything-man, and then upward to the hundred-man. The hundred-man had a duty to control crime locally but in so doing, administered a system of justice that was more consistent with past customary practice, as based on privately negotiated settlements between families. This system for the administration of justice was undoubtedly a more organised version of dispute settlement than the blood feud. However, it still involved customary practice to the extent that accusation and judgment was localised and often familial to the extent that the process of accusation and modes of proof adopted, trial by ordeal by hot irons or cold water, was led by the customary means by which guilt was established (see Holdsworth, 1903–38, 2: 221, 283). Trial by fire involved the placing of hot stones or irons on the skin of the accused. If the resultant wound healed, the accused would be not guilty. If the wound festered, the accused would stand convicted. Clearly, most individuals subject to trial by fire were found guilty. However, Hyams (1981: 90–126) suggests that the outcome of the ordeal was suited to trials within small communities as the result, death if guilty or banishment if innocent, was decided on the basis of the opinion that had already formed as to the guilt of the accused. The ordeal was thus interpretive to the extent that it involved judgement and sanction between community members known to one another.

By the end of the twelfth-century, England fell into disorder following the reign of King Stephen. King Stephen was in a long dispute with Empress Matilda, the daughter and heir of King Henry I. Although Empress Matilda ruled England for a brief period, she was never crowned, and so has never been formally recognised as a reigning monarch. Instead, Matilda's cousin, Stephen, acceded the thrown which created an immense rivalry between the two. This resulted in communal unrest and civil war during the reign of King Stephen. This left England in a state of disorder upon the ascent of Henry II to the throne. King Henry II was faced with civil unrest following years of war in which each of the warring camps of Matilda and Stephen gave away the others' land, hiring soldiers to wage war against the other, many of whom instead took to crime in a state generally lacking local government and control. Other problems also abound, including property disputes resulting from the granting of land and the dislocation of traditional or hereditary owners who were at war, or otherwise fighting in the Crusades.

With a lack of local infrastructure for the management and regulation of crime, and in particular, a secular trial process for those suspected of wrongdoing, Henry II went about constituting a process for the centralised regulation of crime and justice. This system, instigated under the Assize of Clarandon 1166 and later consolidated by the Assize of Northampton 1177, nonetheless initiated a trial process that was still very much under the control of local populations, and preserved the system of private prosecution that came be known as the appeal of felony. The Assize of 1166, proclaimed at Clarendon in 1166, took power from the local courts and thus the local nobility established during the reign of King Stephen, returning such power to the Crown.

The Assize of Clarendon 1166 proclaimed:

> In the first place the said King Henry ordained on the advice of all his barons, for preserving peace and maintaining justice, that inquiry be made through the several counties and through the several hundreds by twelve more lawful men of the hundred and by four more lawful men of each vill, upon oath that they will tell the truth, whether in their hundred or in their vill there is any man cited or charged as himself being a robber or murderer or thief or any one who has been a receiver of robbers or murderers or thieves

since the lord king was king. And let the justices inquire this before themselves and the sheriffs before themselves.

And he who shall be found by the oath of the aforesaid cited or charged as having been a robber or murderer or thief or a receiver of them since the lord king was king, let him be arrested and go to the judgment of water, and let him swear that he was not a robber or murderer or thief or a receiver of them since the lord king was king, to the value of five shillings so far as he knows.

And if the lord of him who was arrested or his steward or his men demand him by pledge within the third day after his arrest, let him be given up and his chattels until he make his law.

The significance of the Assize of 1166 lies in the way it sought to transform the criminal law not by correcting or amending the substantive law but by insisting that it be administered according to the King's will. This meant that localised or customary procedures for the testing of guilt or meting out of punishment could be displaced for one procedure for all of England. Although the Assize of 1166 provided for trial by ordeal, a mode of proof that was widely accepted throughout England, it insisted upon it rather than leaving the trial to whatever process had become customary in each county. The requirement that the King's royal justices attend each county to hear past and present accusations brought by presentment also sought to utilise an ancient institution, the presenting jury, as consisting of groups of persons from the hundred, for the purpose of the systematic administration of justice throughout England (see Warren, 1973: 281–285). The sheriff also gained the power to apprehend felons across county lines, and could pass through the lands of local lords to apprehend suspects. Prior to the Assize of 1166 local lords often excluded the sheriff to claim jurisdiction over the felons complained of. The Assize of 1166 thus set in motion a new administrative procedure for the regulation of criminal justice. Its brilliance lay not as an executive order modifying the law, but in utilising it so as to do away with variable custom that made it impossible to control local order given the numerous means by which accusations of wrongdoing were tried. Better still, the Assize of 1166 sought to unite those customary practices most acceptable to local populations with the institutions of the Crown for the maintenance of similar justice throughout England. This saw the coming together of the trial by ordeal of water,[2] the presenting jury, and King's royal justices, for the consolidation of criminal justice for all England. The Assize of 1166 did not therefore do away with customary law *per se*, it utilised it for the benefit of the Crown.

The Assize of Northampton 1177, believed to have been passed at a council held in Northampton in January 1176, was largely based on the Assize of Clarendon 1166. The Assize of 1177 sought to continue the practice of presentment of indictment of felony by 12 men of the hundred, but also expanded the applicable range of felonies from murder, theft and robbery to include falsification or forgery and arson. Later clauses prescribe that the King has a right to bring certain cases within the jurisdiction of his court. The Assize of 1177 represented a strong response to the disorder of the time, by granting additional powers to the King's royal justices by establishing new offences that they could hear and determine, and providing for new punishments, specifically the removal of an offender's right hand. The Assize of 1177 also sought to provide a means by which unresolved property disputes could be determined, and is the first official document to contain details of the assize of *mort d'ancestor* and *novel disseisin*. This helped consolidate the rights of knightly tenants, making possession of land subject to and secured by common law.

The Assize of Northampton 1177 proclaimed:

> If, by the oath of twelve knights of the hundred – or, should knights not be present, by the oath of twelve lawful freemen – and by the oath of four men of every vill in the hundred, any one has been accused in the presence of the lord king's justices of murder or theft or robbery, or of receiving men who have committed such [crimes], or of falsification or arson, he shall go to the ordeal of water; and if he fails [in the ordeal], he shall lose one foot. And to increase the severity of the law, it was added at Northampton that with the foot he should lose his right hand, and that he should abjure the realm and depart from it within forty days. And if he should be cleared by the [ordeal of] water, let him find sureties and remain in the kingdom, unless he has been accused of murder or other disgraceful felony by the community (commune) of the county and the lawful knights of his own countryside (patria). If [now] he has been accused in the aforesaid manner of this [sort of crime], although he has been cleared by the [ordeal of] water, let him nevertheless go out of the kingdom within forty days and take with him his chattels, saving the rights of his lords; and let him abjure the realm [on pain of being] in the lord king's mercy. This assize, moreover, shall hold good for all the time since the assize was made at Clarendon down to the present, and henceforward during the lord king's pleasure, with regard to murder, treason, and arson, and with regard to all [offenses in] the preceding chapters, except minor thefts and robberies

which were committed in time of war, as of horses, oxen, and lesser things.

Trial by assize was further codified in the Magna Carta 1215, which provides:

> Inquests of novel disseisin, of mort d'ancestor, and of darrein presentment shall not be held elsewhere than in their own county courts, and that in manner following; We, or, if we should be out of the realm, our chief justiciar, will send two justiciaries through every county four times a year, who shall alone with four knights of the county chosen by the county, hold the said assizes in the county court, on the day and in the place of meeting of that court.

King Henry II had created, in the Assize of Clarendon 1166 and Assize of Northampton 1177, a system of itinerant justice through which individuals from each hundred were to notify the King's royal justices by presentment of indictment of felony for certain offences prescribed in the Assizes of 1166 and 1177. The royal justices would travel from Westminster in London to each county once every seven years where they would call on the knights of the county to summon freemen to assemble to issue the royal justices with presentments to be tried upon their arrival (Baker, 1990: 16–19). This process essentially established the grand jury, charged with the gathering of information or evidence upon which the accusations of wrongdoing were made. The general commission was the Assize of Eyre, but other commissions of more limited jurisdiction included gaol delivery and oyer and terminer. The commission of gaol delivery issued to the local justices allowed them to try all persons held in custody, deciding whether the prisoner should be put to the ordeal. The commission of oyer and terminer instructed the local justices to hear and determine particular offences in particular areas or counties. The royal justices generally held more expansive commissions, and could take the presentments and decide whether the accused ought to be put to the ordeal and, if so, which type of ordeal.

This new procedure also discontinued the old process of trial known as 'compurgation'. Under compurgation, an accused who pleaded not guilty would be required to swear that they did not commit the offence in question. An accused who found a sufficient number of neighbours to swear that they believed him was acquitted. The presenting jury effectively did away with compurgation although the ordeal remained the favoured mode of proof. The ordeal was essentially a religious test of guilt or innocence presided by minister of the church or cleric. Throughout the early thirteenth century the ordeal was increasingly questioned as a mode of proof and in 1215 the Fourth Lateran Council refused to permit clerics from participating in trial by ordeal. The process of the ordeal leading to some form of punishment – death if guilty or banishment if not – meant that the presenting jury became the main instigator of the criminal process that would lead, in one form or another, to a prescribed punishment. Trial by battle remained available though the jury system instituted by the Assize of 1166 slowly became accepted as the more dominant mode of proof.

The significant changes brought about by the Assizes of 1166 and 1177 did not go unchallenged. Disputes over jurisdiction arose and many clergy demanded, should they be accused of an offence, that they answer to an ecclesiastical court. The Assize of 1166 therefore promulgated a judicial process that alienated a significant proportion of the population from their preferred mode of trial. The Assize of 1166 further resulted in a power struggle between the King and Thomas Becket, Archbishop of Canterbury. Becket argued that secular courts had no jurisdiction over the clergy, as it was the privilege of the clergy to be accused or tried before a ecclesiastical court. However, following the murder of Becket by four of Henry's knights in 1170, public sentiment turned against the King. King Henry II was forced to make a compromise being that clergy could be subject to canon law, with only but a few exceptions. This compromise led to the rise of benefit of clergy, whereby persons robed in ecclesiastical dress would be transferred to an ecclesiastical court. Overtime, the requirement of dress declined for a literacy test, essentially those who could read from the bible would proceed before an ecclesiastical court. In 1351, this benefit was extended to all who could read.

The general eyre

From the middle of the twelfth century, the Crown sent the King's royal justices to hear and determine felonies throughout all England. The judges commissioned to undertake this circuit were drawn from the *curia regis*, or King's court. Known as justices in eyre, or *justucuae errantes*, their commission enabled them to cover the whole realm and hear both criminal and civil cases. The general eyre was an administrative as well as judicial circuit to the extent that it required the royal justices to enquire into the conduct of local officials and take oaths of allegiance to the King. The Assize of Northampton 1177 provides such additional duties, thus:

> from the first Sunday after Easter to the first Sunday after Pentecost, the justices shall receive oaths of fealty to the lord king from all who wish to dwell in the kingdom: namely, from earls, barons, knights, freeholders, and even peasants. And whoever refuses to swear fealty is to be seized as an enemy of the lord king. The justices are also to command that all those who have not yet performed their homage and allegiance to the lord king shall come at the time assigned them and perform homage and allegiance to the king as to their liege lord.

The justices in eyre usually held various judicial commissions. The justices also settled land disputes that had occurred during the previous reign of King Stephen. The judicial commissions included the commission of oyer and terminer, a general commission to hear and determine offences, usually of a particular class at a particular location. The commission of gaol delivery, which was added during King Edward I's reign, allowed the justices to try people held in the local gaols. A commission of *nisi prius* provided that the justices determine civil matters unless they had already been referred to the common pleas in Westminster.

The powers available to the eyre justices were extremely wide. Once they arrived in each county, they took over the county court and summoned people from within the hundred or surrounding area to answer indictments of felony brought by the presenting jury. Serious offenders may be presented by the sheriff, apprehended or imprisoned prior to the justice's arrival. The eyre justices also summonsed others to appear before them, to answer questions regarding the conduct of Crown officers, to inquire into local affairs, taxes owed to the King, to scrutinise the conduct of the sheriff, such as to ensure the King's interests were secured. The commission was *ad omnia placita* – to deal with all kinds of pleas – which included the audit of local affairs and allowed the justices to hear pleas of the Crown and common pleas not otherwise heard at Westminster. Into the fourteenth century, owing to the plenary power of the eyre justices, the general eyre became feared and was generally unpopular, and was gradually replaced by the court of assize, a similar court of itinerant justice concerned with pleas of the Crown or criminal matters. After the decline of the general eyre in the fourteenth century, the commissions of gaol delivery and oyer and terminer became the common commissions under which the local or royal justices dealt with accusations of serious crime.

Commission of oyer and terminer

Oyer and terminer, to hear and determine, was one of the commissions commanding a royal justice to make expeditious and diligent inquiry into all treasons, felonies and misdemeanors committed in the counties specified in the commission. The justices held the duty to determine each matter according to law. The justice of assize would inquire into the crimes committed by summoning the presenting jury. After a true bill of indictment had been determined, the justices proceeded to hear and determine by means of the petit jury (Baker, 1990: 25).

The words oyer and terminer were also used to signal the court which had jurisdiction to try offences, and the jurisdictional limits to which the commission of oyer and terminer extended. Baker (1990: 30) indicates that general commissions of oyer and terminer were issued but it was also common for justices to be limited to the specific commissions to keep the peace, or to hear and determine a list of prescribed offences. Justices could only act according to the extent of the commission held. Commissions to keep the peace allowed justices to arrest suspects and to commit them to gaol, or to require a surety to bind someone over to keep the peace. This commission effectively created the office of justice of the peace. The general commission allowed justices to hear and determine the cases so listed. Thus, general commissions were issued to allow justices to hear and determine those cases not reserved for the assize justices. Such commissions limited the types of offences that could be heard, to be determined collectively before a session of the pace, held four times a year. This limited commission effectively created quarter sessions, the court assigned to deal with misdemeanor cases leaving the gross felonies for the justices of assize. Oyer and terminer distinguished justices from those empowered to try or release prisoners in a specified gaol, who held the commission of gaol delivery.

Commission of gaol delivery

Imprisonment was not a common mode of punishment until the eighteenth century but offenders apprehended on hue and cry or by the sheriff could be remanded until the eyre justices attended on circuit. As gaols became more popular and more offenders were remanded in custody, and with the number of cases before the general eyre or later court of assize increasing, commissions of gaol delivery were issued to relieve the gaols from overpopulation. Commissions of gaol delivery allowed justices to attend a gaol to deliver prisoners to trial. Such commissions specified a particular gaol, or number of gaols, or were limited to prisoners accused of a particular offence.

Reliance on gaol delivery increased during the fourteenth century, with most counties with a gaol being used to remand accused people (see Kimball, 1978: 19–27). Each gaol might have been visited several times a year by a royal justice from Westminster together with justices drawn from the local gentry. The fifteenth century witnessed an increase in the number of commissions of gaol delivery being issued to ensure that offences subject to the King's jurisdiction were dealt with expeditiously. These commissions also enabled the King's royal justices to enquire into the state of gaols, and to order maintenance, repair or the building of new gaols, bridges and the administration of asylums (see Baker, 1990: 20).

From inquisitorial to adversarial justice

The history of the trial is significant as it shows how the trial has been forged out discursive processes that include, rather than exclude, public and private debate. Historically, the victim has been central to the formation of the criminal trial and to institutions of criminal justice, such as policing and prosecutions (see Kirchengast, 2006: 79–96; Doak, 2008: 2–7). The assize trials of the twelfth and thirteenth centuries indicate just how central victims were. Even after the assent of the Assize of 1166 and 1176, royal decrees that sought to formalise prosecution procedure by presentment before the King's royal justices, the victim remained central (Warren, 1973: 284, 355). Prosecution procedure prior to the Assize of 1166 involved the ordeal or trial by combat. The Assizes of 1166 and 1176 encouraged the development of a trial process by presentment of indictment before a jury called from the county in which the alleged offences were committed. Originally, the jury was only ordered to present the indictment, but this soon extended to the determination of liability, after the ordeal was outlawed in 1215 and following the decline of trial by battle.

What is important is that during this process, which significantly established trial procedure at the hands of the Crown, much as it stands today, the victim and community remained central. Indeed, without the victim bringing the accusation in the first instance, and then agreeing to act as prosecutor, most offences would not have been reported nor prosecuted (Klerman, 2001: 8–10). This was observed by Blackstone (1783, 4: 311):

[O]n an indictment, which is at the suit of the King, the King may pardon and remit the execution; on an appeal, which is at the suit of a private subject... the King can no more pardon it than he can remit the damages recovered in an action of battery.

The customary basis of the trial even after 1166 allowed for more than the participation of the victim. It instituted a process that was accessible to the community and the Crown for the management or regulation of local disputes, and for the maintenance of local order. The trial on circuit from Westminster had come to replace frankpledge as the main mode of communal policing and government control. It also dealt with the variability of localised and customary justice to the extent that it was mete out differently between the hundreds. The process instituted by Henry II, moreover, retained the key features of the trial that gave agency to those persons deemed relevant to the conflict or dispute. King Henry II therefore established a similar trial process that retained its key character as a decentralised mechanism of local justice and dispute resolution. The trial also retained the feature that allowed it to be open to modification and reform. The trial was thus established as an institution of social power that adapted to and enabled social change.

For instance, the ordeal declined after 1215 not only out of the questionable result of trial by fire or water, but also due to the fact that the ordeal was best suited to doing justice in small communities where the individual accused, supporting witnesses, and judge, would likely know one another. Hyam (1981) notes that the result of the ordeal would be interpreted consistently with whatever opinion had already been formed as to the guilt of the accused. Clearly, whether an accused sank, or was able to withstand the pain of fire or the hot irons, had little to do with actual guilt as we come to define it today. As the legitimacy of the ordeal was based on communal knowledge of the offence and offender, the tenacity of this model of proof fell into question when the accused was presented before the jury and King's royal justices on circuit from Westminster, who would have a limited knowledge of the offence and offender. Despite its questionable status, however, Assizes of 1166 and 1177 did not abolish this mode of proof but sought to utilise it as the main mode of proof acceptable to the counties of England. Changes in church policy toward its use saw the decline of the ordeal, to be replaced by wager of battle or trial by jury into the thirteenth century. Trial by ordeal could not be simply abolished but was required to be superseded with a mode of proof more acceptable to the community.

For the Assize of 1166 and 117 to succeed, therefore, the trial had to be approved locally as the means by which justice would be done. As such, the victim and community remained central throughout this transformation. Whether in Westminster or on assize in the counties of England, the criminal trial remained democratised because it was accessible to the victim and community as key constituents in its administration and development. Along with the King's sheriffs responsible for the summoning of the presenting jury on assize, the victim would assist in the apprehension of the felon, perhaps keeping them imprisoned to allow the sheriff to bring the accused before the assize, so that the victim could then bring the information before the royal justices to initiate the prosecution unless otherwise informed by the presenting jury.

The assize of eyre and later, the court of assize, provided for a standard process for the meting out of justice in each county of England. This process was significant as it provided for the development of a trial experience that was both democratic and participatory, based on local custom to the extent that the administration of justice to all England would allow. Local government was thus preserved even though a standard trial process began to emerge. The use of different judicial commissions limited the exercise of power to a class of cases such that different justices were required to service different aspects of criminal justice. The use of royal justices from Westminster alongside justices commissioned oyer and terminer or gaol delivery meant that different courts emerged to deal with particular offences in particular places. A decentralised process that allowed for localised justice avoided the fear generated by the general eyre. The rise of quarter sessions as a court of limited jurisdiction with the most serious felonies tried in a court of assize evidences the genesis of a criminal court system that responded to the need to govern locally.

The Assize of 1166 thus set into motion the transformation of the criminal trial from one based on trial by ordeal or wager of battle, to one based on an evidentiary model, in which evidence was collected and then considered by freemen before the royal justices. Although the Assizes of 1166 and 1176 supported trial by ordeal, the result of the ordeal was not considered to be a consistent nor rigorous means of determining guilt. Further, by being called into question and then subject to the ordeal, the offender was to be punished, in one way or another. This opened up the basis for the jury as the means by which evidence was tested against an accusation.

Langbein (2003) indicates that the origins of the altercation trial of circa 1400–1700 saw the emergence of a court that was increasingly concerned with the weighing up of evidence and arguments. This saw the beginning of an era in which the criminal trial could be seen to 'act judicially'. This era, however, came to be seen as one in which the defendant was denied of rights now deemed fundamental to the constitution of the trial in the first instance. The mode of evidence was largely based on confrontation and the prisoner was denied a copy of the indictment until he or she reached court. The accused was also compelled to speak to answer the accusation, and the jury was increasingly drawn from a wider area than the county in which the offence occurred. The accused could test the evidence of the witnesses, but could not call sworn witnesses until 1702. While this period evidenced many deficiencies of fair trial procedure as we know it today, it does indicate the slow and gradual emergence of the key values that characterise the latter period of the trial from circa 1700, the adversarial trial. The period from 1400 thus evidenced the gravitation to the value of 'truth' as a means of determining the guilt of the accused. Throughout this period, the victim still actively prosecuted the offender, especially on circuit at assize, away from the Crown officers who mainly worked in London. The court of assize still provided a mechanism for Crown control, local government and a means of attaining localised justice.

The era of the adversarial trial presented the normative constraints on trial process that characterise the criminal trial today. The development of a legal profession led to the development of a more adversarial trial experience, despite the defendant being granted bail or provided a copy of the indictment to best prepare a defence against the prosecution case. The *Trials for Felony Act 1836* (Imp) (6 and 7 Wm IV c 114) provided that all persons indicted on felony be entitled to make their defence by counsel, despite the fact that it was already commonplace for defendants to be represented (see *Dietrich v The Queen* (1992) 177 CLR 292 at 301 per Mason CJ and McHugh J). Most notably during this period, the role of the victim as necessary to the policing and prosecution process declined following the rise of an organised police force from 1829 in London, and soon thereafter in the counties, and the rise of a ODPP in the later nineteenth century. Prior to that, Crown officers prosecuted notable cases as indicated by the range of cases reported in the Old Bailey from 1674.

The nineteenth century thus saw the emergence of the reconstructive trial, such that the trial emerged as a contest between prosecution and defence, and where procedural and evidentiary safeguards increasingly protected the defendant. The rise of a summary jurisdiction saw the bifurcation of the criminal trial with the judge and jury trial occupying popular conception as to the form the trial takes. Professional police and detectives, in addition to expert evidence made available through the growth of the sciences, meant that more technical evidence was led at trial. Trials thus became lengthy, and it was not uncommon for trials to last more than one day. Trials became less concerned with anecdotal or circumstantial evidence but with the examination of scientific and forensic material that could place the accused at the scene of the crime. Counsel were increasingly required to organise their case and present their arguments. The judge no longer took an active role examining the accused but still sought to organise the evidence and instruct the jury. The judge became arbiter of law and the jury, arbiter of fact.

3
Shifting Boundaries: Recent Changes to Criminal Justice Policy

The modern criminal trial as an institution of justice is in a state of significant transition. Various influences have come to bear upon the scope, function and form of the criminal trial. Many of these influences, such as terrorism, victim rights, and the need for expediency, remain controversial as to the extent to which such influences ought to be entertained as influencing the scope of the adversarial trial. However, modern criminal justice policy is operating in accordance with a number of competing discourses that challenge the adversarial model in various ways. As the previous chapter has indicated, the criminal trial has never taken a particular form or function to the exclusion of social change. As an institution, it has always been open to change. What the present debate over the scope of the criminal trial shows, moreover, is how the criminal trial continues to transform to meet a number of competing needs. This is not to say that the modification of the trial ought to go unchallenged. We should protect the extent to which ill thought out, reactionist, or popular demand may influence the criminal trial. This chapter will demonstrate, however, that various contemporary influences now seek to dislocate the criminal trial from those characteristics that identify it as an institution of adversarial justice exclusively. This, arguably, is consistent with the continued modification of the criminal trial over time. It shows that the criminal trial continues to be shaped through an array of discourses that render the criminal trial a transgressive institution of social justice. This further challenges the assumption that the criminal trial ought to be constituted through a set of normative assumptions that prescribe its form.

The criminal trial is facing various changes brought about by broad shifts in criminal justice policy. By way of selective indication, this chapter will consider the rise of a number of changes within criminal law and justice in order to highlight the broader influences on the modern criminal trial. These include the extent to which the trial ought to be modified, or even circumvented, to allow for expedient justice, in the form of summary justice, committals, plea or charge bargaining, or through the issuing of infringements or penalty notices. Other challenges, such as the requisite need for a jury, or unanimous jury verdicts, indicates how the mode of proof that was increasingly instituted following the Assize of Clarendon 1166 is now being dispensed with for an alternative, usually more expedient, means to justice, including judge alone trials. The law and order debate, or the need to modify institutions of justice, including the police, bail and appropriate punishments, the use of infringements, as well as new court procedures for the handing out of domestic control orders and ASBOs, is increasingly responding to a fear of crime, expediency and the regulation and control of groups of known deviant or 'risky' offenders. The defences available and procedural limitations against double prosecution have also been significantly modified or reconsidered in light of changing perspectives on the balance of rights the trial ought to protect. The abolition or reform of the defence of provocation, and the modification of the rule against double jeopardy, feature as key examples. The rise of victim lawyers also suggests how the traditional ambit of the adversarial criminal trial, as a contest between defence and state, is changing to accommodate a new agent of justice formerly excluded as irrelevant or prejudicial to 'public' justice – the victim of crime. The rise of legislative frameworks for the integration of victims, represented through counsel, now challenges the basic premise that prosecutorial decision-making is exclusive of the victim, and a linear construct of 'community'. Terrorism also responds to our fear of events of mass destruction and has perpetuated expansive policing techniques and the proliferation of new offences and procedures in the form of control orders to target persons suspected of terrorist activity or domestic disorder. Whether control orders are constituted within the criminal law is arguable, however, given the types of restrictions commonly contained in such orders are similar to those forward-looking sentencing options available to the criminal court.

Expedient justice

The criminal trial as an ascribed apparatus of justice for the determination of liability is increasingly circumvented by changes to aspects of the trial process that allow for quicker, more expedient outcomes.

Various forces are said to legitimate this drive for efficiency. Chapter 1 detailed the significant number of cases disposed of in the local court of NSW before a magistrate sitting alone. Similar statistics may be found across the common law world, as parliament prescribe offences to be heard by a magistrate, which would otherwise be disposed of on indictment before a judge and jury. The rise of infringements and penalty notices as a means of disposing of a matter without court proceedings of any sort is also indicative of a movement away from the trial process. Where matters are disposed of on indictment, the traditional institutions of justice that characterise the criminal trial, such as the grand or petty jury, are increasingly being sidestepped for committal proceedings before a magistrate, judge alone trials or jury trials by majority verdict. The role of charge and plea bargaining as a means of subverting the trial for sentencing also suggests an alternative means by which the traditional criminal trial process may be avoided.

Committal proceedings

The decision to send an accused to trial resided in the discretion of the grand jury until the mid nineteenth century. The grand jury came into significance following the Assize of Clarendon 1166 and the requirement to form a jury of freemen to present the eyre justices with accusations or indictments to be tried before them. The presenting jury in the twelfth century was self-informing, in that it investigated the accusations of wrongdoing itself. Over time, the justice of the peace took responsibility for bringing offenders to justice and sought to interrogate them in order to present the grand jury, no longer self-informing, with evidence in support of a true bill of indictment. *Grassby v The Queen* (1989) 168 CLR 1 sets out the early role of the grand jury (at 11):

> It has consistently been held that committal proceedings do not constitute a judicial inquiry but are conducted in the exercise of an executive or ministerial function. See *Ammann v. Wegener* [1972] HCA 58; (1972) 129 CLR 415, at pp. 435–436; *Lamb v. Moss* [1983] FCA 254; (1983) 76 FLR 296, at p. 321; [1983] FCA 254; 49 ALR 533, at p. 559; *Reg. v. Nicholl* (1862) 1 QSCR 42; *In re The Mercantile Bank; Ex parte Millidge* (1893) 19 VLR 527, at p. 539; *Huddart, Parker & Co. Proprietary Ltd. v. Moorehead* [1909] HCA 36; (1909) 8 CLR 330, at pp. 356–357; *Ex parte Cousens; Re Blacket* (1946) 47 SR (NSW) 145; *Ex parte Coffey; Re Evans* (1971) 1 NSWLR 434. The explanation is largely to be found in history. A magistrate in conducting committal proceedings is exercising the powers of a justice of the peace. Justices

originally acted, in the absence of an organized police force, in the apprehension and arrest of suspected offenders. Following the Statutes of Philip and Mary of 1554 and 1555 (1 & 2 Philip & Mary c.13; 2 & 3 Philip & Mary c.10), they were required to act upon information and to examine both the accused and the witnesses against him. The inquiry was conducted in secret and one of its main purposes was to obtain evidence to present to a grand jury. The role of the justices was thus inquisitorial and of a purely administrative nature. It was the grand jury, not the justices, who determined whether the accused should stand trial.

The role of the justice of the peace was largely inquisitorial and administrative. From the advent of an organised police force in 1829 in London, the role of the justice of the peace changed to reflect the practices of modern day magistrates. However, at least in NSW, a magistrate was required to determine whether an accused person be remanded in custody or granted bail. Their original task was not to commit the accused to trial. That role was still preserved for the grand jury. However, in order to determine wither the accused ought to be remanded, they needed to conduct a cursory evaluation of the evidence against the accused (see *Indictable Offences Act 1848* (UK), the 'Sir John Jervis' Act'). In NSW and elsewhere, including England, the grand jury thus became a formality and in 1933 the grand jury was formally abolished pursuant to the *Administration of Justice (Miscellaneous Provisions) Act 1933* (UK). However, as *Grassby v The Queen* (1989) 168 CLR 1 provides, committal proceedings as they are constituted today do not commit the accused to trial in a technical sense. Rather, committals remain an administrative function that determines whether the accused be discharged, or held pending bail (at 13–15):

> Section 5 of the *Australian Courts Act* and s572 of the *Crimes Act* have been repealed by ss4 and 3 and Sched.1 of the *Miscellaneous Acts (Public Prosecutions) Amendment Act 1986* (NSW). Indictable offences are now punishable by information – to be called an indictment – on behalf of the Crown in the name of the Attorney-General or the Director of Public Prosecutions: *Criminal Procedure Act*, s4(1); *Director of Public Prosecutions Act 1986* (NSW), s.7. A Crown Prosecutor, acting in the name and on behalf of the Director of Public Prosecutions, may also find a bill of indictment: *Crown Prosecutors Act 1986* (NSW), s5(1)(b). Thus in New South Wales indictment on behalf of the Crown in the name of the Attorney-General or the

Director of Public Prosecutions takes the place of the grand jury's bill and the indictment founded upon it. The Attorney-General or Director of Public Prosecutions is not bound by the decision of a magistrate to commit or not to commit a person for trial. An indictment may be filed whether or not the accused has been committed for trial upon the charge contained in the indictment, indeed, even if the accused has been discharged in committal proceedings: *Criminal Procedure Act*, s4(2). See *Reg. v. Cummings* (1846) 1 Legge 289; *Reg. v. Walton* (1851) 1 Legge 706; *R. v. Baxter* (1904) 5 SR (NSW) 134.

...

Committal for trial does not in New South Wales determine, as it now effectively does in the United Kingdom, whether a person charged with an offence shall be indicted. He will, of course, ordinarily stand trial if committed, although not necessarily so, and a person discharged may nevertheless be indicted. The powers of a magistrate in committal proceedings are thus, strictly speaking, still confined to determining whether the person charged shall be discharged, committed to prison to await trial or admitted to bail and do not involve the exercise of a judicial function.

The rise of committal proceedings cannot therefore be seen to be an adversarial process leading to the trial of an offender. Although conventionally understood as the process whereby persons with a *prima facie* case to answer will be committed for trial, the committal is, rather, an administrative proceeding to determine whether the accused be discharged. It remains for the ODPP, charged with the common law powers of the Attorney-General, to bring an indictment or not. Abolition of the grand jury has therefore not been replaced with an alternative or equivalent adversarial process. Rather, the power of the grand jury is now held by the ODPP who may bring an indictment even after a magistrate has discharged an accused following a committal hearing. Electing to indict the accused following a committal at which they were discharged, though controversial, is not uncommon. *Jago v District Court of NSW* (1989) 168 CLR 23 further affirms the power of the office of Attorney-General to bring an *ex officio* indictment even where no committal is held. However, once indicted, it is the responsibility of the courts to control proceedings so as to ensure the accused receives a fair trial.

The rise of summary disposal

Summary disposal is made available by the statutory amendment of the common law providing a means for the fast and efficient disposal of matters before a magistrate sitting alone. Summary disposal became increasingly common into the eighteenth century as an alternative to formal court proceedings, where matters were heard 'in chambers', that is, in the less formal environment of the judge's chambers. In chambers determinations were seen to be less formal as they were not public, and did not follow processes of court etiquette nor required a strict adherence to the procedural rules of a sitting court. Matters would be dealt with on the papers or through oral submission from counsel, and only those matters deemed insignificant enough to warrant a departure for the formal process were dealt with in this way (see McBarnet, 1981b: 188–190). Summary process became increasingly popular into the nineteenth century, where the process was reconvened from 'in chambers' to public hearings, but still without the jury. Today, summary jurisdiction is mainly exercised by local or magistrates' courts. Statute now prescribes a range of indictable offences that will be dealt with summarily unless an election is made to the contrary. In NSW, indictable offences to be disposed of summarily are prescribed under Schedule One of the *Criminal Procedure Act 1986* (NSW). Schedule One is divided into two tables – Table 1 provides a list of the more serious indictable offences to be disposed of summarily that can be dealt with on indictment by the election of the prosecution or defence. Table 2 provides a list of less serious indictable offences to be disposed of summarily that can be dealt with on indictment by the election of the prosecution alone. The *Summary Offences Act 1988* (NSW) also prescribes a range of offences that can only be dealt with summarily.

The vast majority of charges brought in the local court result in a guilty plea. The accused will ordinarily plead guilty and go straight to a sentencing hearing because of the advantages of the guilty plea. A court will discount a sentence where an accused pleads guilty, with the largest benefit being gained if they do so at the first opportunity. In NSW, based on the utilitarian benefit of the guilty plea, discounts of between 10–25 per cent are available per *R v Thomson and Houlton* (2000) 49 NSWLR 383. The utilitarian value of the early guilty plea is seen to be an essential part of the proper functioning of local court justice. Should all accused decide to contest their charges, the local court may well 'grind to a haut'. In *R v Thomson and Houlton* (2000) 49 NSWLR 383 Spigelman CJ indicates the utilitarian value as referring to (at 386):

> First, the plea is a manifestation of remorse or contrition. Secondly, the plea has a utilitarian value to the efficiency of the criminal justice system. Thirdly, in particular cases – especially sexual assault cases, crimes involving children and, often, elderly victims – there is a particular value in avoiding the need to call witnesses, especially victims, to give evidence.

As to the benefit of encouraging an early guilty plea, the Chief Justice quotes the then Attorney-General, later Dowd J, who provided a statutory mechanism for sentencing discounts consequent on a guilty plea (John Dowd, Second Reading Speech, Legislative Assembly, 4/4/1990). Dowd J was of the opinion that such a discount will not lead accused persons who are otherwise not guilty to nonetheless enter a guilty plea:

> The aim of this bill is to provide appropriate encouragements to those who are guilty of an offence to plead guilty to that offence. A substantial amount of the time of the courts in this State is taken up in determining the guilt or otherwise of those who plead not guilty. As far less time is involved in sentencing a person than in determining their guilt, even a minor change in a guilty plea rate has a significant effect on court time required. The guilty plea rate would therefore free up court time to deal with the backlog of cases awaiting hearing. I hasten to add that it is not intended that anyone who is not guilty should plead guilty. That is a fairly rare occurrence among people who turn up at court.

An accused person who may otherwise be considering contesting a charge may decide, for the sake of the discount and the fact that an unsuccessfully contested charge will likely result in a heavier penalty, to take the option to plead guilty and put an end to the matter. Police may also engage in over-charging, whereby several related charges are brought only to encourage charge bargaining, or the dropping of one of more of the charges, for a guilty plea on the remaining charge(s).

Infringement and penalty notices

There is an increasing trend to dispose of matters by the issuing of infringement or penalty notices. The issuing of an infringement, or fine, gives the offender the option of conveniently disposing of the matter by paying the fine. Payment of the fine is tantamount to the guilty plea, where the fine is the punishment, ending the matter. Due to the convenience of the disposing of the infringement in this way, most offenders opt to pay the fine and move on. A mechanism exists to contest an infringement, by nominating to have the matter heard in court. If this option is chosen, a court attendance notice will be issued summoning the accused to court. Here, a police prosecutor or government official will prosecute the accused, as like any other summary offence. By electing to have the matter determined by a court, however, the accused exposes themselves to the full sentence available. For example, in NSW as of 2010, where a driver is caught speeding up to 10 km/h over the prescribed speed limit, an infringement totalling AU$82 may be issued. Should the driver elect to have the matter heard by a court, the maximum fine may be increased to AU$2,200. For the benefit of an early guilty plea and dispensing with court proceedings, the nominal fine on an infringement is usually significantly lower than what would otherwise be available to the court.

Most common law jurisdictions utilise the infringement to control an array of regulatory and public order offences, including motor vehicle and driving offences. However, there have been recent moves to broaden the scope of the use of penalty notices to include offences that would traditionally be dealt with by a court of summary jurisdiction. In NSW, the *Crimes Legislation Amendment (Penalty Notices Offences) Act* 2002 (NSW) now allows police to issue an infringement notice for the following offences: larceny (where value of property is less than AU$300); offensive behaviour; offensive language; unlawful entry of a vehicle/boat; obstruct traffic; obtain money etc. by wilfully false representation; and goods in custody. The 2002 Act provides that the police may issue these infringements in their discretion, and that the traditional process of arrest or issuing a court attendance notice to have the matter dealt with by a court is still available.

Dispensing with the jury

Judge alone trials and trials by majority verdict have been said to undermine the institution that allows for community participation and the democratisation of the criminal justice process – the jury. The jury has been the significant mode of proof increasingly replacing the ordeal and trial by battle from the thirteenth century onwards. The outlawing of the ordeal in 1215 meant that the alternative secular modes of proof were trial by battle and trial by jury. The latter came to dominate. Trial by battle remained the popular and customary mode of proof following accusations of private wrongdoing, known as the appeal of felony (see Kirchengast, 2006: 31–33), whereby the person brining the accusation would fight the defendant under judicial supervision. The battle continued until the death or disablement of one of the parties. The winner was essentially the last person standing. Women, the elderly, minors or the infirm were able to appoint a champion to fight in their place. The case of *Ashford v Thornton* (1818) 1 B & Ald 405 was recorded as the last trial by battle before the mode of proof, together with the appeal of felony, were abolished by parliament in 1819 (see Baker, 1990: 87). In *Ashford v Thornton*, Abraham Thornton was charged with the murder of Mary Ashford. Thornton was tried by jury and acquitted. Mary's brother, William Ashford, then appealed to the King's Bench submitting that he had the right to pursue the matter by appeal of felony. The prosecution submitted that the law was not valid as it had not been used in centuries. However, the King's Bench ruled that the right remained and William Ashford was permitted to proceed to trial by battle. In the end, however, Ashford declined to proceed to battle, and Thornton won the case. Bayley J notes that wager of battle was an unusual process by early nineteenth-century standards not for its brutality, but because appeal of felony was a private action at the hands of the appellee, or victim, and thus could be settled privately (see Klerman, 2001: 8–10). Bayley J notes (at 457):

> This mode of proceeding, by appeal, is unusual in our law, being brought, not for the benefit of the public, but for that of the party, and being a private suit, wholly under his control. It ought, therefore, to be watched very narrowly by the Court; for it may take place after trial and acquittal on an indictment at the suit of the King; and the execution under it is entirely at the option of the party suing, whose sole object it may be to obtain a pecuniary satisfaction. One inconvenience attending this mode of proceeding is, that the party who institutes it must be willing, if required, to stake his life in support of his accusation. For the battel is the right of the appellee at his election, unless he be excluded from it by some violent presumption of guilt existing against him.

Lord Ellenborougher CJ ruled (at 460):

> The general law of the land is in favour of the wager of battel, and it is our duty to pronounce the law as it is, and not as we may wish it

to be. Whatever prejudices therefore may justly exist against this mode of trial, still as it is the law of the land, the Court must pronounce judgment for it.

By 1818, however, trial by jury was firmly established as the accepted mode of proof in criminal cases. *Ashford v Thornton* was thus anomalous for its time, but indicative of the way proof was traditionally seen as a process that involved the coming together of the prosecution and accused in a personal, private, and often violent way.[1] The jury was seen, therefore, as the main mode of proof well before the nineteenth century. The process by which trial by jury proceeds is guided by several principles, many of which have now been amended, abolished or eroded. Trial by jury generally requires that 12 persons be assembled from the local community where the offence took place. Today, jurors are empanelled from voter registration rolls from the location in which the offence took place. The requirement that the verdict of the jury be unanimous has largely been eroded so that, depending on the jurisdiction, a majority verdict of at least ten is required.

In Australian law, majority verdicts are allowed in South Australia, Victoria, Western Australia, Tasmania, the Northern Territory and NSW. Queensland and the Australian Capital Territory require unanimous verdicts. Majority verdicts were introduced in NSW in 2005 (see s55F *Jury Act 1977* (NSW)). In NSW, a majority verdict may be reached after deliberations for a period of time, at least eight hours, which the court considers reasonable given the scope and complexity of the case. The court must be satisfied that it is unlikely that the jurors will reach a unanimous verdict upon further deliberation. Where the jury contains 12 persons, a majority verdict is one that consists of 11 jurors. Different jurisdictions may accept fewer jurors in order to constitute a majority, but the number rarely falls below ten jurors where a full jury of 12 persons is sitting.[2]

The issue of majority verdicts was dealt with by the High Court of Australia in *Cheatle v The Queen* (1993) 177 CLR 541. In this case, the High Court rules that s80 of the Australian Constitution provides that a verdict of guilty to an offence against the Commonwealth tried on indictment requires a unanimous verdict.[3] Their honours indicate that 'history, principle and authority' combine to compel them to maintain the rule in favour of unanimity, despite recognising, throughout their judgement, the various benefits of majority verdicts.

The court indicates the history of unanimity in jury trials thus (at 550–552):

> As a matter of history, the common law's insistence that the verdict of the petty jury on a criminal trial be by agreement of all the jurors can be traced back at least to the judgment of the Common Bench, delivered by Thorpe CJ, in an *Anonymous Case* in 1367 when 'it was finally settled... that [the] verdict must be unanimous'. The origin of that requirement of unanimity would seem to lie not in any reasoned development of principle but in a requirement of the concurrence of twelve jurors in the verdict in the early days when jurors performed the function of local witnesses in trial by compurgation. Be that as it may, the common law has, since the fourteenth century, consistently and unequivocally insisted upon the requirement of unanimity. The requirement was, at one stage, subjected to some distinguished criticism, mainly for the reason that it constituted the foundation and explanation of the practice in earlier times of carrying the jurors around 'in a wagon' with the assize – 'without meat or drinke, fire or candle' – until they were starved or frozen into agreement. In more recent times, however, the requirement has commonly been seen as constituting 'an essential and inseparable part' of the right to trial by jury and an important 'protection' of the citizen against wrongful conviction. It is unnecessary for present purposes to trace the steps by which the common law institution of criminal trial by jury was initially introduced in New South Wales and Van Diemen's Land and subsequently established as the method of trial of serious criminal offences in the Australian colonies. It suffices to say that, by 1900, trial by jury was firmly established by legislation in each of the federating Colonies as the universal method of trial of serious crime. In the legislation of each Colony, some of the traditional characteristics of the common law institution of criminal trial by jury were assumed rather than specifically prescribed. That was certainly the case as regards the requirement of unanimity. Notwithstanding the absence of any specific legislative provision in that regard, it was recognized, as a basic principle of the administration of criminal justice in each of the Colonies, that the verdict of a criminal jury could be returned only by the agreement of all the jurors. Indeed, in the case of the New South Wales, Victorian, Queensland and Tasmanian legislation, the assumption of the requirement of unanimity was underlined by express provision authorizing the discharge of the jury in the event that the

jurors were not agreed – in most cases, only after a specified minimum period of deliberation.

It follows from what has been said above that the history of criminal trial by jury in England and in this country up until the time of Federation establishes that, in 1900, it was an essential feature of the institution that an accused person could not be convicted otherwise than by the agreement or consensus of all the jurors. It is well settled that the interpretation of a constitution such as ours is necessarily influenced by the fact that its provisions are framed in the language of the English common law, and are to be read in the light of the common law's history. In the context of the history of criminal trial by jury, one would assume that s80's directive that the trial to which it refers must be by jury was intended to encompass that requirement of unanimity.

In *Kingswell v The Queen* (1985) 159 CLR 264, Deane J indicates the origins of the jury trial (at 299–300):

> Regardless of whether one traces the common law institution of trial by jury to Roman, Saxon, Frankish or Norman origins, the underlying notion of judgment by one's equals under the law was traditionally seen as established in English criminal law, for those who had the power to be heard, at least by 1215 when the Charter of that year provided, among other things, that no man should be arrested, imprisoned, banished or deprived of life otherwise than by the lawful judgment of his equals ('per legale judicium parium suorum') or by the law of the land. Modern scholarship would indicate that much of the traditional identification of trial by jury with Magna Carta was erroneous. It is, however, clear enough that the right to trial by jury in criminal matters was, by the fourteenth century, seen in England as an 'ancient' right. In the centuries that followed, there was consistent reiteration, by those who developed, pronounced, recorded and systematized the common law of England, of the fundamental importance of trial by jury to the liberty of the subject under the rule of law (see, e.g., Co. Inst., Part II, 45ff.; *Black. Comm.* (1st ed., 1966 rep.), Book III, pp. 379–381, Book IV, pp. 342–344, and, generally, *Singer v. United States* (1965) 380 US 24, at p. 27 (13 Law Ed 2d 630, at p. 633); Mr. Justice Evatt, 'The Jury System in Australia', Australian Law Journal, vol. 10 (1936), Supplement, 49, at pp. 66–67, 72). When British settlements were established in other parts of the world, trial by jury in criminal matters

was claimed as a 'birthright and inheritance' under the common law and as an institution to be established and safeguarded to the extent that local circumstances would permit (cf. the passage from Story's Commentaries on the Constitution quoted in *Patton v. United States* [1930] USSC 74; (1930) 281 US 276, at p. 297 [1930] USSC 74; (74 Law Ed 854, at p. 862); Kent's Commentaries, Lecture 24, pp. 1–6; Rutland, The Birth of the Bill of Rights, 1776–1791 (1983), p. 19; *United States ex rel. Toth v. Quarles* [1955] USSC 15; (1955) 350 US 11, at pp. 16–17, n.9 [1955] USSC 15; (100 Law Ed 8, at p. 14, n.9), and, as to Australia, J.M. Bennett, 'The Establishment of Jury Trial in New South Wales', Sydney Law Review, vol. 3 (1959–1961), 463).

Kingswell, by majority, rules that s80 of the Australian Constitution guarantees trial by jury on indictment. It does not stop the legislature creating summary offences, or prescribing indictable offences to be disposed of summarily, in order to avoid trial by jury. Though instructive as to the history of trial by jury, Deane's J decision is in the minority, his Honour ruling that s80 guarantees trial by jury as a matter of substance over form, in that any 'serious offence' prescribed by the Commonwealth ought to be tried before a jury. As to what may constitute a 'serious offence', Deane J sets as a guide any offence punishable by more than one year of imprisonment (at 318–318):

> The conclusion to which I have finally come is that, notwithstanding the contrary trend in subsequent judgments in this Court, the views expressed by Dixon and Evatt JJ. in Lowenstein, as qualified in the manner which I have mentioned, should be accepted as a correct statement of the effect of the reference to 'trial on indictment' in s80 of the Constitution. On that construction, the guarantee of the section is applicable in respect of any trial of an accused charged with an offence against a law of the Commonwealth in circumstances where the charge is brought by the State or an agency of the State and the accused will, if found guilty, stand convicted of a 'serious offence'. As has been said, a particular alleged offence will, for the purposes of characterizing a particular trial as a 'trial on indictment', be a 'serious offence' if it is not one which could appropriately be dealt with summarily by justices or magistrates in that conviction will expose the accused to grave punishment. It is unnecessary, for the purposes of the present case, to seek to identify more precisely the boundary between offences which are not and offences which are capable of being properly so dealt with. I have,

however, indicated the tentative view that that boundary will ordinarily be identified by reference to whether the offence is punishable, when prosecuted in the manner in which it is being prosecuted, by a maximum term of imprisonment of more than one year.

Deane's J dicta as to the significance of trial by indictment invites consideration of the increased movement towards summary disposal, discussed above. It provides a commentary not only as to the questions confronting the High Court of Australia with regard to the interpretation of s80 of the Australian Constitution, but the movement away from the principles of adversarial justice and the institutions constitutive of the adversarial criminal trial more generally. That accused persons ought to be afforded trial by jury for serious offences, offences punishable by imprisonment for a year or more, is increasingly questioned in an era of justice characterised by expedient resolution before a tribunal that, arguably, only gives the 'appearance' of the adversarial criminal trial (see McBarnet, 1981a, 1981b).

Charge bargaining

The charge bargaining process is at the discretion of the prosecuting officer laying the charge in the first instance. Those authorities bringing the prosecution, usually the police, CPS or ODPP, have a wide discretion to bring charges to be determined by a court. The discretion to charge in the first instance, to continue or withdraw a charge, or to offer no evidence, is a matter of discretion that lies with the executive and, is embodied in the office of Attorney-General. *Gouriet v Union of Post Office Workers* [1978] AC 438 settles this principle in English law, per Viscount Dilhorne (at 487):

> The Attorney-General has many powers and duties. He may stop any prosecution on indictment by entering a *nolle prosequi*. He merely has to sign a piece of paper saying that he does not wish the prosecution to continue. He need not give any reasons. He can direct the institution of a prosecution and direct the Director of Public Prosecutions to take over the conduct of any criminal proceedings and he may tell him to offer no evidence. In the exercise of these powers he is not subject to direction by his ministerial colleagues or to control and supervision by the courts.

As the prosecution process is a discretionary one, the police have a wide discretion to deal with alleged wrongdoing by laying a charge or not (see *Wright v McQualter* (1970) 17 FLR 305 at 318). As a matter of tactics, it is possible for the police to over-charge a suspect by either laying a charge that is higher than that which is appropriate against the circumstances of the offence, or by laying numerous charges that speak to same or similar circumstances. A police officer may do this in order to facilitate a charge bargaining process whereby the police prosecutor agrees to drop various charges, or reduce the charge to a lesser offence, on the basis that the accused enter a guilty plea to one or more charges, or the lesser charge. This practice is highly questionable in an ethical sense, given the power of the police against any one individual, but remains lawful. *R v Andrew Foster Brown* (1989) 17 NSWLR 472 indicates why such discretion is central to the exercise of executive power (at 479):

> There may be circumstances in which it is appropriate to characterise a decision by the prosecuting authorities to charge a person with one offence, to which he is prepared to plead guilty, rather than another and more serious offence which he has apparently committed, as an abuse of the process of the court. We do not accept that the Director of Public Prosecutions has an absolute and uncontrolled discretion which empowers him to charge an accused person in whatever way he pleases, regardless of the gravity of the conduct of the accused, and then to require the court to give effect to his decision in that regard. There are substantial practical limitations upon the power of courts to control the exercise by prosecuting authorities of the wide discretion which they undoubtedly enjoy, and in practice the most important sanctions in this regard are likely to be political rather than legal. Nevertheless, in an appropriate case a court, paying due regard to the prosecuting authority's rights in relation to the formulation of charges, may need to give effect to its own right to prevent an abuse of its process.

The High Court of Australia has further clarified the centrality of the role of executive discretion in the charging process in *GAS v The Queen; SJK v The Queen* (2004) 217 CLR 198. The High Court of Australia has outlined the fundamental principles affecting plea agreements. These include (at 210–211):

> First, it is the prosecutor, alone, who has the responsibility of deciding the charges to be preferred against an accused person. The

judge has no role to play in that decision. There is no suggestion, in the present case, that the judge was in any way a party to the 'plea agreement' referred to. The appellants, through their counsel, evidently indicated to the prosecutor that, if a charge of manslaughter were to be substituted for the charge of murder, they would plead guilty, and the prosecutor filed a new presentment on that understanding. However, the charging of the appellants was a matter for the prosecutor.

Secondly, it is the accused person, alone, who must decide whether to plead guilty to the charge preferred. That decision must be made freely and, in this case, it was made with the benefit of legal advice. Once again, the judge is not, and in this case was not, involved in the decision. Such a decision is not made with any foreknowledge of the sentence that will be imposed. No doubt it will often be made in the light of professional advice as to what might reasonably be expected to happen, but that advice is the responsibility of the accused's legal representatives.

Thirdly, it is for the sentencing judge, alone, to decide the sentence to be imposed. For that purpose, the judge must find the relevant facts. In the case of a plea of guilty, any facts beyond what is necessarily involved as an element of the offence must be proved by evidence, or admitted formally (as in an agreed statement of facts), or informally (as occurred in the present case by a statement of facts from the bar table which was not contradicted). There may be significant limitations as to a judge's capacity to find potentially relevant facts in a given case. The present appeal provides an example. The limitation arose from the absence of evidence as to who killed the victim, and the absence of any admission from either appellant that his involvement was more than that of an aider and abettor.

Fourthly, as a corollary to the third principle, there may be an understanding, between the prosecution and the defence, as to evidence that will be led, or admissions that will be made, but that does not bind the judge, except in the practical sense that the judge's capacity to find facts will be affected by the evidence and the admissions. In deciding the sentence, the judge must apply to the facts as found the relevant law and sentencing principles. It is for the judge, assisted by the submissions of counsel, to decide and apply the law. There may be an understanding between counsel as to the submissions of law that they will make, but that does not bind the judge in any sense. The judge's responsibility to find and apply the law is not circumscribed by the conduct of counsel.

The High Court of Australia goes some way toward settling issues as to plea deals that then lead to the sentencing process as based on an 'agreed' set of facts. Although sentencing is for the judge alone, the judge cannot sentence the accused based on facts that remain unproven, although a judge is otherwise free to determine an appropriate sentence notwithstanding the limited case presented to them. The charge bargaining process is a key indication as to how the criminal trial may be circumvented for an alternative process of agreement and deal making between accused and prosecution. Though judicial discretion remains, it is limited to those facts in evidence before the court which, in any event, is not led by the nominal adversarial process of open examination of all relevant facts in issue.

The law and order debate

The law and order debate has led to the significant growth in policing power for the control of public space. This has included expanded stop and search powers for police, new offences, and new penalties and modes of initiation, such as the expanded use of penalty notices for offences otherwise dealt with by a court, as discussed above. Taken together, these changes evidence the expansion of police power for the promise of increased public order. In NSW, the *Law Enforcement (Powers and Responsibilities) Act 2002* (NSW) and in England and Wales, the *Police and Criminal Evidence Act 1984* (UK), may be considered as an intention to consolidate and extend police power at common law in order to secure threats to the 'public peace' and to provide police the means to control gross public disorder. The *Criminal Justice and Public Order Act 1994* (UK) also provides for extended police stop and search powers and certain public order offences, and specifically seeks to limits an individual's right to silence. Critical perspectives assume that such legislation is a draconian response to the government's fear of large crowds, or in the case of the 1994 Act, a 'moral panic' as to alternative music festivals. Combined with the use of orders to restrain anti-social behaviour, the above legislation may been seen as a positive attempt to consolidate police power into the one legislative instrument for the better organisation, amendment and control of an otherwise diverse set of laws.

Many of the amendments to police search and arrest powers have also resulted in modifications to bail law and procedure. The right to bail generally follows the premise 'innocent until proven guilty', whereby an accused person will be bailed without restriction or conditionally, unless they are unlikely to show for their next appearance, or otherwise exhibit a continuing risk of offending. Recently, however, bail law has been reformed to increase the number of offences for which there is a presumption against bail, and to strengthen procedural measures, including the number of times the accused may apply for bail and a court's ability to review bail decisions.

Concern over specific types of offenders, such as sex offenders, has seen the curtailment of defendant rights in most jurisdictions through the registration of prescribed sex offenders, or through the continued imprisonment of offenders deemed to be highly recidivist. In the context of victim rights and the need to ensure the continued control of dangerous offenders, the state has increasingly sought the control of offenders beyond the scope of their original sentence as determined at trial. *Fardon v Attorney-General (Qld)* (2004) 223 CLR 575, discussed in Chapter 1, demonstrates how such process are now modifying what it means to be 'guilty' of a crime and subject to imprisonment. Concern over organised motorcycle gangs or bikies had also resulted in association restrictions, or control orders, limiting the movement of members in declared organisations. *Totani and Anor. v The State of South Australia* [2009] SASC 301, also discussed in Chapter 1, demonstrates the tensions that have resulted from this new means of restricting the liberty of persons not subject to traditional criminal trial processes. In a similar way, the English equivalent to the domestic control order in the form of the ASBO provides for a modified civil standard that evidences the traversing of the criminal and civil jurisdictions for the rise of a new 'trial' experience.

Extending policing power

The *Police and Criminal Evidence Act 1984* (UK) consolidates police power into the one legislative instrument and also provides for a code of practice for the exercise of those powers, as issued by the Home Secretary. The 1984 Act, known as 'PACE', proscribes police power to search an individual or premises, including powers to enter premises, the handling of exhibits seized, and the treatment and interrogation of suspects in custody. The *Criminal Procedures and Investigation Act 1996* (UK) also contains provisions in relation to police investigative powers. PACE has been substantially modified by the *Serious Organised Crime and Police Act 2005* (UK), which replaced the existing powers of arrest, including the category of arrestable offences, with a new general power of arrest for all offences.

Several cases have emerged that suggest that the courts are reluctant to afford the police powers broader than those reasonably proscribed in the Act. In *Osman v Southwark Crown Court* [1999] EWHC Admin 622, the police search of Osman was deemed to be unlawful as the police officers seeking to search him failed to give their names and station, at the time of the search. Section 60(4)(5) of the *Criminal Justice and Public Order Act 1994* (UK) allows the police to search persons in a declared area. Osman was stopped to be searched though, by Crown admission, the police failed to follow the requirements of s2 of PACE. In the course of this search it was further contended that the police were assaulted. Lord Justice Sedley indicates (at par 10):

> What happened in this case, on the Crown Court's findings of fact, was, as the Crown Court accepts, a breach of sub-sections 2(2) and (3) of the Police and Criminal Evidence Act 1984. From this, without more, it followed that the search which was initiated by the officers was not a lawful search and that, even though they may have been assaulted, they were not assaulted in the execution of their duty.

In *O'Loughlin v Chief Constable of Essex* [1997] EWCA Civ 2891, the court ruled that the entry of a premises under s17 of PACE to arrest O'Loughlin's wife for smashing her neighbours' car window was unlawful as PACE required that any person at the premises be given the reason for police entry. Failure to indicate the reasons for entry then call into question the use of reasonable force by the arresting officer. Lord Justice Roch suggests the significance of the issues at play (at 6):

> This case concerns the balancing of conflicting interests. The statutory power of a police constable to enter premises for the purposes which Parliament has identified in various statutory provisions such as s17 of the Police and Criminal Evidence Act, 1984 and the public interest in effective policing on the one side, and the right of the home owner that the privacy and security of his home should not be invaded and that he should be entitled to protect that privacy and security on the other.

R v Longman [1988] 1 WLR 619, however, provides that the police may enjoy greater power than *Osman* and *O'Loughlin* suggest. In *Longman*, plain clothes police obtained a warrant under s23(3) of the *Misuse of Drugs Act 1971* (UK) to search the defendant's home. It was held that the police's use of deception to gain entry was lawful, despite the fact that the police had not identified themselves nor shown the warrant providing for their entry.

In NSW, the *Law Enforcement (Powers and Responsibilities) Act 2002* (NSW) or 'LEPRA', sought to consolidate the common law relating to various policing powers, including the powers of entry to prevent a breach of the peace and use of force to effect arrest, while also creating new statutory powers, such as the power to create a 'crime scene'. There are details as to the requirements of personal searches, including strip searches. Police powers of arrest are now largely prescribed by LEPRA as are other provisions relating to detention after arrest, search warrants, in-car video recording, drug searches, special powers to prevent public disorder, entry powers for domestic violence disputes, and associated powers relating to vehicles and traffic.

Under LEPRA, the police may enter premises and stay for a 'reasonable time' to arrest a person. They may only do so if they believe on reasonable grounds that the person is in the dwelling. A police officer that enters premises under this section may search the premises for the relevant person. This section extends the common law powers of entry for effecting arrest without warrant, by relaxing the conditions of entry specified in *Lippl v Haines* (1989) 18 NSWLR 620. In *Haines*, the standard specified by Gleeson J of 'reasonable and probable grounds' has been reduced to just one of 'reasonableness'. The other condition in *Haines*, properly announcing the search to give the occupants time to consent to it, has been removed. However, s201 of LEPRA does require that the police announce their office and the reason for the exercise of their power, if reasonably practicable, before or at the time of entry.

The movement to modes of pre-emptive crime control through the codification and expansion of police power has significant implications for the way justice is mete out (see Zedner, 2006, 2007; Lee and Herborn, 2003). Pre-emptive crime control removes the locus of control from the courts and places it with, *inter alia*, the police. It does this by expanding the range of policing powers to stop and search persons, at time without warrant or on reasonable suspicion, for the regulation of persons who may, at some point in the future, commit an offence. The development of increased police power therefore signifies the movement toward the management of crime by limiting opportunities for future offending. This is achieved through strategies that create offences out of the failure to follow police direction, such as move along powers, which allow for judgement and sanction without the need to proceed to trial. The combination of increased police powers and the use of infringement notices also relocates the trial and sentencing process to the present act of policing.[4] Ultimately, the trial is reduced to an incident of police discretion.

Bail

The right to bail pending a full hearing or trial of the charges brought has been modified in recent years, largely in response to the growing concern over public disorder. In NSW, this has seen the modification of bail law in two key ways. The first, by increasing those number of offences for which there is a presumption against bail, and secondly, by restricting the power to apply for bail, or have a previous application reviewed. *The Law Enforcement Legislation Amendment (Public Safety) Act 2005* (NSW) inserted s8D into the *Bail Act 1978* (NSW) providing a presumption against bail for offences committed during a gross civil disturbance. The section specifically refers to s93D of the *Crimes Act 1900* (NSW), the offence of riot, or any other offence that is punishable by imprisonment for 2 years or more, which is alleged to have been committed either in the course of the accused person participating in a large-scale public disorder, or in connection with the exercise of police powers to prevent or control such a disorder or the threat of such a disorder. Such amendments characterise the modification of a range of criminal laws following the December 2005 Cronulla Riots in Sydney. On an 'emergency' sitting of Parliament following the riots, the then Premier of NSW, Morris Iemma (Legislative Assembly, Second Reading Speech, 15/12/2005), said is passage of the Bill:

> Twenty-three rioters charged over Sunday's riots have been granted bail, one of whom had been granted bail days earlier for assault and destroying property. It is unacceptable that such thugs and morons are automatically granted bail, just to be given the chance to wreak further havoc. This bill will help shut that revolving door by creating a presumption against bail for riot and for any other offence that is punishable by imprisonment for two years or more, where that offence is committed in the course of the person participating in a large-scale public disorder, or in connection with the exercise of police powers to prevent or control such a disorder or the threat of such a disorder. That way the police can do their jobs knowing that they will be backed up.
> That is an important point – backing the police. The police can be assured that they have our full support to use these new laws to rid

our streets of the violence, the thugs, the hooligans and the criminals who have been responsible for the actions we have seen. Frontline police should not need to look over their shoulder wondering if sound policing decisions will be second-guessed. They will not be. Police will be free to use these powers as intended by this Parliament. Good, firm, effective policing will be rewarded, not questioned.

A revised s22A has also been inserted into the *Bail Act 1978* (NSW). This section allows a court to refuse to entertain an application for bail if an application has already been dealt with by the court. There are some exceptions to this general rule, specifically, where the accused was not legally represented at the first application, or where new facts or circumstances have come to light since the initial application. Section 22A thus limits a court's ability to hear repeat bail applications, where a court 'is to refuse' to entertain a bail application if an application has already been determined. A court may also refuse frivolous or vexatious bail applications. Obligations are also imposed on lawyers who cannot apply for bail on behalf of a client where a court has already made a determination, unless the lawyer is satisfied that the accused was not already represented by a lawyer or because new facts or circumstances have arisen. The Attorney-General, John Hatzistergos, justified the amendments by reference to the cost of entertaining unnecessary and repeated applications. He also referred to the trauma caused to victims by repeated applications and 'magistrate shopping'. The Attorney-General (Legislative Assembly, Second Reading Speech, 17/10/2007) said in recommending the Bill to the House:

> New South Wales has the toughest bail laws in Australia. Over the last few years we have cracked down on repeat offenders... Those types of offenders now have a much tougher time being granted bail under our rigorous system. These extensive changes have delivered results. There is no doubt that the inmate population, particularly those on remand, has risen considerably... In fact the number of remand prisoners has risen by 20 per cent in the last 3 years alone and new gaols are being opened to accommodate the increase.

Section 22A, however, only applies to prevent new or fresh applications for bail. It does not limit a court from reviewing a previous decision. However, Reynolds J in *R v Hammill* (1986) 25 A Crim

R 316, speaking to an earlier version of the *Bail Act 1978* (NSW), has indicated:

> The Act gives to an accused the right to make any number of applications for bail and that right is contained in s22(1). An accused can also make applications to have a bail determination reviewed: s48. Any such application by an accused has, in my view, because of the presence of s48(1)(b) and s48(5), the same effect as a fresh application.

The law of bail has thus expanded in recent years to allow for the pre-trial management and regulation of persons deemed to be a continuing risk to society. While there is nothing new about the need to secure persons accused of wrongdoing by remanding them in custody or by way of surety or bond, the growth in law and order and the fear of social disorder, especially gross disorder beyond the control of the police, has led to the limiting of the granting of unrestricted bail indicating that bail law is now more than a mere means of pre-trial administration. Arguably, bail is now a new mode of punitiveness allowing for the control of accused persons without the full benefit and protection of the trial process.

Control orders, ASBOs and domestic order

New South Wales and South Australia have each introduced legislation providing for the issuing of control orders involving a non-association restriction for persons in outlaw motorcycle organisations. The State of South Australia is seeking to challenge the ruling before the High Court of Australia, following the full court decision of the South Australian Supreme Court in *Totani and Anor. v The State of South Australia* [2009] SASC 301, discussed in Chapter 1. In a two to one majority, Bleby J, with whom Kelly J agreed, ruled that s14(1) of the *Serious and Organised Crime (Control) Act 2008* (SA) was an invalid exercise of state power. White J ruled otherwise. Section 14(1) of the 2008 Act prescribes:

> The Court must, on application by the Commissioner, make a control order against a person (the 'defendant') if the Court is satisfied that the defendant is a member of a declared organisation.

Bleby J indicates the principles at stake (at par 139):

> The fact that Parliament has conferred a limited jurisdiction on the Magistrates Court with a direction that an order must be made if

certain things are proved does not mean that, in exercising that jurisdiction, the Court is doing no more than effecting a directed outcome in a way which compromises its integrity as a court. What is relevant to that question is the extent to which, if at all, Parliament has perversely directed the Court how it is to go about deciding the issue or issues that have been committed to it.

The High Court of Australia has enunciated the principles of judicial independence in a series of cases including *Kable v Director of Public Prosecutions for the State of New South Wales* (1996) 189 CLR 51, *Forge v Australian Securities and Investments Commission* (2006) 228 CLR 45, *Gypsy Jokers Motorcycle Club Inc v Commissioner of Police* (2008) 234 CLR 532 and *K-Generation Pty Ltd v Liquor Licensing Court* (2009) 83 ALJR 327. These cases develop the principle that state Supreme Courts must act judicially with independence, as Gleeson CJ explains in *Forge* (at 67–68):

> It follows from the terms of Ch III that State Supreme Courts must continue to answer the description of 'courts'. For a body to answer the description of a court it must satisfy minimum requirements of independence and impartiality. That is a stable principle, founded on the text of the Constitution. It is the principle that governs the outcome of the present case. If State legislation attempted to alter the character of a State Supreme Court in such a manner that it no longer satisfied those minimum requirements, then the legislation would be contrary to Ch III and invalid. For the reasons given above, however, Ch III of the Constitution, and in particular s72, did not before 1977, and does not now, specify those minimum requirements, either for State Supreme Courts or for other State courts that may be invested with federal jurisdiction.

This line of authority leads Bleby J to consider the control orders available under s14(1) an invalid exercise of judicial power on the basis that such orders follow determinations of the Attorney-General, and not a independent magistrate or judge (at par 155–156):

> The effect of the Control Act is therefore that the Magistrates Court is required by the Act to act on what is, in effect, the certificate of the Attorney-General... The Attorney-General is not subject to or bound by the rules of evidence or any standard of proof. He can

act on whatever information he pleases and give it whatever weight he pleases. The Attorney-General's findings are unreviewable. They are, in effect, binding on the Court.

That fact in itself would, in my opinion, be sufficient to undermine the institutional integrity of the Court, as the most significant and essential findings of fact are made not by a judicial officer but by a Minister of the Crown.

White J ruled that the 2008 Act was valid to the extant that s41(1) does afford the court some evaluative and adjudicative role when handing down a control order with regard to the content of that order (at par 187):

> Although the decision of the Magistrates Court under s14(1) is constrained both as to the making of the order, and as to its content, s14 does have features indicating that the Court is to exercise an evaluative and adjudicative role of a well-recognised judicial kind before making the order.

In NSW, the relevant legislation is the *Crimes (Criminal Organisations Control) Act 2009* (NSW). A control order may restrict the individuals to which the order relates from associating with other members of declared organisations. An organisation may become a 'declared organisation' after an eligible judge of the Supreme Court of NSW orders so. Only those judges of the Supreme Court of NSW that take up the offer to become an eligible judge may make such determinations. An individual subject to a control order may not associate with another controlled member. Where such association has occurred, the prosecution need not prove that the defendant associated with another person for any particular purpose, or that the association would have led to the commission of any offence. The *Criminal Organisations Legislation Amendment Act 2009* (NSW) further provides that a controlled member may not recruit another person into a declared organisation. Section 27 provides that any prescribed activity may not be undertaken by an individual subject to a control order:

(a) operating a casino within the meaning of the Casino Control Act 1992, or being a special employee within the meaning of Part 4 of that Act,
(b) carrying on a security activity within the meaning of the Security Industry Act 1997,

(c) carrying on the business of a pawnbroker within the meaning of the Pawnbrokers and Second-hand Dealers Act 1996,
(d) carrying on business as a commercial agent or private inquiry agent within the meaning of the Commercial Agents and Private Inquiry Agents Act 2004,
(e) possessing or using a firearm within the meaning of the Firearms Act 1996 or carrying on business as a firearms dealer within the meaning of that Act,
(f) operating a tow truck within the meaning of the Tow Truck Industry Act 1998,
(g) carrying on business as a dealer within the meaning of the Motor Dealers Act 1974,
(h) carrying on business as a repairer within the meaning of the Motor Vehicle Repairs Act 1980,
(i) selling or supplying liquor within the meaning of the Liquor Act 2007,
(j) carrying on the business of a bookmaker within the meaning of the Racing Administration Act 1998,
(k) carrying out the activities of an owner, trainer, jockey, stable-hand, bookmaker, bookmaker's clerk or another person associated with racing who is required to be registered or licensed under the Thoroughbred Racing Act 1996,
(l) carrying out the activities of an owner, trainer or other person associated with greyhound or harness racing who is required to be registered under the Greyhound and Harness Racing Administration Act 2004,
(m) any other activity prescribed by the regulations.

The then premier of NSW, Nathan Rees, said in support of the Crimes (Criminal Organisations Control) Bill 2009 (Legislative Assembly, Second Reading Speech, 2/5/2009):

> Once these laws take full effect, the Commissioner of Police will be able to seek a declaration from a Supreme Court judge that a bikie gang is a declared criminal organisation. An eligible judge may make a declaration if they are satisfied that an organisation's members associate for the purpose of organising, planning, facilitating, supporting or engaging in serious criminal activity and that the organisation represents a risk to public safety and order in New South Wales. Once the organisation is declared, the commissioner may then seek control orders from the Supreme Court in respect of

one of more persons on the basis that those persons are members of a declared criminal organisation and there are sufficient grounds for making the order. The controlled member will not be able to associate with another controlled member of that gang. If they do, they will risk two years jail for the first offence. Do it again and they will risk five years in jail. To help take these gang members off the streets there will be no presumption in favour of bail for this offence.

The English version of the domestic control order is contained in the *Crime and Disorder Act 1998* (UK). This Act originally introduced the ASBO, a civil order with a modified standard of proof, taken out against persons whose conduct 'caused or was likely to cause harassment, alarm or distress to one or more persons not of the same household as himself', and where such an order is necessary to protect persons in the local government area from further anti-social acts by the defendant. A magistrate satisfied that an order should be made may then make an order which essentially prohibits the defendant from doing anything listed in the order for not less than two years. Although the order is constituted as a civil order, breach of an ASBO, without reasonable excuse, may leave the offender liable to imprisonment for six months if disposed of summarily, or up to five years if proceeded upon by indictment. Applications for ASBOs are determined in a magistrates' court. The 1998 Act provides that the proceedings must be determined by a modified civil standard. *R (on the application of McCann and others) v Crown Court at Manchester; Clingham v Kensington and Chelsea Royal London Borough Council* [2002] 4 All ER 593, provides, per Lord Steyn (at 603–604):

> There is no doubt that Parliament intended to adopt the model of a civil remedy of an injunction, backed up by criminal penalties, when it enacted s1 of the CDA. The view was taken that the proceedings for an anti-social behaviour order would be civil and would not attract the rigour of the inflexible and sometimes absurdly technical hearsay rule which applies in criminal cases. If this supposition was wrong, in the sense that Parliament did not objectively achieve its aim, it would inevitably follow that the procedure for obtaining anti-social behaviour orders is completely or virtually unworkable and useless. If that is what the law decrees, so be it. My starting point is, however, an initial scepticism of an outcome which would deprive communities of their fundamental rights (see *Brown v Stott (Procurator Fiscal, Dunfermline)* [2001] 2 All ER 97 at 115, 118,

128–129, [2001] 2 WLR 817 at 836, 839, 850 (per Lord Bingham of Cornhill, my judgment and Lord Hope of Craighead respectively)).

The standard of proof that emerges is similar to the criminal standard of beyond reasonable doubt. Technically, the court must be persuaded 'to be sure' that the defendant acted in a manner considered to be anti-social. Pursuant to *In re H (Minors) (Sexual Abuse: Standard of Proof)* [1996] AC 563 at 586, per Lord Nicholls of Birkenhead, reference to the heightened civil standard would ordinarily apply. *M v Director of Public Prosecutions* [2007] EWHC 1032 (Admin) further ruled that the high standard of proof would be difficult to meet if the accusation of anti-social behaviour was based entirely on hearsay evidence.[5]

The rise of control orders for the regulation of domestic 'law and order' suggests the use of a novel order for the control of certain persons as an extension to nominal police power. Demonstrated in *Clingham*, the control order departs from a standard criminal process to bind persons over to modes of conduct that do not offend the order of the court. While such orders are not tantamount to a criminal trial, they do evidence the tendency to usurp the trial for alternative means to justice. Controversial though they are, such orders now seem to be part of the machinery of justice for the control of identified individuals. Further, such orders are now part of a judicial process that traverses the jurisdictional limits of the criminal and civil process.

Modifying the criminal trial

Several recent policy changes have led to the questioning of certain aspects of the adversarial criminal trial. These include the availability of certain defences and restraints to prosecution, as a response to a growing awareness of the various competing interests in the trial process. These interests include those of the community and state in ensuring justice is served on those who are culpable, but also extends to discrete victim interests where certain forms of victimisation may have formerly been excluded as irrelevant to judicial determinations of offence liability. The abolition of the defence of provocation on the ground that it mitigates the culpability of individuals prone to a violent loss of self-control, and the removal of the rule against double jeopardy as a restraint to double prosecution, have been issues of significant debate in recent years. As for provocation, Victoria, Tasmania and New Zealand have abrogated the defence from the common law out of the realisation that it may mask intimate partner homicide.

Various jurisdictions, including NSW and England and Wales, have opted to remove double jeopardy for a class of serious offences where new evidence emerges implicating a formerly acquitted accused.

Defences: Provocation

The defence of provocation has been abolished in Tasmania, Victoria and New Zealand *(Criminal Code Amendment (Abolition of Defence of Provocation) Act 2003* (Tas); *Crimes (Homicide) Act 2005* (Vic); *Crimes (Provocation Repeal) Amendment Act 2009* (NZ)). England and Wales and NSW have considered the defence but have chosen to retain it, making amendments where desirable (see LCEW, 2004; NSWLRC, 1997). The Victorian Law Reform Commission recommended that the defence of provocation be abolished on the basis that it privileges those who lose self-control and kill in the face of some provoking circumstance (see VLRF, 2004). Despite the requirement that the accused needed to have so far lost self-control as would the ordinary person, various criticisms remain as to the biased nature of the offence. In particular, the defence has been subjected to broad feminist critique. Such perspectives are critical of the defence out of recognition that it privileges male violence against women (see Brown, 1999; Tolmie, 2005). The gendered history of the defence was considered by the House of Lords in *R v Smith* [2000] 4 All ER 289. In this case, the Lord Hoffman outlined the history of the defence, indicating that it evolved as a largely subjective test based on the expected loss of self-control of the seventeenth century gentleman when subject to an insult to his reputation or property. Lord Hoffman indicates this history thus (at 299–300):

> The researches of Dr. Horder (Provocation and Responsibility, (1992)) show that although the doctrine has much earlier roots, it emerged in recognisably modern form in the late 17th and early 18th centuries. It comes from a world of Restoration gallantry in which gentlemen habitually carried lethal weapons, acted in accordance with a code of honour which required insult to be personally avenged by instant angry retaliation and in which the mandatory penalty for premeditated murder was death. To show anger 'in hot blood' for a proper reason by an appropriate response was not merely permissible but the badge of a man of honour. The human frailty to which the defence of provocation made allowance was the possibility that the man of honour might overreact and kill when a lesser retaliation would have been appropriate. Provided that he did not

grossly overreact in the extent or manner of his retaliation, the offence would be manslaughter and execution avoided.

The defence developed throughout the nineteenth century to include two main additional elements. The first element sought to test whether the provocative response was proportionate to the provocative conduct, whilst the second element sought to test whether the ordinary or reasonable person would have lost self-control to the extent that they would kill (at 300):

> The 19th century judges had to adapt this law to a society of Victorian middle-class propriety. They changed it in two ways. First, they generalised the specific situations which the old law had regarded as sufficient provocation into a rule that whatever the alleged provocation, the response had to be 'reasonable.' In *Reg. v. Kirkham* (1837) 8 C. & P. 115, 119 Coleridge J. told the jury that 'though the law condescends to human frailty, it will not indulge human ferocity. It considers man to be a rational being, and requires that he should exercise a reasonable controul over his passions.' The 'reasonable man', as a test of the appropriate response, first appeared in *Reg. v. Welsh* (1869) 11 Cox C.C. 336, 339 in which Keating J. said that provocation would be sufficient if it was 'something which might naturally cause an ordinary and reasonably minded man to lose his self-control and commit such an act.'

Provocation was therefore established as a gendered defence of human, or perhaps more accurately, masculine frailty. The resort to violence was considered a natural reaction when a man of honour was faced with provocative conduct of a type that would ordinarily cause the reasonable person to retaliate in 'hot blood'. Such defendants were therefore less culpable, and should be spared a conviction of murder, and in the nineteenth century a death sentence, for conviction for manslaughter.

Provocation has thus been held as a defence that affords men an excuse for killing when their pride is injured or insulted. This has led some to claim that men are more likely to raise the defence successfully where they kill their female partner following an infidelity on the woman's part. Women may thus not be able to benefit from the defence to the same degree as they have no masculine pride to protect. Provocation may also be stratified along heterosexual lines, such that gays or lesbians faced with a provocative act may not be afforded the same concession as the straight man, again out of recognition that gays or lesbians are not bound to the same gender assumptions that provide that a straight man will lose self-control to the point that he will kill when faced with a cheating partner. On a similar point, the majority in *Green v The Queen* (1998) 191 CLR 334 indicate that the ordinary person may lose self-control to the point that they would kill or inflict grievous bodily harm when faced with an unwelcome homosexual advance.

Other less gender specific explanations have also emerged. Such perspectives suggest, *inter alia*, that the defence of provocation promotes a culture of blaming the victim, and seeks to privilege those who lose self-control to the extent that they are then driven to kill. On this basis, the Victorian Law Reform Commission (VLRC) has recommended that the defence be abolished. Victoria passed the Crimes (Homicide) Bill 2005 (Vic) abolishing the common law defence of provocation (Rob Hulls, Attorney-General, Legislative Assembly, Second Reading Speech, 18/10/2005):

> The commission found that the law of provocation has failed to evolve sufficiently to keep pace with a changing society. By reducing murder to manslaughter, the partial defence condones male aggression towards women and is often relied upon by men who kill partners or ex-partners out of jealousy or anger. It has no place in a modern, civilised society.

Where a defendant is faced with provocative circumstances that mitigate his or her culpability, this should be reflected in sentencing. Where a woman would seek to utilise the defence, they should rely on excessive force self-defence, diminished responsibility or substantial impairment, defensive homicide, or manslaughter. The availability of an alternative charge after abolition of provocation will turn of the specific nature of the killing and the particular elements of the alternative defence or charge.

Double jeopardy

Several jurisdictions have modified the common law rule against double prosecution in the form of autrefois acquit and autrefois convict (see Roberts, 2002; Corns, 2003; Kirchengast, 2006: 198–201). The rules have been modified in Tasmania, NSW, Western Australia, and England and Wales (see *Criminal Code Act 1924* (Tas) s401(2)(b); *Criminal Code 1913* (WA) ss13,688(2)(b); *Crimes (Appeal and Review) Amendment (Double*

Jeopardy) Act 2006 (NSW); *Crimes (Appeal and Review) Amendment (Double Jeopardy) Act 2009* (NSW); *Criminal Justice Act 2003* (UK) Pt 10; also see *The Queen v Carroll* (2002) 213 CLR 643; *Daniels v Thompson* [1998] 3 NZLR 22; *Hudson v United States* (1997) 522 US 93; *Franz Fischer v Austria* [2001] ECHR 37950/97). Other jurisdictions, including New Zealand, have chosen to retain the protection following the recommendation of the New Zealand Law Commission in 2001 (see NZLC, 2001; *Bill of Rights Act 1990* (NZ) s26(2)).

In NSW, the *Crimes (Appeal and Review) Amendment (Double Jeopardy) Act 2006* (NSW) provided for the retrial of acquitted offenders in three situations. Firstly, where the accused is acquitted of an offence that carries a life sentence (in NSW, such offences include murder, violent gang rapes, large commercial supply or production of illegal drugs) where there is 'fresh and compelling' evidence of guilt. Secondly, where the accused is acquitted of an offence which carries a sentence of 15 years or more, and where the acquittal was tainted (by perjury, bribery or perversion of the course of justice). Thirdly, where the accused was acquitted in a judge alone trial, or where a judge directed the jury to acquit. In passing the 2006 Act, the then Premier of NSW, Morris Iemma, said (Legislative Assembly, Second Reading Speech, 19/9/2006):

> There will sometimes be cases where diligent police and prosecutors will still fail to find all the possible evidence. Perhaps it is being concealed from them deliberately, or perhaps developments in forensic technology will reveal new evidence or new conclusions to be drawn from existing evidence. In such cases, there may well be grounds to bring the accused back to trial. In fact, not to do so risks perpetrating a major injustice by allowing a guilty person to walk free even when there is compelling evidence of his or her guilt and this can bring the justice system into disrepute.
>
> There are other cases where an acquittal is obtained by subverting the trial by threatening witnesses, by tampering with the jury, or by perjury by defence witnesses. Where such cases come to light the double jeopardy law can stand in the way of justice. For these reasons the government is proposing reforms to the double jeopardy rule in a measured way by creating exceptions framed with precision and containing appropriate safeguards. These reforms will ensure that justice can be done in our courts.

In 2009, NSW parliament made further amendments to account for the need to prosecute an accused following several tainted trials, and also sought to modify the rule against autrefois convict, or double punishment. These changes included removing the prohibition where an accused faces retrial following a tainted acquittal in the first trial or on any subsequent trial, and where the prosecution seeks to appeal against sentence, that the appellate court not discount the new sentence based on the accused's double exposure to sentencing. Thus, where an accused presents for re-sentencing based on a manifestly inadequate or inconsistent sentence, it is common for the appellate court to find sentencing error but dismiss the appeal on the basis that a new sentence is not warranted given the requirements of autrefois convict, that an accused ought not be exposed to the sentencing process more than once. Such modifications speak to the tendency to modify the trial process to allow for changes in forensic procedure and the shifting community expectations of punishment following appeal. This requirement may adhere to the law and order ideology that requires the actual punishment of persons convicted, rather than respect to the notion of sentencing jeopardy whereby the process itself is factored into a proportionate punishment.

Victims' lawyers

Since the 1970s various groups have increasingly criticised the power of the state. The victim rights movement, for example, specifically sought to criticise the removal of the victim from the criminal justice process. Victims became critical of the way they were silenced following an offence, removed from the policing, prosecution and punishment process. Seeking ways in which this removal could be practically redressed, victims formed grassroots movements to lobby government in support of greater victim's services, such as state based compensation. Since the 1970's, each common law jurisdiction has responded to the needs of victims by offering compensation and other modes of support to help satisfy the medical, emotional and financial needs of victims following an offence. The need for redress, however, has now gone beyond the development of support services peripheral to the criminal trial. Each common law jurisdiction now offers victims the opportunity to present a victim impact statement (victim personal statement in England and Wales) that affords victims the opportunity to participate in the sentencing phase of the trial. The needs of discrete groups of victims such as rape victims have also been addressed with the modification of defendant rights in rape trials to allow for the protection of vulnerable victims from the trauma of criminal trials. This has emerged in the form of limitations on the defendant's access to the victim, prohibition on the defendant cross-examining the victim personally, and the prohibition of the examination of the victim's past sexual conduct. This suggests a movement away from traditional defendant rights for the sake of victim interests.

In the context of seeking further reforms integrating the victim in the criminal process, various common law jurisdictions and the International Criminal Court (ICC) allow for the representation of the victim in court. Known as victims' advocates or lawyers, such counsel may represent the interests of the victim at each stage of the criminal trial process – pre-trial hearings, the trial and during sentencing. Such reforms have proven controversial, and debate abounds as to the extent such lawyers may jeopardise the defendant's right to a fair trial. While it is commonly agreed that the various parts of the criminal trial process, such as bail applications, may significantly impact upon the victim and their family, the extent to which the victim ought to be able to contribute to decision-making processes or contest substantive principles of law through counsel remains controversial.

England and Wales

The Secretary of State for Constitutional Affairs and Lord Chancellor, Lord Falconer, issued a consultation paper in 2005 proposing an innovative approach incorporating victim interests by providing family victims an opportunity to be heard before sentencing in homicide cases. The 2005 proposal established a process whereby victims were provided a direct voice in proceedings for homicide offenders (Ministry of Justice, 2005). This policy has now moved through a pilot program in which family victims were given the option to instruct private counsel, known as Victims' Advocates, of the trauma they have suffered as a result of the offence. The Victims' Advocate, a publicly funded lawyer, could be retained by family victims to represent their interests in any proceeding dealing with the charge. Further, the Victims' Advocate would submit the victim personal statement after conviction. Such submissions would ordinarily focus on the stress suffered by each family victim as a result of the loss of the deceased. Family victims would also be able to address the court. The Victims' Advocate presents independently of the prosecution and only represents the victim's interests. As such, they present alongside the prosecutor, who continues to represent the public interest. The Victims' Advocate is limited to the pre-trial and sentencing hearings, and would not play a part in the trial of the offender. It was envisaged that their role would also be extended to plea deals or the downgrading of charges, withdrawal of charges by the prosecution, and discontinuance of proceedings (Secretary of State for Constitutional Affairs and Lord Chancellor, 2006: 16).

Consultation of the government's plans to introduce a Victims' Advocate scheme indicated, of those responding to the consultation paper, that most were in favour of the proposed pilot, with victims groups showing strong support (Secretary of State for Constitutional Affairs and Lord Chancellor, 2006: 5). Some respondents noted that the proposals would do little more than raise a victim's expectation that their personal statements would actually impact sentence. The fear was that many sentencing judges determined sentence prior to any submission made by the Victims' Advocate. Formalising the procedure to be adopted during the pilot, the President of the Queen's Bench Division established a protocol indicating the functions of the Victims' Advocate, particularly in the sentencing process (President of the Queen's Bench Division, 2006). This protocol is written in accordance with the Consolidated Criminal Practice Direction (UK) setting out a victim's right to present a victim personal statement to a sentencing court, and for that court to actually consider it prior to passing sentence. This direction appeared to limit the formal role of the Victims' Advocate to the sentencing phase alone, excluding bail applications and other pre-trial proceedings, despite the policy recommending they be available to advise family victims following charge by the police. Contact between the CPS was emphasised, however, consistent with new duties of prosecutors requiring them to consult with victims in the first instance (CPS, 2007).

The Victims' Advocate scheme was piloted from 24 April 2006 to 23 April 2008 in the Old Bailey in London and the Crown Courts in Birmingham, Cardiff, Manchester (Crown Square) and Winchester. In June 2007, following the announcement in February 2007 that the Victims' Advocate pilot would be extended for a further 12 months, the Attorney-General Lord Goldsmith announced that a variation of the pilot scheme would be made available to all England and Wales (Office for Criminal Justice Reform, 2007: 8). The new program, 'Victim Focus', does not provide for private counsel and is restricted to the sentencing phase following conviction. Under the scheme, family victims are not given any power to address the court personally although such a personal capacity was recognised in the Protocol of the President of the Queen's Bench Division with regard to the Victims' Advocate pilot. However, the ambit of the current scheme seems to guide victims toward

CPS prosecutors who tender the victim's personal statement during the sentencing hearing. Victim Focus is available to family victims where the offender has been charged with murder; manslaughter; corporate manslaughter; familial homicide; causing death by dangerous driving; causing death by careless driving while unfit through drink or drugs; aggravated vehicle taking where death is caused.

The Ministry of Justice has announced plans to continue to evaluate the modified scheme now delivered by the CPS. Specifically, Victim Focus limits the availability of counsel to representation provided by the CPS, removing the possibility of additional private counsel presenting alongside the public prosecutor. The CPS indicate that the scope of the Criminal Practice Direction of the Lord Chief Justice is narrow, where it is suggested that family statements 'cannot affect the sentence that the Judge may pass' (CPS, 2007: Pt 23):

> The effect of an impact statement has subsequently been considered by Lord Justice Judge in relation to the Victim Advocate pilot where a family impact statement may be given. The Family Impact Statement is analogous to a VPS save that the content is limited to the impact of the crime. In the direction provided by Judge LJ, the Family Impact Statement cannot affect the sentence that the Judge may pass and the family will not be able to comment on what they think the sentence should be. However, the Family Impact Statement may help to provide a fuller understanding of the nature and impact of the crime when passing sentence.

While this nuance may provide greater balance between prosecution and defence by limiting a family victim's capacity to intervene in any proceeding against the defendant, it may effectively restore the status quo where victims proceed through the prosecutor, acting in the public interest *a priori*, and where victim impact evidence is given little to no weight in sentencing proceedings. Whether Victim Focus provides an enhanced experience for family victims through the inclusion of their perspectives as to the harms occasioned as a result of the offence thus requires further examination and assessment.

United States

The United States provides substantive rights of participation to victims of crime under federal law. These rights of participation were enacted under the *Justice For All Act 2004*, Pub. L. No. 108–405, 118 Stat. 2260, which came into effect on 30th October 2004. Victims of federal crimes were prescribed rights of participation pursuant to the Scott Campbell, Stephanie Roper, Wendy Preston, Louarna Gillis, and Nila Lynn Crime Victims' Rights Act (CVRA). Although the CVRA does not provide for direct representation by a lawyer, victims are afforded the right to be provided with information and to participate in key decision-making processes in the pre-trial, trial and sentencing phases. Although victims gain participation rights, they are not party to proceedings until they appear in a motion contesting their rights under the CVRA. The CVRA prescribes these rights under 18 USC s3771 that places a duty on the federal courts to ensure that victims are afforded those rights. Section 3771 effectively replaces 42 USC s10606, repealed by the CVRA, which included a list of non-enforceable victims' rights. The CVRA provides that victims are entitled to be present at public court proceedings under s3771(a)(2),(3) CVRA, which includes the right to be 'reasonably heard at any public proceeding in the district court involving release, plea, sentencing, or any parole proceeding' pursuant to s3771(a)(4) CVRA. Most states also provide a means by which victims may participate in various aspects of the criminal trial process. The CVRA, as proscribed under 42 USC s3771 provides for the following substantive rights:

(a) Rights of crime victims. A crime victim has the following rights:
   (1) The right to be reasonably protected from the accused.
   (2) The right to reasonable, accurate, and timely notice of any public court proceeding, or any parole proceeding, involving the crime or of any release or escape of the accused.
   (3) The right not to be excluded from any such public court proceeding, unless the court, after receiving clear and convincing evidence, determines that testimony by the victim would be materially altered if the victim heard other testimony at that proceeding.
   (4) The right to be reasonably heard at any public proceeding in the district court involving release, plea, sentencing, or any parole proceeding.
   (5) The reasonable right to confer with the attorney for the Government in the case.
   (6) The right to full and timely restitution as provided in law.
   (7) The right to proceedings free from unreasonable delay.
   (8) The right to be treated with fairness and with respect for the victim's dignity and privacy.

(b) Rights afforded:
  (1) In general. In any court proceeding involving an offense against a crime victim, the court shall ensure that the crime victim is afforded the rights described in subsection (a). Before making a determination described in subsection (a)(3), the court shall make every effort to permit the fullest attendance possible by the victim and shall consider reasonable alternatives to the exclusion of the victim from the criminal proceeding. The reasons for any decision denying relief under this chapter shall be clearly stated on the record.

Issues arising under the CVRA include whether an individual may be considered a victim for the purpose of the Act. In *US v Sharp* (2006) 463 F Supp 2d 556 at 561–567, the defendant entered a guilty plea for conspiracy to possess with intent to distribute marijuana. The partner of one of the defendant's customers alleged that she was abused as a result of her partner's use of the drug sold by the defendant, rendering her a victim of the offence charged. The court discussed the meaning of 'directly and proximately harmed' and ruled that she was not a victim of the defendant's offence under the CVRA. The court ruled that a partner of a drug user was not proximately connected to the supplier of that drug in a way envisioned by the CVRA. Linking a partner's suffering to a supplier was too attenuated, either temporally or factually, to confer 'victim' status on the present claimant. A victim needs to be able to demonstrate a sufficient nexus between the defendant's acts and the consequences resultant upon them.

The victim's right to participate in trial processes includes the right to be reasonably heard as determined in *Kenna v US District Court* (2006) 435 F 3d 1011. In *Kenna*, the Ninth Circuit Court of Appeals ruled that the right to be reasonably heard included the right to provide oral or written statements during sentencing. Victims thus enjoyed a right to allocution, to read their victim impact statement to the court, granting victims similar rights of address as held by the defendant. *Kenna* thus affirmed the intent of Congress to provide for the participation of victims in the criminal trial process. The court rules (at 1016):

> Our interpretation advances the purposes of the CVRA. The statute was enacted to make crime victims full participants in the criminal justice system. Prosecutors and defendants already have the right to

speak at sentencing, see Fed. R. Crim. P. 32(i)(4)(A); our interpretation puts crime victims on the same footing. Our interpretation also serves to effectuate other statutory aims: (1) To ensure that the district court doesn't discount the impact of the crime on the victims; (2) to force the defendant to confront the human cost of his crime; and (3) to allow the victim 'to regain a sense of dignity and respect rather than feeling powerless and ashamed.' Jayne W. Barnard, Allocution for Victims of Economic Crimes, 77 Notre Dame L. Rev. 39, 41 (2001). Limiting victims to written impact statements, while allowing the prosecutor and the defendant the opportunity to address the court, would treat victims as secondary participants in the sentencing process. The CVRA clearly meant to make victims full participants.

In re Antrobus (2008) 519 F 3d 1123, however, the defendant entered a guilty plea to the illegal transfer of a handgun to a juvenile, who, after reaching the age of 18, killed several people at a shopping centre. The gunman was also killed. The parents of one of the victims at the shopping centre petitioned the court to have their daughter recognised as a victim of the transfer of handgun offence, assuming her rights under s3771(e) CVRA. This would have allowed the parents of the deceased to be heard at the defendant's sentencing hearing. The Tenth Circuit Court of Appeals ruled that the transfer of a handgun was not a direct and proximate cause of their daughter's killing. As such, the daughter was not a 'victim' of the handgun sale pursuant to s3771(e) CVRA. The parents did not gain the right to be heard at sentencing. The court ruled (at 1131):

> If we were to hold, on this record, that petitioners' daughter is a crime victim within the meaning of the CVRA, we would effectively establish a per se rule that any harm inflicted by an adult using a gun he or she illegally obtained as a minor is directly and proximately caused by the seller of the gun. In the instant case, and on this record, Mackenzie Glade Hunter knew only that Sulejman Talovic was a minor at the time the gun changed hands; the record before us is silent on the question whether Mr. Hunter had knowledge of Mr. Talovic's intentions with the firearm, see January 11, 2008 Order at 5, and Mr. Talovic was apparently an adult when he committed his terrible crimes. Id. at 6; Appellee's Response to Petition for Writ of Mandamus, Ex. B at 2. To be sure, some courts hold that the seller of a gun to a minor in violation of a statute is

per se the proximate cause of harm inflicted by the minor (during his or her minority) with that gun. And to be sure, there are courts that refuse to apply a *per se* rule, but will hold sellers liable for harm inflicted by minors (again, during their minority) when there is some indicia that the seller of the gun knew of the minor's intent to misuse it. But petitioners have directed us to no authority of any kind suggesting that harm inflicted by an adult with a gun purchased during the adult's minority is, without more, *per se* directly and proximately caused by the seller of the gun.

Other notable aspects of the CVRA allow the victim to seek judicial review of the prosecution's capacity to make a plea deal with the defendant. Victims have the ability to participate in all stages of the criminal trial although most often seek to participate in pre-trial decision making processes or in sentencing. As to pre-trial matters, victims have the right to be kept informed and to make representation and to prepare for their appearance at each hearing leading to the plea hearing, in particular. In this regard, the first case to arise under the CVRA amendments sought to limit the victim's capacity to litigate under the CVRA despite affirming that the requisite test for the issuing of a writ to the prosecution to revise a plea deal made with the defendant ought to be issued under an ordinary standard of review. *In re Huff Asset Management Co.* (2005) 409 F 3d 555, the Second Circuit Court of Appeals ruled that a writ of mandamus may be issued according to the ordinary standards of review (at 562):

> Under the plain language of the CVRA, however, Congress has chosen a petition for mandamus as a mechanism by which a crime victim may appeal a district court's decision denying relief sought under the provisions of the CVRA. See 18 USC s3771(d)(3) ('the movant may petition the court of appeals for a writ of mandamus'); s3771(d)(5)(B) ('A victim may make a motion to re-open a plea or sentence only if... the victim petitions the court of appeals for a writ of mandamus within 10 days....'). It is clear, therefore, that a petitioner seeking relief pursuant to the mandamus provision set forth in s3771(d)(3) need not overcome the hurdles typically faced by a petitioner seeking review of a district court determination through a writ of mandamus.

The test for the issuing of a mandamus was revised, however, *In re Antrobus* (2008) 519 F 3d 1123 at 1124–1126. The Tenth Circuit

Court of Appeals found that a stricter standard should prevail, in particular, over the nominal standard for the issuing of a writ of mandamus. Given the extraordinary nature of such a writ, the court ruled that the appropriate standard ought to be the stricter standard, acknowledging that the term mandamus 'is a well worn term of art in our common law tradition' (at 1127). As clarified in *In re Dean* (2008) 527 F 3d 391 at 393–394, discussed below, such a writ ought to be issued where the petitioner has 'no other adequate means' of relief, that the petitioner has demonstrated a right to the issuance of a writ which is 'clear and indisputable' and where the issuing court, in the exercise of its discretion, is satisfied that the writ is 'appropriate under the circumstances' (see *In re Antrobus* (2008) 519 F 3d 1123 at 1130; also see *United States v Roberts* (1996) 88 F 3d 872; *Dalton v United States (In re Dalton)* (1984) 733 F 2d 710).

In *United States v BP Product North America* (2008) WL 501321 (SD Tex), an explosion at a BP Products refinery in Texas in 2005 caused a significant amount of damage resulting in 185 victims, a civil action and criminal charges. Prior to filing criminal charges, the government obtained an order from the district court allowing it to reach a plea deal with the defendant. The victims were to be notified following the reaching of the plea arrangement. The prosecution did not think it practical to approach such a large number of victims, which in itself would have attracted significant media attention, to negotiate a plea deal. After agreement was reached, however, the prosecution was required to inform the victims of the court order and to ensure that the victims would be able to attend the plea hearing and exercise their right to be heard. An agreement was soon reached between prosecution and defence. Notice of the agreement was then forwarded to the victims. However, before the plea hearing lawyers for the victims filed motions in opposition to the plea agreement. At the hearing, the defendant entered a guilty plea and counsel representing the victims argued that the court ought to reject the plea agreement.

Following the initial hearing, victims further filed that the agreement be rejected on the basis that the prosecution did not avail itself of obligations under the CVRA, essentially that the prosecution had failed to extend to victims a reasonable right to confer with the prosecution, to be treated with fairness and to use its best efforts to notify the victims of these rights. The court ruled that the prosecution acted lawfully under the CVRA by meeting the s3771(a)(2) requirement of a 'right to reasonable, accurate, and timely notice of any public court proceeding'. The prosecution had issued three mailings to victims informing them of the court hearings, had established a website and telephone contact, and made a victim-witness coordinator available for consultation. The court found that the victims had participated in the plea hearing either personally or through counsel. Importantly, the right to confer was subject to differing interpretations based on case law, legislative history, and Department of Justice guidelines. In *United States v BP Product North America* the court ruled (at 20):

> In this case, the record shows that the unusual circumstances of the presence of multiple victims and the intense media coverage made it impracticable for the victims to receive notice of the plea negotiations and to confer with the government before the negotiations concluded. The record also shows that the government had been in communication with many of those affected by the explosion well in advance of any plea negotiations. (Docket Entry No. 26 at 31–32; Docket Entry No. 63 at 5). The government's extensive investigation had allowed it to learn much from the victims before any plea negotiations. The government knew before it agreed to the plea that the families of those who died, the individuals injured in the explosion and their families, and others affected by the explosion, had strong views that BP Products should receive the maximum available punishment. The government had the victims' opinions about the need for a criminal charge and a severe sanction. To read the right to confer as an inflexible right to express an opinion on specific terms that the government and defendant are negotiating would both endanger the confidentiality of plea negotiations and suggest that crime victims have a right to join in plea negotiations and to approve the proposed terms, inconsistent with the CVRA recognition of prosecutorial discretion.

However, in *In re Dean* (2008) 527 F 3d 391 victims from *United States v BP Product North America* petitioned the Fifth Circuit Court of Appeals for a writ of mandamus following the district court's ruling dismissing their motion to reject the plea agreement. The Court of Appeals agreed that the victim's rights under the CVRA had been violated although it denied the petition as it failed to meet the strict standards for granting a writ of mandamus. The court first held that it agreed with *In re Antrobus*, that the strict standards for obtaining a writ of mandamus should apply, rather than the ordinary standard as applied in *Kenna* and *In re Huff*. *In re Dean*, the court ruled (at 393–394):

> The parties dispute the standard of review. The victims assert that despite the fact that the CVRA states that '[i]f the district court denies the relief sought [by a *394 victim], the movant may petition the court of appeals for a writ of mandamus,' 18 USC s3771(d)(3), the ordinary appeal standards (instead of the stricter standards for obtaining a writ of mandamus) apply. Two circuits agree with the victims. See *Kenna v. United States Dist. Court*, 435 F. 3d 1011, 1017 (9th Cir. 2006); *In re W.R. Huff Asset Mgmt. Co.*, 409 F. 3d 555, 563 (2d Cir. 2005).
>
> The Tenth Circuit, however, taking the view that '[m]andamus is a well worn term of art in our common law tradition,' most recently has held that mandamus standards apply. *In re Antrobus*, 519 F. 3d 1123, 1127 (10th Cir. 2008) (per curiam) (on petition for rehearing and rehearing en banc). We are in accord with the Tenth Circuit for the reasons stated in its opinion.
>
> ...
>
> A writ of mandamus may issue only if (1) the petitioner has 'no other adequate means' to attain the desired relief; (2) the petitioner has demonstrated a right to the issuance of a writ that is 'clear and indisputable;' and (3) the issuing court, in the exercise of its discretion, is satisfied that the writ is 'appropriate under the circumstances'.

The Fifth Circuit Court of Appeals went on to suggest, however, that 185 victims were not too many for the government to contact prior to negotiating a plea deal. The appellate court was also critical of the district court's concern that the early notification of victims could harm the plea negotiation, attract undue media attention and thereby prejudice the case should no deal be reached. The court ruled (at 395):

> The real rub for the government and the district court was that, as the district judge who handled the *ex parte* proceeding as a miscellaneous matter reasoned, "'[d]ue to extensive media coverage of the... explosion..., any public notification of a potential criminal disposition resulting from the government's investigation... would

prejudice BP... and could impair the plea negotiation process and may prejudice the case in the event that no plea is reached.'" BP Prods., 2008 WL 501321 at *2, 2008 US Dist. LEXIS 12893, at *6–*7. In making that observation, the court missed the purpose of the CVRA's right to confer. In passing the Act, Congress made the policy decision-which we are bound to enforce-that the victims have a right to inform the plea negotiation process by conferring with prosecutors before a plea agreement is reached. That is not an infringement, as the district court believed, on the government's independent prosecutorial discretion, see id. 2008 WL 501321, at *11–12, 2008 US Dist. LEXIS 12893, at *37–*38; instead, it is only a requirement that the government confer in some reasonable way with the victims before ultimately exercising its broad discretion.

The Fifth Circuit Court of Appeals, however, denied the writ because it was appropriate to do so under the circumstances given that victims were notified and were allowed substantial and meaningful participation at the plea hearing. The appellate court noted that although it denied relief on this occasion, that the district court will take note that to this point, the victims were not accorded their full rights pursuant to the CVRA and is required to consider the objections of victims as the matter proceeds.

Australia

In Australian law, victims do not have a prescribed right to appoint a lawyer to representing them in proceedings in the criminal justice system. A victim may participate in sentencing proceedings of their own motion by presenting a victim impact statement, generally recognised throughout the states and territories and for Commonwealth offences prosecuted in state courts. Victims may seek the services of a lawyer to assist with an application for victims' compensation, although such schemes exist outside the ambit of the criminal law and trial process (Kirchengast, 2009). However, there may exist two limited bases upon which a victim may appoint counsel to represent them in the criminal justice system: through private prosecution or by challenging the ODPPs decision to prosecute in the first instance.

The power of private prosecution resides in the common informant and is available to any individual seeking to inform a court of an offence. The current procedure for NSW allows a individual to seek a court attendance notice from the registrar of the Local Court. The registrar will conduct a cursory review of the charge and the evidence in support of it. Should the registrar decline to issue the court attendance notice, the individual, represented by counsel, may challenge the decision before a magistrate. Should the court attendance notice be issued, the defendant will be summonsed to court to answer the change in the usual way (see s49 *Criminal Procedure Act 1986* (NSW)). The police prosecutor or ODPP solicitor would be replaced by the victim themselves or their counsel. Note that under NSW law, the ODPP may step in at any time to take over the matter pursuant to s9 *Director of Public Prosecution Act 1986* (NSW). This effectively gives the ODPP the power to undertake any prosecution initiated by the police, victim or other person and includes the power to discontinue proceedings.[6] Consents to prosecute increasingly fetter the power of the common informant such that any individual attempting to inform a court of a prescribed offence (such as incest and incest attempts, see s78F *Crimes Act 1900* (NSW)), now requires the sanction of the Attorney-General.

The individual's right to seek review of a decision to prosecute, a decision ordinarily reserved for the state, is a right expressed by the common law. *Maxwell v The Queen* (1996) 184 CLR 501 is authority for the proposition that decisions of the ODPP as to whether or not to proceed on indictment is generally not reviewable, save in the most exceptional circumstances. *R v DPP, Ex parte C* [1995] 1 Cr App R 136 provides, however, that where the decision to prosecute is contrary to law, jurisdictional error or not made in accordance with the Code for Crown Prosecutors (CCP), a stay could be lifted for want of procedural fairness. *Ex parte C* is thus a significant decision affirming the basis upon which individual victim rights may be displaced by a decision of the state. However limited, the challenging of prosecutorial decision-making by victims or other interested parties, otherwise deemed outside the scope of the criminal trial at common law, suggests that the common law may provide a limited means by which prosecutorial decision-making may be challenged by private counsel.

The International Criminal Court

The ICC provides a mechanism by which victims may address the court personally, so long this does not compromise the defendant's right to a fair trial (see art. 68(3) Rome Statute, A/CONF.183/9):

> Where the personal interests of the victims are affected, the Court shall permit their views and concerns to be presented and considered at stages of the proceedings determined to be appropriate by the Court and in a manner which is not prejudicial to or

110 *The Criminal Trial in Law and Discourse*

inconsistent with the rights of the accused and a fair and impartial trial. Such views and concerns may be presented by the legal representatives of the victims where the Court considers it appropriate, in accordance with the Rules of Procedure and Evidence.

The Rome Statute of the ICC contains provisions that allow victims to participate in all stages of proceedings before the ICC. Article 68(3) of the Rome Statute allows victims to articulate their views and perspective in accordance with the Rules of Procedure and Evidence of the ICC (ICC-ASP/1/3). The Office of Public Counsel for Victims was established under Reg. 81, and provides representation for victims appearing before the ICC, free of charge (Regulations of the International Criminal Court (ICC-BD/01-01-04), Reg. 81). These provisions ensure a measure of balance between retributive and restorative justice that also provides for a level of reconciliation by allowing the victim to participate in proceedings in a formal way. Article 75 provides for reparation from one individual to another. The lawyer may seek reparation by way of restitution, indemnification or rehabilitation. The ICC may grant individual or collective reparation, to a group of victims or to an entire community. If collective reparation is ordered, then this may be paid to a state or non-government organisation.

The rise of terrorism

The rise of terrorism as a significant threat to the state justifies, for some, the shifting of the previous protections provided to suspects and defendants. Those persons now suspected of terrorist offences may be detained, in certain cases without cause, for days or weeks at a time. Such suspects may be interrogated without access to a lawyer and their detention may be continued with minimal grounds for judicial review. The executive may now detain or control certain suspects or others convicted of terrorist offences long after they have been released from prison. This illustrates the expanded use of state power against the rights of the individual. Such rights have previously been held in check by the criminal trial in that it was principally through this tribunal that such restrictions could be lawfully prescribed.

Control orders – A criminal charge?

In *Secretary of State for the Home Department v MB and AF* [2008] 1 AC 440, Lord Bingham of Cornhill answers the question as to whether a non-derogating control order is a criminal charge, as conventionally understood. His Lordship ultimately determines that proceedings for a non-derogating control order do not involve the resolution of a criminal charge. The distinction is found in the purpose or rationale of a control order. Such orders are preventative, not punitive or retributive. In this sense, they are forward looking, and not a reflective exercise of criminal punishment. Arguably, the line distinguishing control orders and charges under the criminal law may be extremely fine. The sentencing options available to criminal courts include many orders that look forward in time, to control or regulate the conduct of the accused, which may include preventing or minimising the chance of re-offending. Bonds are one such order. Although Lord Bingham of Cornhill was not inclined to conflate the process leading to the granting of a control order with a criminal charge, his Lordship highlights the requirement under art. 6 of the ECHR, that an accused person is entitled to a level of procedural fairness commensurate with the gravity of the consequences of the order (at 473):

> I would on balance accept the Secretary of State's submission that non-derogating control order proceedings do not involve the determination of a criminal charge. Parliament has gone to some lengths to avoid a procedure which crosses the criminal boundary: there is no assertion of criminal conduct, only a foundation of suspicion; no identification of any specific criminal offence is provided for; the order made is preventative in purpose, not punitive or retributive; and the obligations imposed must be no more restrictive than are judged necessary to achieve the preventative object of the order. I would reject AF's contrary submission. This reflects the approach of the English courts up to now: *A v Secretary of State for the Home Department* [2002] EWCA Civ 1502, [2004] QB 335, para 57. But I would accept the substance of AF's alternative submission: in any case in which a person is at risk of an order containing obligations of the stringency found in this case, or the cases of JJ and others and E, the application of the civil limb of article 6(1) does in my opinion entitle such person to such measure of procedural protection as is commensurate with the gravity of the potential consequences. This has been the approach of the domestic courts in cases such as B, Gough and McCann, above, and it seems to me to reflect the spirit of the Convention.

Gleeson CJ in *Thomas v Mowbray* (2007) 233 CLR 307 considers the examples of bail and apprehended violence orders as powers similar to those available to a court under the *Anti-Terrorism Act (No. 2) 2005* (Cth). Such powers, it was held, are not foreign to the exercise of judicial power. Gleeson CJ likens such orders to those available under Australian criminal law.[7] Although the High Court of Australia is not called upon to determine whether control orders are tantamount to a criminal charge *per se*, the court is asked to determine whether such orders, being punitive in character, are in fact a criminal punishment to the extent that such orders should only be available following a criminal conviction. Gleeson CJ disagrees (at 330):

> Alternatively, it was argued that the restriction on liberty involved in the power to make a control order is penal or punitive in character, and the governmental power involved exists only as an incident of the exclusively judicial function of adjudging and punishing criminal guilt... We are concerned with preventive restraints on liberty by judicial order. *Fardon* was an example of preventive detention in custody pursuant to judicial order. Apprehended violence orders made by judicial officers also involve restrictions on liberty falling short of detention in custody. It is not correct to say, as an absolute proposition, that, under our system of government, restraints on liberty, whether or not involving detention in custody, exist only as an incident of adjudging and punishing criminal guilt.

Given the similarities between powers of control used in the criminal jurisdiction and those available under the *Prevention of Terrorism Act 2005* (UK) and *Anti-Terrorism Act (No. 2) 2005* (Cth), a question remains as to their true 'jurisdictional' character. It is not enough to dismiss control orders as not 'backward looking' to the extent that a sentence following a criminal conviction is based on a retrospective of the seriousness of the offence and offender. Gleeson CJ attacks the issue in the opposite way, by likening control orders to criminal processes such as bail, a well recognised criminal procedure. Gleeson CJ and Lord Bingham of Cornhill seem to come to the same point by a different path of analysis; his Lordship ruling that control orders are not criminal as 'the order made is preventative in purpose, not punitive or retributive' while his Honour rules that restraints on liberty may result from applications other than those 'adjudging and punishing criminal guilt'.[8] Ashworth (2009: 96) remarks that control orders and other 'civil' orders involving a form of restraint may be a hybrid of the civil and criminal law to the extent that the orders initially imposed may be supported by a regime of criminal punishments, including imprisonment.⁹

Non-derogating control orders and the ECHR

This section extends upon the discussion of the *Anti-Terrorism Act (No. 2) 2005* (Cth) in Chapter 1 where, in the case of *Thomas v Mowbray* (2007) 233 CLR 307, the High Court of Australia determined that control orders that allow for the restricted liberty of the controlled person were constitutional. This may be contrasted to the English situation where the initial version of 'control orders', as prescribed under s23 of the *Anti-Terrorism, Crime and Security Act 2001* (UK), provided for the indefinite detention of non-British nationals suspected of terrorist activity. In *A v Secretary of State for the Home Department* [2005] 2 AC 68 the House of Lords declared s23 of the *Anti-Terrorism, Crime and Security Act 2001* (UK) incompatible with articles 5 and 14 of the ECHR. Lord Scott of Foscote, making the orders of Lord Bingham of Cornhill, said of the legislation (at 148):

> Section 23 constitutes, in my opinion, a derogation from article 5(1) at the extreme end of the severity spectrum. An individual who is detained under section 23 will be a person accused of no crime but a person whom the Secretary of State has certified that he 'reasonably… suspects… is a terrorist' (section 21(1)). The individual may then be detained in prison indefinitely. True it is that he can leave the United Kingdom if he elects to do so but the reality in many cases will be that the only country to which he is entitled to go will be a country where he is likely to undergo torture if he does go there.

As a result, parliament enacted the *Prevention of Terrorism Act 2005* (UK), which now makes provision for derogating and non-derogating control orders. The explanatory notes for the *Prevention of Terrorism Act 2005* (UK) distinguishes derogating from non-derogating control orders (at par 5):

> Control orders that do not involve derogating from the European Convention on Human Rights (ECHR), called 'non-derogating control orders', will be made by the Secretary of State. The Secretary of State must seek permission from the court to make a non-derogating control order. However, in cases of urgency, the Secretary of State can make an order without first seeking the permission of the court but he must refer it immediately to the court for confirmation.

Control orders that do involve derogating from the ECHR will be made by the court itself on application from the Secretary of State. Such control orders are called 'derogating control orders'. All control orders will be subject to full hearings by the High Court or Court of Session. There will be a right of appeal on a point of law from a decision of the High Court or Court of Session.

Section 2(1) of the 2005 Act provides the power to make a control order against an individual so long as the Secretary of State:

(a) has reasonable grounds for suspecting that the individual is or has been involved in terrorism-related activity; and
(b) considers that it is necessary, for purposes connected with protecting members of the public from a risk of terrorism, to make a control order imposing obligations on that individual.

The *Prevention of Terrorism Act 2005* (UK) provides a means by which a non-derogating control may be made by the Secretary of State. The issue that continues to emerge for resolution before the House of Lords concerns the mode of hearing, and the extent to which the defendant may be privy to the intelligence of the Secretary of State, in particular. Whether it is fair to make a non-derogating control order under circumstances where a defendant may be deprived of the intelligence against them is at issue. The rules that govern a s3(10) hearing under the *Prevention of Terrorism Act 2005* (UK) were summarised by Lord Bingham of Cornhill in *Secretary of State for the Home Department v MB and AF* [2008] 1 AC 440 (at 474–475):

> The Schedule to the 2005 Act provides a rule-making power applicable to both derogating and non-derogating control orders. It requires the rule-making authority (paragraph 2(b)) to have regard in particular to the need to ensure that disclosures of information are not made where they would be contrary to the public interest. Rules so made (paragraph 4(2)(b)) may make provision enabling the relevant court to conduct proceedings in the absence of any person, including a relevant party to the proceedings and his legal representative. Provision may be made for the appointment of a person to represent a relevant party: paragraphs 4(2)(c) and 7. The Secretary of State must be required to disclose all relevant material (paragraph 4(3)(a)), but may apply to the court for permission not to do so: paragraph 4(3)(b). Such application must be heard in the absence of

every relevant person and his legal representative (paragraph 4(3)(c)) and the court must give permission for material not to be disclosed where it considers that the disclosure of the material would be contrary to the public interest: paragraph 4(3)(d). The court must consider requiring the Secretary of State to provide the relevant party and his legal representative with a summary of the material withheld (paragraph 4(3)(e)), but the court must ensure that such summary does not contain information or other material the disclosure of which would be contrary to the public interest: paragraph 4(3)(f). If the Secretary of State elects not to disclose or summarise material which he is required to disclose or summarise, the court may give directions withdrawing from its consideration the matter to which the material is relevant or otherwise ensure that the material is not relied on: paragraph 4(4).

CPR Pt 76 gives effect to the procedural scheme authorised by the Schedule to the 2005 Act. Rule 76.2 modifies the overriding objective of the Rules so as to require a court to ensure that information is not disclosed contrary to the public interest. Rule 76.1(4) stipulates that disclosure is contrary to the public interest if it is made contrary to the interests of national security, the international relations of the United Kingdom, the detection or prevention of crime, or in any other circumstances where disclosure is likely to harm the public interest. Part III of the Rule applies to non-derogating control orders. It is unnecessary to rehearse its detailed terms. Provision is made for the exclusion of a relevant person and his legal representative from a hearing to secure that information is not disclosed contrary to the public interest: rule 76.22. Provision is made for the appointment of a special advocate whose function is to represent the interests of a relevant party (rules 76.23, 76.24), but who may only communicate with the relevant party before closed material is served upon him, save with permission of the court: rules 76.25, 76.28(2). The ordinary rules governing evidence and inspection of documents are not to apply (rule 76.26): evidence may be given orally or in writing, and in documentary or any other form; it may receive evidence which would not be admissible in a court of law; it is provided by rule 76.26(5) that 'Every party shall be entitled to adduce evidence and to cross-examine witnesses during any part of a hearing from which he and his legal representative are not excluded'.

The process for issuing a non-derogating control orders under the *Prevention of Terrorism Act 2005* (UK) with the assistance, where applicable, of a special advocate in relation to the use of 'closed material' which, for security reasons, may be unable to be personally disclosed to the defendant to whom the control order relates, was discussed by Lord Bingham of Cornhill in *Secretary of State for the Home Department v MB and AF* [2008] 1 AC 440, 474. These provisions, enacted so as to afford the defendant a measure of procedural fairness in dealing with the intelligence that lead to the control order against them, have since been declared as undermining a fair trial following the decision of ECtHR in *A v UK* (2009) 268 BHRC 1 (see *Secretary of State for the Home Department v AF* (No 3) [2009] 3 WLR 74).

Lord Bingham of Cornhill in *Secretary of State for the Home Department v MB and AF* [2008] 1 AC 440, raises some salient point as to the granting of a non-derogating control order where the defendant is not privy to the intelligence against them. In this case, AF (with MB) was the subject of a non-derogating control order issued by the Secretary of State under ss2 and 3(1)(a) of the *Prevention of Terrorism Act 2005* (UK). The order was made on the basis that AF was suspected of associating with Islamist extremists, some of whom were affiliated with the Libyan Islamic Fighting Group, a prescribed terrorist organisation. After a full hearing under s3(10), Ouseley J quashed the order but dismissed an application by AF for a declaration that the order was incompatible with the ECHR.

Lord Bingham of Cornhill summarised the impact of the non-derogating control order to which AF was subject (at 468–469):

> By the 11 September control order AF was required to remain in the flat where he was already living (not including any communal area) at all times save for a period of 10 hours between 8 am and 6 pm. He was thus subject to a 14 hour curfew. He was required to wear an electronic tag at all times. He was restricted during non-curfew hours to an area of about 9 square miles bounded by a number of identified main roads and bisected by one. He was to report to a monitoring company on first leaving his flat after a curfew period had ended and on his last return before the next curfew period began. His flat was liable to be searched by the police at any time. During curfew hours he was not allowed to permit any person to enter his flat except his father, official or professional visitors, children aged 10 or under or persons agreed by the Home Office in advance on supplying the visitor's name, address, date of birth and photographic identification. He was not to communicate directly or indirectly at any time with a certain specified individual (and, later,

several specified individuals). He was only permitted to attend one specified mosque. He was not permitted to have any communications equipment of any kind. He was to surrender his passport. He was prohibited from visiting airports, sea ports or certain railway stations, and was subject to additional obligations pertaining to his financial arrangements.

Lord Bingham of Cornhill concludes that the process open to AF (and MB) afforded little chance to know the actual case against them to the point where it may compromise their right to a fair hearing (at 482):

> The judge accepted, at para 146, without qualification, submissions by counsel for AF that no, or at least no clear or significant, allegations of involvement in terrorist-related activity were disclosed by the open material, that no such allegations had been gisted, that the case made by the Secretary of State against AF was in its essence entirely undisclosed to him and that no allegations of wrongdoing had been put to him by the police in interview after his arrest, affording him an idea by that side wind of what the case against him might be.
> ... If, as I understand the House to have accepted in *Roberts*, above, the concept of fairness imports a core, irreducible minimum of procedural protection, I have difficulty, on the judge's findings, in concluding that such protection has been afforded to AF. The right to a fair hearing is fundamental. In the absence of a derogation (where that is permissible) it must be protected.

In *Secretary of State for the Home Department v AF* (No. 3) [2009] 3 WLR 74 three appellants, AF, AN and AE were subject to non-derogating control orders under s2 of the *Prevention of Terrorism Act 2005* (UK). The control orders were made on the basis that the Secretary of State had reasonable grounds for suspecting that the appellants were, or had been, involved in terrorist activity. The issue raised in this present appeal concerns whether the process that led to the making of the non-derogating control order conformed with the appellant's right to a fair hearing pursuant to art. 6 of the ECHR. Lord Hope of Craighead remarked (at 105):

> The principle that the accused has a right to know what is being alleged against him has a long pedigree. As Lord Scott of Foscote

observed in *A v Secretary of State for the Home Department,* a denunciation on grounds that are not disclosed is the stuff of nightmares. The rule of law in a democratic society does not tolerate such behaviour. The fundamental principle is that everyone is entitled to the disclosure of sufficient material to enable him to answer effectively the case that is made against him. The domestic and European authorities on which this proposition rests were referred to by Lord Bingham in *Roberts v Parole Board*. In Secretary of State for the Home Department v MB he drew attention to McLachlin CJ's observation for the Supreme Court of Canada in *Charkaoui v Canada* (Minister of Citizenship and Immigration) that a person whose liberty is in jeopardy must know the case he has to meet and to *Hamdi v Rumsfeld* where it was declared by O'Connor J for the majority in the US Supreme Court that for more than a century it has been clear that parties whose rights are to be affected are entitled to be heard and that in order that they may enjoy that right they must first be notified.

The jurisprudence that has emerged around the rights of the accused subject to a non-derogating control order is drawn from an established body of doctrine that gives the accused the right to know their accuser. In Chapter 5 this issue is discussed in the context of the use of out of court evidence and the confrontation clause of the Constitution of the United States and the extent to which courts may be willing to entertain new approaches to evidence in order to meet the competing interests of victim rights and due process. As is the case in *Secretary of State for the Home Department v AF,* the requirements of a fair hearing are not easily overcome, save those matters where countermeasures are in place to offset any prejudicial effect to the accused. Chapter 4 examines those causes where the courts have sought to balance the rights of the accused against those of the victim by evaluating the appropriateness of the countermeasures undertaken to preserve the defendant's right to a fair trial.

4
The Transformative Criminal Trial Emerges

> According to the popular image, in a British criminal trial witnesses give evidence before a robed judge and a jury and they are examined and cross-examined by bewigged counsel for the Crown and for the defence. Inevitably, that image is over-simplified. The vast majority of trials take place before magistrates; the representatives of both sides may be solicitors rather than counsel and, in exceptional cases, in England – but not in Scotland – even trials for serious offences may proceed in the absence of the accused. Where children are involved, in the Crown Court wigs and gowns are discarded and various other steps are taken to make the proceedings less formal. In the Youth Court the proceedings are always relatively informal, being tailored to the requirements of the children who appear there. Historically, also, the popular image does not tell the whole story. For centuries, in England the parties in a criminal trial usually had no professional representation. The prosecutor and his witnesses would put their side of the story and the accused would try to discredit it. In that world, cross-examination and formal rules of evidence were unknown: they are the products of the adversarial form of trial that emerged when, in the course of the eighteenth and early nineteenth centuries, it became common for counsel to be instructed. *Since the forms of trial have evolved in this way over the centuries, there is no reason to suppose that today's norm represents the ultimate state of perfection* or that the procedures will not evolve further, as technology advances.
>
> Lord Rodger of Earlsferry, *R v Camberwell Green Youth Court* [2005] 1 All ER 999 at 1004–1005. (emphasis added)

This chapter will argue that the modern criminal trial is less adversarial and increasingly decentralised than is currently realised. The criminal trial is emerging as an institution of transformative justice. As Lord Rodger of Earlsferry indicates, the criminal trial need not be organised around the principles of adversarialism to the exclusion of other pathways to justice. As demonstrated in Chapter 3, this decentralisation takes effect through a range of criminal justice policies that challenge the notion that the adversarial trial takes a prescribed form. Such policies not only come to affect the scope of the conventional trial by indictment before a 'judge and jury', but affect the pre-trial and sentencing processes as well. The need for expediency, the law and order debate, the rise of terrorism, victim's rights, and the rise of new court procedures to bind persons over to prevent offending, have each challenged the conventional means by which persons are being held to account for their wrongdoing. The liability of the offender is now dealt with through an array of processes, across a number of tribunals, each of which dislocate the trial experience from a nominal adversarial process. A number of common law jurisdictions are therefore modifying the conventional approach to the adversarial criminal trial to connect individuals, such as victims, and groups, such as the community and service organisations, to effect a different, perhaps less centralised criminal process.

This notion of the transformative trial is not based on any normative or prescribed account of what the trial ought to be. It is transgressive to the extent that it seeks to break some of the rules of criminal procedure, while holding onto others. This chapter will further argue that the transformative criminal trial is neither normative nor prescriptive. As such, it is impossible to map the strictures through which this notion of the trial seeks to operate. Rather, the notion of the transformative criminal trial merely reminds us that the criminal trial is not a normative institution that functions according to a prescribed set of rules and principles. It is not that rules and processes of general application constitute particular aspects of the criminal trial. Trial processes and rules of evidence are of application between trials. The point is that the social institution of the criminal trial is not restricted to a set adversarial process before judge and jury. Adversarial processes may vary, or be more inquisitorial, or be modified to include different agents of justice, such as the victim. The adversarial criminal trial as a normative experience is being increasingly sidestepped for alternative means to justice. This, arguably, is consistent with the genealogy of the trial discussed in Chapter 2.

Findlay and Henham (2005: 322–323; also see Findlay and Henham, 2010: 5–9) suggest that such a transition, in the context of integrating the victim into international criminal justice, may occur through the reconsideration of relationships within the normative framework of the trial. This is consistent with the development of a variety of new institutions, such as problem-solving courts, and the modification of established institutions, through the inclusion of the victim and the community in sentencing proceedings, or through the consideration of human rights discourse, such that the trial becomes 'experimental' to the extent that it seeks to break some of the rules within a network of established, normative, or given processes:

> The essence of trial transformation following on from an ideological shift in justification could be achieved by considering how trial relationships can be reconsidered within a normative framework that facilitates change. Such a framework would reflect the rebalancing of victims' interests and suggests the possibilities for mediation, diversion and multi-agency pathways to be developed within the trial process. These institutional reforms would provide victims with an active processual role in terms of initiation, negotiation and participation. Consequently, existing decision relationships, such as that between prosecutor and defence advocate, would be directed towards the establishment of a different kind of evidential truth, whilst the formative and instrumental focus for the process, would be maintained by the judiciary.

The modern criminal trial, however, is non-prescriptive, decentralised and transformative to the extent that (i) trials are increasingly taking an alternative form (take, for instance, the rise of problem-solving courts, proceedings leading to the issuing of control orders), and (ii) the sources of information and evidence from which courts draw is increasingly derived from non-standard sources (for example, victim impact evidence, government intelligence, victims lawyers, community panels, human rights discourse). This chapter will consider the effect of human rights discourse, movements in European civil law, problem-solving courts, and challenges in sentencing and punishment, to demonstrate how the adversarial criminal trial is being dislocated for a transformative criminal trial experience.

Rethinking the public/private dichotomy

Various authors have commented on the separation of the public and private spheres, and most agree that these boundaries are at the very least shifting. Law, and indeed criminal law and procedure more specifically, relies on the separation of these notions of public and private in order to define the territory or jurisdiction of the criminal law as excluding private interests. Cotterrell (1992: 300) identifies the polemic of the shifting boundaries of public and private, thus:

> The uncertainty of boundaries between public and private spheres, state and civil society, law and administration, legal principle and public policy is seen as undermining law's integrity and dissolving away its specific competencies.

The isolation or exclusivity of the criminal trial is often affirmed by its manifest concern over public ideals removed from any particular private or sectarian interest. Its function is to test the prosecution case and to arrive at a version of the truth through a strategic contest between prosecution and defence, under the law of evidence. The criminal trial is thus considered to be an institution that does not submit to any particular politics or power. Its form, scope and content is considered to be consistent, objective, and construed in the public interest out of application of a fair and transparent trial process focussed on testing the prosecution case within the constraints of adversarialism. The texts of trial procedure indicate how this rhetoric is perpetuated to student and practitioner (see, for example, Cross, 1979; Tanford, 2009; Mauet, 2007). The criminal trial thus comes to be seen as a tribunal through which accusations of wrongdoing are made in the public interest, by public officials, to be tested against standards of liability and seriousness that are generally construed in terms of what the community deems to be appropriate standards of liability or punishment. Within this context, there is little room for considerations that are private in nature. Opinions from persons connected to the offence, such as the victim, are deemed to be irrelevant and even prejudicial to the interests of an objective assessment of the scope of the offending. In criminal law, the victim, for example, comes to be seen as unreliable, emotive and inconsistent. The case of *R v P* (1992) 64 A Crim R 381 obverses this principle (at 384):

> ... because in our adversarial system of criminal justice the victim is not directly represented and has no more right to be heard in the sentencing process than in the trial, a difficulty arises as to how information relating to the effect on the victim is to be gathered and presented to the court. That reliable information of that nature

should be presented is in the public interest, not only in the interest of the injured victim (or of the accused, if the victim has escaped relatively unharmed), since a proper sentence should not be based on a misconception or ignorance of salient facts. There is not necessarily any unfairness or impropriety in the representative of the Crown assisting in this regard. The prosecutor appears in the public interest and has the role of assisting the court in reaching a fair decision rather than exclusively advocating a particular interest: see *Whitehorn v The Queen* (1983) 152 CLR 657; *R v Apostilides* (1984) 154 CLR 563.

The victim is thus relegated to the status of unreliable because they may introduce perspectives that cannot be coalesced with what we understand to be objective or public. It is inconceivable, following this rhetoric, that the victim may be able to supply particulars in the criminal trial process that may indeed be relevant to that process. Doak (2005a: 299–302) questions the extent to which we ought to entertain a clear separation between public and private. Realising the criminal justice system is governed by rules and standards that call for objectivity and consistency, victims are largely excluded out of the fear that victims will only introduce subjective and personal motives that call for retribution and vengeance. Being risked is the 'judicially made law', codified to the requirements of system of public rather than private accountability (see Weisstub, 1986: 203–205). Where the victim desires relief they ought to be directed to tort to pursue personal damages. However, as Doak (2005a: 300) indicates, the distinction between tort and contract remains artificial and tort often contains the corollary offence of criminal law, at least in terms of the intentional torts such as assault. Standards of negligence, however, also inform both jurisdictions. Doak (2005a: 300) notes Goldstein's (1982: 530) argument that criminal and civil liability is generally founded upon similar notions of fault, recklessness and strict liability. As such, the theoretical reasons why victims need be excluded from the criminal law may indeed be limited.

The genealogy of the criminal law as a 'state' enterprise also tells a different story when one considers it from the perspective of the victim (Kirchengast, 2006; Goldstein, 1982). Goldstein (1982: 549) indicates that the '"monopoly" of criminal prosecution by the district attorney is more the result of a misunderstanding of history than of explicit legislative direction'. Further, the English Attorney-General was not a public prosecutor in the true sense of the word, given, as Goldstein

(1982: 549) argues, that almost all prosecutions were brought by victims in the form of a private prosecution. This genealogy suggests that the victim may indeed be more integral to the development of criminal law and justice than is otherwise realised through a conventional history of the criminal law as an institution that emerged as a response to the need to secure state interests alone.

There are several reasons why criminal law and procedure, and the criminal trial in particular, cannot be considered a public institution *a priori*. Most common law countries provide a variety of statutory rights in the form of compensation, assistance, the right to fair treatment in the criminal justice system, participatory rights in the criminal trial, and even the ability to participate in the sentencing process. Various authors have traced these developments in both domestic and international law (Doak, 2005a, 2008; Kirchengast, 2006; Goldstein, 1982; also see Wemmers, 2009: 395–397, 411–413). Supporting the right to fair treatment, the police and ODPP of most common law countries have guidelines for the inclusion of victims, to be kept informed, where possible, of key decision-making processes. Programs of restorative justice that allow for greater participation of the victim in intervention programs or other novel sentencing arrangements, such as circle or forum sentencing, whereby the victim participates in the sentencing decision-making process, evidences a continued movement toward the increased participation of the victim on a substantive level. Victims are also able to participate in conferencing and mediation, bringing victim and offender together in a way that supports a process of personal restoration and healing. On the international front, the rights of victims have been recognised under the art. 6 and 8 of the ECHR affording victims some protection in the trial process, especially where they are identified as a vulnerable victim. States, including those in Australia, that are not constituted under a bill of rights, have provided for similar measures by way of statutory amendment of domestic law. Novel procedures, contained more broadly in European civil law but enacted under the Rome Statute, now inform the practices of the ICC to allow the victim direct party participation alongside the state prosecutor.

It is possible that the criminal law and adversarial trial more precisely are amenable to the participation of victims, albeit in a measured and carefully organised way. The realisation that there is nothing inherent in the notion of the 'public good' that essentially excludes a private perspective evidences that we need not preclude private perspectives where they help inform publicly accepted notions of wrongdoing and standards of liability. Furthermore, the recognition of the private needs of victims may help inform a fair trial process. This is evidenced by the realisation that certain victims, such as rape or sexual assault or child victims, are particularly vulnerable to the techniques of examination and cross-examination in the adversarial context.[1] For some time now, since 1981 in NSW, common law jurisdictions have recognised the status of rape victims as especially vulnerable.[2] The trial process, providing as it does for the cross-examination of the victim, has been limited to the circumstances of the sexual assault or rape as charged. Numerous enactments in both domestic and international law now limit the defence's ability to ask questions about the sexual history and reputation of the victim (see, for example, s293 *Criminal Procedure Act 1986* (NSW)). Reforms to this area of law are ongoing, with vulnerable victims being further protected through provisions that afford witnesses the ability to provide their testimony via remote means, or behind a screen, and limit the accused's ability to cross-examine the victim personally, should they appear as litigant in person. Further amendments limit the court's ability to require that a victim's accusation be corroborated or to classify them as an unreliable witness, or to provide a warning to the jury regarding a delay in complaint. Victims are also entitled to a support person when testifying (see ss293–294C *Criminal Procedure Act 1986* (NSW)).

Emerging human rights discourse: Victims' rights, human rights and due process

Victim rights have been identified as significantly detracting from the adversarial criminal trial. Such proponents have argued that despite the importance of appeasing the victim following an offence, that victim issues ought to be dealt with outside the normative constraints of the trial and sentencing process. Victim's needs should thus be addressed by means of welfare assistance, state based compensation or, where applicable, through the introduction of victim impact evidence during the sentencing phase of the trial. It is not surprising then that the victim, in the context of recent calls for the greater inclusion of the victim in the trial and sentencing process, test the extent to which the trial is able to change and adapt to meet emerging social needs. This point is emphasised when one considers the increased focus on victim rights in the context of human rights frameworks that promote the consideration of fundamental rights to protection amongst key stakeholders of justice, including defendants and victims, in the attempt to render the trial process more transparent, fair and responsive to those involved. In the context of the defendant's right to a fair trial, a particular focus is placed on preventing re-victimisation, especially for sexual assault complainants and child witnesses. A critical examination of the inclusion of the victim in the broader context of emerging human rights discourse suggests how the trial is indeed an institution constituted by at times highly competitive discourses of fairness, voice and participation.

Human rights under the ECHR

Significant changes to the criminal trial have emerged through the integration of human rights discourse. As discussed in Chapter 1, the ECHR provides a means of modifying trial processes to accommodate the interests of the victim as well as the defendant. Article 2 of the ECHR provides the right to life.[3] Although not impacting on the scope of the criminal trial in a direct way, this right does raise the status and primacy of the victim as important to the rights agenda. Article 6 of the ECHR provides the right to a fair trial.[4] This right has been interpreted in terms of criminal trials and civil hearings. The right to a fair trial in the criminal jurisdiction refers to the proportionality requirements of defendant rights. Article 8 provides the right to privacy.[5] The cases seeking to integrate the rights of the victim into the adversarial trial have generally been brought under art. 6 and 8 of the ECHR. Where the victim has been incorporated under art. 6, the ECtHR has done so under the proportionality requirement to the defendant's right to a fair trial (see *Doorson v The Netherlands* (1996) 22 EHRR 330 at 350).

The case of *McCann and Ors v United Kingdom* (1995) 21 EHRR 97 puts at the forefront of human rights discourse the positive obligation to protect all human life. It is not enough, under art. 2 of the ECHR, to refrain from taking life. States must act to protect life from threats made by third parties. *Osman v United Kingdom* (1998) 29 EHRR 245 is another case in point. In this case, Osman was killed by his son's former teacher, following a complaint that the teacher had made threats to Osman's family. Osman's widow claimed that the police had failed to act to protect Osman following complaints about the teacher, contrary to art. 2 and the duty to protect life. The English courts followed the precedent of *Hill v Chief Constable of West Yorkshire Police* [1999] AC 53, holding that the police did not owe the applicant a duty of care to prevent the crime. As a matter of public policy, therefore, the police were immune from allegations of negligence arising from their investigation and suppression of crime. The ECtHR reasoned that art. 2 did not provide a positive obligation for the police to act in the circumstances. Although decided on strong policy grounds, the ECtHR did outline a number of measures sensitive to the plight of the victim (at 304–305):

> The Court notes that the first sentence of Article 2 s1 enjoins the State not only to refrain from the intentional and unlawful taking of life, but also to take appropriate steps to safeguard the lives of those within its jurisdiction (see the *L.C.B. v. the United Kingdom* judgment of 9 June 1998, Reports of Judgments and Decisions 1998–III, p. 1403, s36). It is common ground that the State's obligation in this respect extends beyond its primary duty to secure the right to life by putting in place effective criminal-law provisions to deter the commission of offences against the person backed up by law-enforcement machinery for the prevention, suppression and sanctioning of breaches of such provisions. It is thus accepted by those appearing before the Court that Article 2 of the Convention may also imply in certain well-defined circumstances a positive obligation on the authorities to take preventive operational measures to protect an individual whose life is at risk from the criminal acts of another individual. The scope of this obligation is a matter of dispute between the parties.
>
> For the Court, and bearing in mind the difficulties involved in policing modern societies, the unpredictability of human conduct and the operational choices which must be made in terms of priorities and resources, such an obligation must be interpreted in a way which does not impose an impossible or disproportionate burden on the authorities. Accordingly, not every claimed risk to life can entail for the authorities a Convention requirement to take operational measures to prevent that risk from materialising. Another relevant consideration is the need to ensure that the police exercise their powers to control and prevent crime in a manner which fully respects the due process and other guarantees which legitimately place restraints on the scope of their action to investigate crime and bring offenders to justice, including the guarantees contained in Articles 5 and 8 of the Convention.
>
> In the opinion of the Court where there is an allegation that the authorities have violated their positive obligation to protect the right to life in the context of their above-mentioned duty to prevent and suppress offences against the person (see paragraph 115 above), it must be established to its satisfaction that the authorities knew or

ought to have known at the time of the existence of a real and immediate risk to the life of an identified individual or individuals from the criminal acts of a third party and that they failed to take measures within the scope of their powers which, judged reasonably, might have been expected to avoid that risk.

The positive obligations placed on the state, however, do little to afford the victim greater participation in the criminal trial. *Osman* is significant to the extent that it places victim rights on the agenda.

However, challenges under art. 6 and 8 of the ECHR demonstrate the consideration of the status of the victim in the criminal trial in a way that, as some have argued (see Wolhunter et al., 2009: 173), compromises defendant rights by encouraging a dangerous law and order ideology affecting the status of the defendant, and their right to a fair trial. Much like the NSW situation advocating rape reform in the late 1970s, notable cases under the ECHR have flowed from sexual assault or rape matters where the victim themselves is often called as a witness to personally testify their lack of consent to sexual intercourse. These cases indicate that other than by statutory modification of the common law, that human rights discourse may directly challenge the scope of the criminal trial by introducing a new perspective on an agent of justice normally excluded from the consideration of the courts. Human rights cases under the ECHR recognise that rape victims are particularly vulnerable (see Ellison, 2002: 78–79). The harm caused to the victim of crime as a result of giving personally distressing evidence would be something generally beyond the purview of the courts given the primacy that the defendant be able to face their accuser, and challenge each element of the prosecution case against them. The limitation of a defendant's capacity to cross-examine and challenge the victim's accusation of wrongdoing would be seen as denying the defendant a fundamental due process right, determinative of a 'fair trial' in the first instance. The cases before the ECtHR demonstrate the interplay of 'voices' between defendant, victim and state that call for the balancing of the rights of the victim against the requirement that the defendant receives a 'fair trial'.[6]

In *Baegen v The Netherlands* (1994) 16696/90 (20 October 1994), a rape victim was granted anonymity following threats of a reprisal attack made against her. The applicant complained that he could not personally examine the victim, who wished to remain anonymous. In this instance, the ECtHR found no breach of art. 6 on the basis that measures were in place granting the accused a procedural fairness, in particular, the ability to put questions to the victim at several key points of the trial and appeal. The victim's right to anonymity was preserved under art. 8, this being a positive right to protect vulnerable victims and witnesses, provided that there are measures in place to reconcile these protections with the rights of the defence at trial. The availability of evidence corroborating statements given by the victim may also be significant to reaching a balance between victim and defendant. The ECtHR found (at par 78 and 79):

> The Commission observes that, during the preliminary judicial investigation, the applicant failed to avail himself of the offer of the investigating judge to put written questions to Ms. X, that in the proceedings before the Regional Court he did not request an examination of Ms. X either before this court or the investigating judge, and that the applicant did not request the prosecution authorities to summon her as a witness for the hearing of 6 September 1988 before the Court of Appeal. It was only in the course of that last hearing that he requested the court to order an examination of Ms. X.
> The Commission further observes that the applicant's conviction did not rest solely on the statements of Ms. X. The Court of Appeal also used in evidence statements of police officers, the statement of Ms. X's mother, and the statement of K. All those statements, more or less, corroborated the version of events Ms. X had given. They were not, however, consistent with the applicant's statements on a number of points. In the course of the proceedings before the trial courts, the applicant never requested an examination of these persons.

The victim was anonymously questioned by the examining magistrate, but did not give evidence at trial. The ECtHR found that the applicant had the ability to put questions to the victim at several points but availed himself of the opportunity.

The case of *Bocos-Cuesta v The Netherlands* (2005) 54789/00 (10 November 2005) provides another example of the ECtHRs willingness to recognise the rights of the victim in a substantive way. This case applies an earlier decision of *Finkensieper v The Netherlands* (1995) 19525/92 (17 May 1995), providing that anonymous testimony may be provided by victims so long as adequate counter measures existed to maintain the defence's right to access the accused. In *Bocos-Cuesta,* the applicant alleged that he did not receive a fair trial under art. 6(1),(3)(d) of the

ECHR in criminal proceedings taken against him. In particular, statements given by four minors were used in evidence without the opportunity for the defence to question them directly. The ECtHR ruled (at par 7.1–7.2):

> The remaining question is whether the statements of the four children can be used in evidence although the suspect has not had the opportunity to question them himself. The court's first consideration is the fact that Article 6 [of the Convention], particularly in the light of some recent [Strasbourg] decisions given on applications brought against the Netherlands, does not unconditionally oppose the use in evidence of statements given by witnesses whom a suspect has not been able to question. There is room for the balancing of interests. In its judgment of 26 March 1996 in the case of *Doorson v. the Netherlands*, the European Court [of Human Rights] considered in this respect that the principles of a fair trial also require that, in appropriate cases, the interests of the suspect in questioning [witnesses] are to be balanced against the interests of witnesses and victims in the adequate protection of their rights guaranteed by Article 8 [of the Convention]. In the opinion of the European Court, briefly summarised, in balancing these interests much weight must be given to the question whether the handicaps under which the defence labours on account of the inability to questioning a witness in an indirect manner are compensated, and whether a conviction is based either solely or to a decisive extent on the statement of this witness. In its report of 17 May 1995 [in the case of *Finkensieper v. the Netherlands*, no. 19525/92], the European Commission [of Human Rights] adopted an essentially similar opinion.
>
> In the light of these decisions, the following can be said. As already found by the court, the interests of the four children in not being exposed to reliving a possibly traumatic experience weighs heavily. With that, as also already found by the court, stands the fact that the confrontations of these four witnesses with the suspect have been carried out with the required care, and that the results thereof, as already found earlier, are particularly reliable. As regards the acts themselves of which the suspect stands accused, the court finds it established that the four children have all been questioned by (or assisted by) investigation officers of the Amsterdam Juvenile and Vice Police Bureau with extensive experience in questioning very young persons. It has become plausible from the records drawn up by them and from the oral evidence given in court by these civil

servants that the four children have been questioned in an open, careful and non-suggestive manner.

The extent to which the ECtHR is willing to modify criminal procedure to cater for the needs of the victim is limited to the extent which is strictly necessary to afford the victim protection. In *Kostovski v The Netherlands* (1989) 12 EHRR 434, for instance, anonymous evidence was tendered at trial but in hearsay form through a magistrate who was available to the defence for questioning. The ECtHR found that this measure provided insufficient protection for the rights of the accused. The ECtHR maintained the principle that evidence ought to be tendered at a public hearing, in the presence of the accused, providing the defence the opportunity to challenge the evidence directly. Statements obtained at an initial examination of witnesses may be tendered at trial, but the defence would nonetheless require an opportunity to challenge the evidence, and put questions to the witnesses. The ECtHR ruled (at 477–448):

> In principle, all the evidence must be produced in the presence of the accused at a public hearing with a view to adversarial argument. This does not mean, however, that in order to be used as evidence statements of witnesses should always be made at a public hearing in court: to use as evidence such statements obtained at the pre-trial stage is not in itself inconsistent with paragraphs (3)(d) and (1) of Article 6, provided the rights of the defence have been respected.
>
> As a rule, these rights require that an accused should be given an adequate and proper opportunity to challenge and question a witness against him, either at the time the witness was making his statement or at some later stage of the proceedings.

The fundamental right of the accused to challenge the prosecution case against them, in an adequate way, is well supported in English domestic law. In *R v Camberwell Green Youth Court* [2005] 1 All ER 999, Baroness Hale of Richmond examines s21 of the *Youth Justice and Criminal Evidence Act* 1999 (UK) in the context of the jurisprudence of the ECtHR and the right of the accused to examine witnesses 'with a view to adversarial argument'. In *R v Camberwell Green Youth Court*, a question was put to the House of Lords as to whether s21 was compliant with art. 6 of the ECHR insofar as the section prevented the individualised consideration of the necessity for a 'special measures' direction. The 'special measures' mentioned referred to the examination of witnesses under seventeen years of age, in relation to sexual offences and crimes of violence, by a live television link and video recording. Supporting such mechanisms for the tenure of evidence to accord a measure of protection for child witnesses, Lady Hale rules (at 1015–1016):

> It is difficult to see anything in the provisions of the 1999 Act with which we are concerned which is inconsistent with these principles. All the evidence is produced at the trial in the presence of the accused, some of it in pre-recorded form and some of it by contemporaneous television transmission. The accused can see and hear it all. The accused has every opportunity to challenge and question the witnesses against him at the trial itself. The only thing missing is a face to face confrontation, but the appellants accept that the Convention does not guarantee a right to face to face confrontation. This case is completely different from the case of anonymous witnesses. Even then the Strasbourg Court has accepted that exceptions may be made, provided that sufficient steps are taken to counterbalance the handicaps under which the defence laboured and a conviction is not based solely or decisively on anonymous statements (see *Doorson v Netherlands* (1996) 22 EHRR 330, 350, para 72; *Van Mechelen v Netherlands* (1997) 25 EHRR 647, 673, paras 54, 55; *Visser v Netherlands*, Application No 26668/95, Judgment 14 February 2002, para 43).

A similar issue was raised in *Van Mechelen and Ors v The Netherlands* (1998) 25 EHRR 647. In *Van Mechelen v The Netherlands*, the applicants were convicted of attempted manslaughter and robbery on the basis of statements made by anonymous police officers. The investigating judge arranged hearings such that the anonymous witnesses were in one room, with the applicants, together with their lawyers, in another room. An audio connection was all that was provided. The ECtHR determined that there had been a breach of art. 6 since the defence was unable to observe the anonymous police present their evidence, and therefore could not test its reliability. The ECtHR is particularly guided by trial process over any particular rule of evidence or procedure. Thus, the court is guided not by the particularities of a specific code or law but by the requirement of procedural fairness in general terms. This means that the ECtHR is focused on the nature of the trial taken as a whole (see Doak, 2008: 74), over any substantive law that prescribes a particular part of its form. Such perspectives provide for the argument that the ECtHR is promulgating an international criminal procedure that overcomes normative assumptions as to the usefulness of adversarial vs inquisitorial justice (see Summers, 2007).

The ECtHR has moved toward the interpretation of art. 6 as a right to a fair trial for all involved in the criminal trial process. As *Kostovski v The Netherlands*, demonstrates, it is not that victim rights prevail over those of the defence. A careful balancing of the rights of all parties is required such that the trial becomes 'fair' to all parties. As provided in *SN v Sweden* (2004) 39 EHRR 13, this extends to the admission of victims' lawyers or auxiliary prosecutors, which, have been deemed to be compatible with the accused's right to a fair trial. The extent to which the victim may be accommodated is determined with reference to the proportionality requirement balancing the rights of the victim against the defendant's right to a fair trial.

Human rights and statutory reform

Throughout the course of the latter part of the twentieth century, the trial process has been increasingly shaped by human rights discourse as it is integrated into statute on a domestic level. The modification of defendant rights in favour of victim interests can be demonstrated most strikingly in the case of rape law reform. Most common law jurisdictions now specifically cater for the vulnerable victim of rape out of the need to recognise the sensitive nature of rape prosecutions. Rape victims are a particularly vulnerable class of victim, not only because rape is such a private offence, but because consent to sex in rape trials is largely determined on the basis of conflicting points of view between victim and defendant. It is out of the realisation that rape victims are especially vulnerable in the adversarial context of the trial that most governments have now moved to protect rape victims by directly modifying trial process. As indicated above, numerous common law jurisdictions now cater for the needs of rape victims in the trial process out of recognition of the significant impact of the trial upon them, leading to their potential re-victimisation on the witness stand. In NSW, for instance, rape victims have been increasingly protected as vulnerable witnesses since the 1981 reforms abrogating the common law offence of rape for sexual assault (see above discussion, ss293–294C *Criminal Procedure Act 1986* (NSW)).

Out of the need to preserve the autonomy of the person, various rights and privileges available to the defendant at common law have been restricted or limited. This is out of recognition of the gendered and sexualised nature of common law rape, the underreporting of rape as a serious offence, and the re-victimisation most witnesses experience through exposure to police and court processes. The defendant's right to cross-examine the victim on their sexual history as evidence potentially relevant to the victim's tendency to consent to intercourse has been significantly limited out of need to respect the integrity of the victim and to re-focus the trial away from the character of the victim, and on the incident in question. In the NSW context, reform to the law of rape has continued into the twenty-first century.

The most recent reforms allow the victim to provide testimony behind a screen or via video-link; limit the defendant's capacity to cross-examine the rape victim personally, without counsel; and, quite controversially, provides for the re-trial of offenders on the basis of the tendering of the transcript of the evidence in chief where the NSW Court of Criminal Appeal overturns a conviction and orders a re-trial. The tendering of the original trial transcript essentially removes the victim from the re-trial altogether, saving the victim from having to testify all over again, but denying the defendant the ability to face their accuser and cross-examine them, via counsel, on their original testimony (see ss306A–306G *Criminal Procedure Act 1986* (NSW); as to the sentence following application of such special provisions protecting vulnerable rape victims see *R v Skaf*; *R v Skaf* [2006] NSWSC 394, also see special leave to appeal to the High Court of Australia, *Skaf v The Queen* (S170 of 2004); *Skaf v The Queen* (S406 of 2004); see Warner, 2004; as to child victims see Friedman and Jones, 2005; Powell, Roberts and Guadagno, 2007; also see Corns, 2004).

Human rights otherwise foreign to the common law, including those now relevant to victims, defendants, witnesses and others involved in the criminal prosecution process, now inform the very processes by which we determine the guilt of the accused. It is not that the common law is not concerned with certain human rights prescribed under the ECHR. To a significant extent, the right to a fair trial under art. 6 of the ECHR mirrors the requirements of a right to a fair trial at common law: *Barton v The Queen* (1980) 147 CLR 75; *Maxwell v The Queen* (1996) 184 CLR 501; *Cheung v The Queen* (2001) 209 CLR 1. The ECHR has, however, affirmed new directions in trial procedure beyond that previously informed by common law. It is not that interests other than those traditionally secured under an adversarial criminal trial cannot be attended to at common law, or inserted into the common law by statutory modification. However, the modification of the accused's right to a fair trial at common law by the introduction of special measures to protect the integrity of the victim from, for example, giving evidence of a distressing or embarrassing nature, indicates how human rights discourse may effectively modify the orthodox boundaries of the common law to allow for the inclusion of interests generally not considered as rights protected at common law, as rights material to the defendant, the key stakeholder of the adversarial criminal trial.

In England and Wales, modification of the criminal trial by the incorporation of the rights and interests of the victim alongside those of the defendant have largely followed the jurisprudence of the ECtHR. In *R v Camberwell Green Youth Court* [2005] 1 All ER 999, s21 of the *Youth Justice and Criminal Evidence Act* 1999 (UK) was found to be consistent with art. 6 of the ECHR. Child witnesses, under a list of particular offences, may give their testimony via live video link or by recording. Lord Roger of Eearlsferry indicates that the ECtHR has not interpreted art. 6 as allowing the accused the right to be present in the same room as the witness testifying so long as the accused is given a proper opportunity to question and challenge the prosecution witness. In a similar way, s23 of the *Criminal Justice Act 1988* (UK) allows courts to accept hearsay evidence where the witness is classed as a frightened witness. In *R v Sellick and Sellick* [2005] 2 Cr App R 15, the Court of Appeal of England and Wales held that where the witness would not testify because the accused had caused them to be in fear, the witness's statement could be tendered without the accused being able to cross-examine them in court. This was the case even where the statement formed the decisive evidence against the accused. Lord Justice Waller, with whom Mr Justice Owen and Mr Justice Fulford agreed, held, dismissing the appeal (at par 57):

> Our view is that certainly care must be taken to see that sections 23 and 26, and indeed the new provisions in the Criminal Justice Act 2003, are not abused. Where intimidation of witnesses is alleged the court must examine with care the circumstances. Are the witnesses truly being kept away by fear? Has that fear been generated by the defendant, or by persons acting with the defendant's authority? Have reasonable steps been taken to trace the witnesses and bring them into court? Can anything be done to enable the witnesses to be brought to court to give evidence and be there protected? It is obvious that the more 'decisive' the evidence in the statements, the greater the care will be needed to be sure why it is that a witness cannot come and give evidence. The court should be astute to examine the quality and reliability of the evidence in the statement

and astute and sure that the defendant has every opportunity to apply the provisions of Schedule 2. It will, as section 26 states, be looking at the interests of justice, which includes justice to the defendant and justice to the victims. The judge will give warnings to the jury stressing the disadvantage that the defendant is in, not being able to examine a witness.

However, in *R v Martin* [2003] 2 Cr App R 21, the Court of Appeal of England and Wales did not allow the statement of an intimidated witness because it found that the statement was unreliable and that as the accused was unfit to stand trial, he could not testify to his defence. Lord Justice Potter, Mr Justice Mackay, and His Honour Judge Mellor, rule (at par 61):

> ... we find ourselves unable to support the judge's exercise of his discretion to admit the statement of Tamba Bona. It is not in dispute that the entire case for the prosecution rested upon Tamba Bona's statement. Thus, while it was plainly in the interests of justice so far as the prosecution was concerned that the statements should be before the jury, it was also in the interests of justice from the point of view of the defendant that he should not be unduly disadvantaged by admission of the statements in circumstances where they could not be made the subject of cross-examination.

In 2003, the *Criminal Justice Act 2003* (UK) was amended to allow admission of hearsay in circumstances that frees an intimidated witness from the experience of being cross-examined. Under s116(1) a statement, not made in oral evidence in proceedings, is admissible as evidence of any matter stated if (a) oral evidence given in the proceedings by the person who made the statement would be admissible as evidence of that matter, (b) the person who made the statement (the relevant person) is identified to the court's satisfaction, and (c) any of the five conditions mentioned in subsection (2) are satisfied. Sub-section 2(e) provides the condition:

> that through fear the relevant person does not give (or does not continue to give) oral evidence in the proceedings, either at all or in connection with the subject matter of the statement, and the court gives leave for the statement to be given in evidence.

Section 116 of the 2003 Act provides for a broader set of circumstances in which statements of witnesses too afraid to testify would be admissible. Unlike the previous provisions under s23 of the 1988 Act, s116 applies to oral and written evidence. Such statements do not need to be made to a police officer. The term 'fear' is also construed broadly, to encompass a range of possible reasons for not wanting to testify, including anecdotally, the suggestion that the a witness is intimidated by the court in which they are called to give evidence. As Lord Justice Waller said in *Sellick* (at par 53):

> In our view, having regard to the rights of victims, their families, the safety of the public in general, it still cannot be right for there to be some absolute rule that, where compelling evidence is the sole or decisive evidence, an admission in evidence of a statement must then automatically lead to a defendant's Article 6 rights being infringed. That would lead to a situation in which the more successful the intimidation of the witnesses, the stronger the argument becomes that the statements cannot be read. If the decisive witnesses can be 'got at' the case must collapse. The more subtle and less easily established intimidation provides defendants with the opportunity of excluding the most material evidence against them. Such an absolute rule cannot have been intended by the European Court in Strasbourg.

Human rights discourse as enacted by statute allows for the reconsideration of the adversarial trial process to protect the needs of victims and witnesses when giving evidence. Such provisions allow for the modification of processes that would otherwise be seen to be constitutive of a fair trial in the first instance including the accused's right to confront and cross-examine their accuser. Resistance to such change has mounted, however, and the United States Supreme Court has held that the confrontation clause of the Constitution of the United States affords the accused access to their accuser in open court. Such resistance is discussed in Chapters 5 and 6.

Criminal procedure in European civil law

The criminal trial process in European civil law is inquisitorial, with the exception of certain countries, such as Sweden, the Netherlands, Denmark, Portugal, Spain and Italy, each of whom have adversarial aspects to their trial process. Goodey (2005: 180) has remarked that the incorporation of victim and defendant rights presents avenues for the development of the criminal trial. The rights of all agents to justice – defence, prosecution, victims, and state – may be incorporated into a model of procedural fairness that presents a new perspective on the usefulness of European civil law and procedure for the further development of a hybrid adversarial-inquisitorial process that better serves the competing needs of the stakeholders of criminal justice.[7] At the very least, this 'hybrid' model provides a means by which persons traditionally excluded from the criminal law, such as victims and their families, may be able to gain rights of audience before the criminal law and participate legitimately in decision-making processes.

The International Criminal Court

The model adopted by the ICC provides for the incorporation of both adversarial and inquisitorial approaches. The ICC contains a pre-trial examining or investigative division, similar to the examining magistrate that works alongside the police and the prosecution to review the material relevant to the charge in domestic inquisitorial jurisdictions. Knoops (2007: 8) suggests that the hybrid approach is key to the functions of the ICC, thus:

> A significant aspect of the ICC Statute is that, during its drafting stage, delegates made a conscious effort to negotiate a statute and set of RPE [rules of procedure and evidence] that were acceptable to all. One could say that the battle between common law and civil law was there replaced by an agreement on common principles and civil behaviour. It can therefore be said that the ICC Statute and RPE represent a truly international set of procedures, acceptable to the major legal systems of the world and drawing on the experiences of the ICTY [International Criminal Tribunal for the former Yugoslavia] and ICTR [International Criminal Tribunal for Rwanda]. Some novel procedures were created with predominantly civil law features, these being:
>
> - admissibility of evidence and defences;
> - pre-trial proceedings;.
> - supervisory responsibility of the ICC over arrested individuals; and
> - rights of victims and witnesses.

Reflecting on the European tradition of auxiliary prosecutions, Sanders (2002) argues that a process that allows for the participation of both victim and defendants increases the opportunity for dialogue and understanding. This reduces secondary victimisation by being excluded from the criminal justice system altogether, or by being called to participate against the will of the witness.

Auxiliary prosecution in adversarial criminal trials

The Council of Europe's 'Recommendation of the Committee of Ministers to the Member States on the Position of the Victim in the Framework of Criminal Law and Procedure', R 85(11), guideline 7, provides a right to review a decision not to prosecute, or to institute private proceedings. Joutsen (1987) indicates that the victim holds various rights of review in the continental European system. This includes the right to private prosecution, which may be initiated independently of the state as in the case of Sweden, discussed below. In such circumstances, the victim may join the state as auxiliary prosecutor, as Joutsen (1987: 109) indicates:

> There are four basic methods of victim intervention in the prosecutorial decision. These are: (1) requesting that the decision-maker review the decision; (2) appealing to the decision-maker's superior or to an independent board of complaints; (3) appealing to the court; or (4) personally bringing the case to court. All four are subsumed in one of the guidelines of the Council of Europe's Recommendation, which simply states: 'The victim should have the right to ask for review by a competent authority of a decision not to prosecute, or the right to institute private proceedings'.

Auxiliary prosecution is a method adopted in civil law jurisdictions that affords the victim actual participation and standing alongside the state prosecutor. Auxiliary prosecution is generally only available for serious offences. It is widely available across civil law jurisdictions, including Sweden, Denmark and Portugal, which have adversarial trials. An auxiliary prosecutor differs from a victim's lawyer in that the former is only available where the state brings a prosecution. The latter, discussed in Chapter 3, may be appointed by the victim to challenge a decision of the prosecution to, for example, make a plea-deal with the defendant. Most civil law jurisdictions grant the victim rights of participation in the pre-trial process, which allows them to seek information, be kept informed, and to appoint a lawyer to advocate their position to the state prosecutor, examining magistrate and trial judge. A victim may be able to challenge a decision of the prosecution to not proceed with a matter. Should the state not wish to proceed with a matter the victim may initiate a private prosecution. The exact nature of these rights varies between the jurisdictions (see Wolhunter et al., 2009: 187–189; Herrmann, 1996; as to Swedish law generally, see Ortwein, 2003: 420–422, 427–433; as to juvenile justice proceedings, see Feld, 1994: 639–646).

Ortwein (2003: 431–432) provides a useful overview of the adversarial characteristics of the Swedish criminal trial, an example of an inquisitorial system with an adversarial trial process:

> Similar to a number of civil law systems, the Swedish trial court has no lay jury but, instead has a mixed panel of professional and lay judges. This mixture of judges acts as a single body, simultaneously deciding issues of both law and fact as well as guilt and punishment. Any judgement made must be based on evidence presented to the court on the day of trial. Similar to Anglo-American adversarial trials, both defense and prosecution in Sweden follow a standard fixed trial progression including open speeches, presentation of evidence, and closing addresses. In addition to the prosecutor and defense counsel, the injured party in the matter may also be present, with or without counsel, and is entitled to testify, examine witnesses, and present evidence for the court to consider. Neither the defendant nor the injured party testify under oath at trial. No other witnesses area allowed in the courtroom while the defendant and the injured party testify.
>
> After presenting evidence of guilt or innocence, the parties will immediately present evidence relating to the punishment to be imposed upon conviction and make closing arguments on both issues.

At trial, the Swedish procedure for the prosecution of offences provides for auxiliary prosecution by allowing the injured victim to join the prosecutor as an injured party. There are three categories of victim in the Swedish system, specifically, a brottsoffer, a victim in a broad or general sense; a målsägande, a victim that does not enter a compensation claim nor supports the prosecution case; and a målsägande, a victim that either presents a compensation claim or appears as auxiliary prosecutor alongside the state (Brienen and Hoegen, 2000: 890). The målsägande that presents alongside the prosecutor is a victim in a legal sense as well as an emotional sense, and may otherwise be identified as an injured party. The injured party is thus distinct from an injured person, who may still qualify as målsägande, but who does not join proceedings as adhesive prosecutor, although they may still come to court to give a statement. The brottsoffer is a broad term referring to victim of crime, but it is not a term used in Swedish legislation and the Code of Judicial Procedure, in particular. The Code of Judicial Procedure (s8 ch. 20 RB) identifies an injured person as 'the one against whom the offence was committed, or who was affronted or harmed by it'.

An injured party may institute proceedings on their own motion without the assistance of the prosecution service. Private prosecutions occur occasionally (see Zila, 2006: 293). However, if the state prosecutor decides not to proceed with a case, the målsägande, or injured party, may seek to continue the case. If the injured party wishes to prosecute privately, they would ordinarily seek review of the state prosecutor's decision not to proceed with the matter, by writing to the prosecution service. A higher ranked prosecutor would then review the matter (Brienen and Hoegen, 2000: 891). Should the injured party seek to pursue a private prosecution they run the risk of having to pay the costs of the trial, and of being sentenced for an unfounded prosecution, should the judge decide that there was no probable reason to prosecute in the first instance.

The injured party may support the prosecution by indicating in court that they wish to join the prosecution. Once this is made clear to the court, the injured party may participate in the preliminary examination and at trial by putting questions to witnesses. The injured person has the right to a state-funded legal adviser, a målsägandebiträde, for sexual or other serious offences. Such an adviser will not be appointed where the prosecution seeks to withdraw or discontinue a case. The role of the legal adviser is to protect the interests of the injured person throughout the preliminary examination and at trial. This will ordinarily involve attending police questioning, helping the victim prepare their claim for compensation, presenting claims in court, and assistance in the preparation of an appeal. The legal adviser is appointed by the court at the request of the injured person. Such advisers are usually drawn from a pre-prepared list of advocates or assistant lawyers already known to the court. The court may not appoint a legal advisor in all cases, depending on the seriousness of the offence, but such appointments are usual in sexual assault matters. Should the court refuse to appoint a legal adviser, a stödperson, or support person, may be permitted. A stödperson is a volunteer who is usually affiliated with a victim's support agency, and will help the injured person fill out paperwork for compensation claims (see Brienen and Hoegen, 2000: 891).

The Swedish trial process differs from other European civil law jurisdictions, such as the German or French systems of prosecution, in that the trial phase is adversarial. At trial, the charge is read and the defendant pleads, the målsägande testifies first, then the defendant, followed by witnesses to the crime. The målsägande, defendant and witnesses give narrative evidence, as based on their version of events, unlike witnesses called in common law jurisdictions, who are generally confined to particular questions going to the elements of the offence in dispute. Witnesses are examined by the counsel that call them to testify, and then followed by the other counsel present and then the judge. This mode of examination may be likened to cross-examination, though such examination is not usually done aggressively. The judge will ensure that the victim is not subject to improper or irrelevant questioning. After the witnesses have each been examined and the judge decides that no further questions are necessary, the court retires to consider the verdict. The målsägandebiträde is therefore entitled to the following rights of participation: to be present throughout the trial; to speak for the injured victim; to object to questions put by other counsel, including the prosecution and defence; to cross-examine the defendant; to call witnesses; and to address the court as to the liability of the defendant and to make submissions as to a relevant sentence (see Wolhunter et al., 2009: 192–193; Brienen and Hoegen, 2000: 890).

Adhesion proceedings

Various European jurisdictions allow the injured victim to institute adhesion proceedings for a claim of compensation alongside criminal proceedings. In England and Wales and in South Australia (see below), the victim is afforded the ability to be provided compensation and reparation as part of the sentencing process. Where the victim is not afforded the power of auxiliary prosecution, as in Dutch law, adhesion proceedings become an important adjunct to participation in the prosecutorial phase of trial. As such, victims enjoy the ability to raise a claim for compensation and may do so during the pre-trial investigative phase or during the actual trial of the defendant. Once adhesion proceedings are afoot, the victim gains the status of the injured party. Relatives of the injured party may also present. If the prosecution is discontinued at this point, the victim, now recognised with rights as an injured party, may seek an explanation as to why the proceedings have been discontinued from the state prosecutor.

The injured party seeking compensation has the right to appoint a legal advisor at both preliminary investigation and trial phases, and has a right to pre-trial discovery of the dossier of evidence used to establish the prosecution in the first instance. If the state prosecutor refuses such discovery, the injured party has the right to appeal the decision. The prosecutor may refuse discovery on the basis that the investigation is ongoing, to protect the rights of the defendant, or because of arguments of general interest (Brienen and Hoegen, 2000: 901–902). In practice, trial judges may refer the more complex parts of the claim for compensation to a civil court for determination following the trial. Awards of compensation must follow the conviction of the defendant, who must be sentenced to a penal sanction. The injured party may not appeal any acquittal of the defendant, but may appeal the claim for compensation determined by the trial judge.

Therapeutic jurisprudence and problem-solving courts

Problem-solving courts first appeared in Florida in the United States in 1989 in the form of a drug court. Since then, problem-solving courts have emerged throughout the United States and the common law world. Certain states, such as the State of New York, have significantly developed their use of problem-solving and specialist courts (see Berman and Feinblatt, 2005; Kaye, 2004; Berman, 2000). Therapeutic justice takes a divergent path to traditional legal problem-solving, which is more concerned with the argumentative nature of orthodox processes (Wexler, 1999). The rise of problem-solving courts in the State of New York as a means of including all agents of justice, specifically, the defendant, state, community, victim, and support organisations, was briefly discussed in Chapter 1. This section details the rise of the therapeutic courts in the context of innovative approaches to justice that see the specific needs of offenders and victims dealt with in a non-adversarial way (see King et al., 2009: 138–169). As discussed earlier, problem-solving courts vary depending on the needs of offenders or victims and the therapeutic outcomes sought. Some courts are available only where the offender pleads guilty, while others are constituted as trial courts that seek to divert all offenders from normal adversarial proceedings. As a starting point, problem-solving courts seek to use the authority of the court to address a range of practical and policy issues, specifically, the needs of individual defendants, and the structural issues of the criminal justice system, in the context of the broader problems of communities (Berman and Feinblatt, 2001).

The community court of the State of New York is one such court. This style of court provides for an interesting case study that focuses on the how this type of court dislocates and fragments traditional or 'narrow' judicial functions in order to better serve its local community. King et al. (2009: 158) remark that such courts can be complex and tenuous, in that such courts may be linked to the community by focussing on specific offences or by problems within the community generally. Such programs are currently being piloted in England and Wales (see Ministry of Justice, 2009: 1; as to the Melbourne experience, see King et al., 2009: 160), and forms the basis of the case study towards the end of this section. Problem-based justice may be seen as an important complement or adjunct to orthodox adversarial processes and should not be seen as replacing such processes within the broader criminal justice system (Feldthusen, 1993). It is therefore important that we examine the processes that bring adversarial and problem-solving justice together into the one judicial system as alternating pathways to justice.

Origins of problem-solving courts

Problem-solving justice may have its origins in problem based policing (Goldstein, 1987). Such practices seek to engage community members in the pursuit of crime, by examining patterns of crime within community areas and by utilising the community as a crime prevention entity and as a site of restoration following an offence. Such perspectives helped give rise to concepts such as community prosecution, community courts, and problem-solving punishments, including the first generation of problem-solving courts, such as drug courts. These courts, generally only available to an accused who enters a guilty plea, sought to keep drug dependant offenders out of gaol by enrolling them into a course of supervised treatment that may also involve a community reparation or service order. Offenders who would otherwise face a custodial sentence would thus be directed out of prison by attending to their drug rehabilitation needs while making amends to the community in which their offending took place (also see King et al., 2009: 138–139).

These first problem-solving courts gained popularity throughout the 1990s and sought to make new and innovative connections between the court, judiciary, the community, and service organisations. Rather than simply turn the offender over to corrections, these courts sought the continued supervision of the offender. Offenders engaging in such alternative treatments would ordinarily come back before the supervising court several times before the program of treatment was deemed completed. Such perspectives are far removed from the notion of the trial judge 'handing down' a final sentence, perhaps never to see the prisoner again. Problem-solving courts may thus become a vital part of the recovery of the offender, including the reintegration of the offender back into the community (see *Lee v State Parole Authority of New South Wales* [2006] NSWSC 1225 at par 69).

Problem-solving courts, or problem-solving justice more broadly, seeks to utilise the positioning of the court in the community. Rather than understand the court and the sentencing of the accused as a sovereign institution of control, which corrects the conduct of the accused by threat or force, problem-solving courts seek to place themselves amongst other services and service providers to provide for an integrated approach to the management of all agents of justice in the disciplinary arena of the criminal justice system. Thus, in sex offence courts, the offender is referred to relevant treatment programs that refer the offender back to the court, who may also organise referral of the victim to counselling and welfare services to aid in their recovery. A different perspective is thus promulgated – one which disassociates the court from strict adversarialism that constitutes the court as a removed arbiter of law and fact.

The principles of problem-solving courts

Several principles guide a problem-solving approach to justice. Enhanced information, community engagement, collaboration, individualised justice, accountability and an outcomes focus are important policy markers for problem-solving courts. Problem-solving courts will seek to reverse the tendency to dehumanise the justice experience by making connections with service providers and the community to reconnect offenders and victims with professionals from relevant disciplines (King et al., 2009: 139–142, 209–214; also see Kaye, 2004: 143–150). Judith S. Kaye (2004: 129), the Chief Judge of the State of New York, indicates:

> Conventional case processing may dispose of the legal issues in these cases, but it does little to address the underlying problems that return these people to court again and again. It does little to promote victim or community safety. In too many cases, our courts miss an opportunity to aid victims and change the behaviour of offenders.

Most criminal courts hear a range of matters and the magistrate or judge may not have a specialised knowledge of the issues facing victims or defendants throughout the range of offences they deal with.

Sexual assault complaints, for instance, may be affected by a range of factors, including the trauma of proceeding with a prosecution and giving evidence, or of the problems such a prosecution will cause to a relationship, especially where the victim is in a relationship with the offender. A detailed knowledge of the range of issues facing sexual assault offenders and their victims, including the gross under reporting of such offences, may assist the problem-solving court by increasing the pre-trial monitoring of the defendant and to encourage the prosecution to seek corroborating evidence in support of the victim's claims. A case manager may be appointed to collect information about the defendant, their victim, and counsel to draft a service plan for the defendant to assist the court when making decisions as to appropriate treatment. King's (2006a, 2006b) study of non-adversarial approaches in the higher courts, however, suggests that such approaches requires further development and it is altogether rare to find such courts giving significant weight to therapeutic or problem-solving approaches.

Community engagement also features as a significant rationalising principle of problem-solving justice. Engaging members of the community in the rehabilitation of offenders or the support of victims may also reconnect the business of the courts with the local community. Offenders and victims who can relate to others in a supportive environment are more likely to overcome or move beyond the effects of the crime. Offenders are less likely to re-offend when constructively supported. Community engagement may also be important on an informational basis, specifically in terms of the expectations of the community and the courts when dealing with specific types of offences. Community courts, for instance, may have advisory panels of members of the local community who may inform the court of the types of offences that concern the community. This information may then assist the court in forming appropriate community based sentences, such as graffiti removal.

The courts are well positioned to connect a variety of key agencies. The role of a problem-solving court as a collaborative agent is significant to its successful placement of the offender and victim in a therapeutic and community context (Gil, 2008: 501). Courts have access to other government agencies and community groups. Courts may also bring stakeholders together in an official way, for instance, judges, prosecutors, defence counsel, corrections, and probation, may each play a role in the management of the offender. Court officers may also be brought together to offer their expertise. These officials may then further engage others in the community, such as social services, victims groups, and support networks. Such connections may encourage trust in the judicial process, and foster new outcomes for offenders, including placement programs or intervention support.

Problem-solving courts do not mete out standardised sentences, such as imprisonment, only then to leave the nature of the confinement of the prisoner to corrections alone. Such courts seek to use evidence-based risk and needs assessment to link an offender to suitable community based services. These may include intervention programs, counselling, job training, drug treatment, safety planning, and mental health counselling (see, for instance, the focus on mediation between key agents pursuant to ss27–30 *Sentencing Act 1995* (WA)). The key here is the realisation that the offender is an individual who needs to be engaged in networks of care and assistance that reconnect and restore the offender within their community.

By engaging the offender within a matrix of community stakeholders, a problem-solving court can emphasise personal accountability, raising the consciousness of the offender to the outcomes of their offending (Gil, 2008: 501). Even minor offences will have consequences, especially on the community, and offenders ought to be aware of them. By maintaining a high level of person accountability, the offender can also approach their treatment with responsibility and purpose, with the aim of successfully completing their program. Offenders can be actively engaged in their own recovery and rehabilitation, although this will invariably be supported by the requirement that offenders undergo monitoring and compliance testing, such as regular drug testing. These strategies combined will ensure that offenders have a better idea of the consequences of non-compliance. Guiding offenders toward a specific outcome of a set therapy or treatment is an important gaol of problem-solving justice. The court is also guided by outcomes, in particular, the outcomes of particular intervention programs or courses of treatment, including their costs and benefits to all stakeholders involved.

Case study: The community court

The community court provides a venue for 'community prosecution'. In the State of New York, community prosecution is based on the notion that although prosecutors ought to respond to particular cases, they continue to have a broader responsibility to public safety, crime prevention, and to develop public confidence in the justice system. Community prosecution requires prosecutors to work differently, and with different people, than is traditionally the case. Prosecutors thus work with residents, victims, community groups and other government agencies (see Berman and Fox, 2001: 205–206; King et al., 2009: 158–163). The main difference involves the accountability of the prosecutor. Rather than report success in terms of cases disposed of, or length of sentence, community prosecutors measure the effect of their work on neighbourhood 'quality of life', community attitudes and crime rates.

The English pilot 'Engaging Communities in Criminal Justice' is rationalised on the basis of making new connections between key criminal justice stakeholders, within a community context. The Ministry of Justice (2009: 1) provides that the scheme be established:

> To ensure that all the agencies in the criminal justice services engage with the public in a way that is joined up, better co-ordinated and more productive by better understanding their needs. To ensure that the service delivered to local communities is based on the needs of, and issues faced, by those communities, and contributes towards solving local problems. To better inform and involve local people, in particular to encourage more people to become involved through various types of community engagement including volunteering. The intended effects are to improve confidence.

The consultation document *Engaging Communities in Criminal Justice* follows the Cabinet Office Review 'Engaging Communities in Fighting Crime' by Louise Casey (the Casey Review) (Casey, 2008: 78), which determined that:

> It is important that citizens are engaged in ways that are quick, easy and reasonable. The public should not be expected to understand the 'system' – police, local authorities and the Criminal Justice System should be expected to understand the public. In order to achieve this across so many different and disparate organisations, it is reasonable to expect that there are some common and nationally recognisable structures that everyone can understand and use.

In *Engaging Communities in Criminal Justice,* Casey (2008) centres on four primary aims of stronger, community focused partnerships; community justice projects and the problem-solving approach; intensity and visibility of community payback; and keeping the public better informed. Respectively, these aims seek to bring criminal justice services together to facilitate 'two way' communication between the criminal justice service and local people; to solve problems for the community and to assist in the reform of offenders to reduce re-offending, and enable offenders to make amends; to increase forms of reparation and compensation, so that justice is delivered and seen to be delivered; and by improving the information the community receives on case outcomes, so that the community may understand that a real connection between crime, consequences, and punishment is made.

The pilot seeks to introduce community prosecutors to work with the CPS, together with the police, the courts and other community partners. Community prosecutors will engage directly with their communities, and will be aware of local concerns such that they will better reflect local concerns when making case decisions, which may include local business priorities. Some of this engagement work is already undertaken by the CPS, although community prosecutors will be encouraged to further engage with their local community than is currently the case. Local communities will be able to provide the community prosecutor with information and details of local crime conditions in the form of a community impact statement. It is envisaged that local prosecution 'team leaders' will take on a more visible proactive community prosecutor role within the geographical area assigned to them.

This approach, it is argued, will increase community participation in the decision to prosecute, albeit the formalities of this process are still opaque. Engaging community interaction, in the form of a community impact statement, together with other criminal justice agencies, seeks to raise community involvement in prosecution related decisions. For instance, if offenders are identified pursuant to the Prolific and Priority Offender Program, prosecutors will liaise with probation and police teams to capture the intelligence and information these agencies have on that individual. This pilot thus seeks to move toward Integrated Offender Management, where information sharing will become a routine approach to prosecution decision-making. Local prosecution teams will seek to work with Neighbourhood Policing Teams, Neighbourhood Crime and Justice Coordinators, and probation officers, so as to garner information on community concerns and to also provide feedback to communities. The pilot also calls for prosecutors to live in the area in which they work, to heighten their awareness of local concerns. Community prosecutors engage in local problem-solving, advising the police on priority problems in the community; on evidential issues related to such concerns; and on ancillary orders or out of court disposals which may be suitable in the circumstances. Community prosecutors will be responsible for providing advice on charging for crime and disorder offences, providing continuity of advice and case handling targeting underlying problems, to decrease the harm to the community. Informed decisions as to anti-social behaviour, domestic violence, problematic drug and alcohol use, prostitution or youth crime, will assist communities by harnessing the experience of a prosecutor dealing with like cases, in a particular locality. Community prosecutors will use information gathered from the community and other agencies to help consider the public interest when making prosecution decisions. This pilot thus seeks to complement the CCP, which establishes principles to assist prosecutors make key decisions in the case management and prosecution process.

The use of community impact statements will seek to facilitate an understanding of local issues amongst the police, the CPS, the courts, the judiciary and the probation service. Each stakeholder should understand the concerns of their local community to better inform the decisions they make. Community impact statements provide locals the ability to raise concerns as to offences, offence prevalence, and access to criminal justice services in their particular area. It is envisaged that the community impact statement will be a short report on offences and their contexts, compiled by the police but may include other partner agencies.

The pilot also requires increased interaction between the magistrates' courts and the community. Magistrates' courts will be encouraged to develop their knowledge and understanding of their local community; to maintain regular direct contact with the community; to provide feedback on the work of the courts, to ensure the activities of the court are integrated with other agencies and the community; to strengthen links to community payback schemes to raise awareness and increase visibility of service orders within the community; and to encourage opportunities for local residents to be involved in criminal justice services (including opportunities for volunteer magistrates, members of courts boards, mentors, special constables, or as employed staff).

The Casey Review found that communities held a widespread concern that criminals are largely subject to 'soft' justice, and that many offenders are not punished sufficiently. The pilot also seeks to utilise community payback sentences and to afford communities a say in the work undertaken by offenders in their local areas. This will be achieved by instituting citizens' panels to give locals the opportunity to discuss appropriate work that ought to be undertaken as community payback. The use of such panels will enable members of each community to attend meetings and participate in the identification of relevant work for offenders. The pilot also seeks to make information on crime more available to the public. This controversially includes the publication of individual court outcomes but does not include out of court disposals, such as penalty notices or cautions.

Sentencing and punishment

It is in the context of the removal of the victim from criminal law and justice that, since the 1970s, various groups have criticised the power of the state as monopolising the justice system to the exclusion of the discrete needs of victims. The victim's rights movement, for example, became increasingly critical of the way sentencing and punishment seemed to be rationalised around the interests of the defendant, and views emerged as to the tendency toward lenient sentencing. Arguably, it may not be that the courts are sentencing leniently, but that victims are increasingly sceptical of the business of the courts due to their exclusion from decision-making processes. Seeking ways in which this removal could be practically redressed, courts have been increasingly directed to consider the plight of the community and victim in sentencing.

Victim's rights have been inserted into the law in various ways. Most jurisdictions now offer a charter or declaration of victim's rights detailing the rights and obligations of government agencies in their treatment of victims; modes of criminal injuries compensation which provides standard amounts of compensation for prescribed injuries flowing from an alleged criminal offence; and the ability to adduce into sentencing proceedings a victim impact statement to detail the harms occasioned as a result of the offence, after conviction but before sentencing. While debate ensues as to the extent to which a charter of rights and compensation appropriately restores the victim following an offence (Mawby, 2007: 209–239), the tenure of victim impact statements in sentencing proceedings remains the most contentious. While the use of such statements remains controversial throughout the common law world, it is in NSW where the judiciary has assumed greatest resistance to their use in sentencing, particularly in homicide cases. The arguments for or against such resistance will be canvassed in light of those reasons for the continued exclusion of the voice of the victim in sentencing proceedings, particularly with regard to those normative assumptions that identify the victim as a threat to the stability of the sentencing and punishment process as objective and removed from the emotional interests of sectarian groups, especially victims and their families.

The expansion of defendant's rights and the formation of a trial process testing the prosecution case characterises the advent of the adversarial trial (Duff et al., 2007: 40–50). It was during this period, especially so toward the end of the twentieth century, where police and Crown officers increasingly stood in place of the victim, particularly in sentencing. The personal interests of the victim, either in selecting a relevant charge or as evidencing the harms occasioned to them, were largely replaced by those accounts of harm decided by public officials for the protection of the community. Garkawe (2006: 109) indicates why this assumption may be seen as necessarily limiting the increased participation of the victim in the modern justice system:

> Allowing victims' opinions to have an influence on sentencing provides them with a status of decision-makers, and this would conflict with Edward's and the writer's view that this is not appropriate in an adversarial system of justice. As referred to above, the amount of a criminal penalty should primarily be dependent on the knowledge and awareness of the offender, and the victims' views are not really relevant to this assessment.

The sentencing phase is one that is potentially inclusive, rather than exclusive, to the benefit of both defendant and victim. This could be seen to be the very basis of sentencing doctrine at least in terms of the rule that sentences be objectively proportionate to the harms occasioned to all parties, including victims and society: *The Queen v Veen (No. 1)* (1979) 143 CLR 458 and *The Queen v Veen (No. 2)* (1988) 164 CLR 465. Much has been written on the topic and many agree that given the exclusion of the victim from the trial, sentencing provides an opportunity to allow the victim to participate in common law processes (see Fox, 1994: 489; Kirchengast, 2005: 128).

The following sections indicate how the sentencing process has been reformed to incorporate the interests of the victim and community in new ways. These include the introduction of nuanced programs including intervention, forum and circle sentencing; victim impact statements; and through the incorporation of compensation and reparation as part of the sentence of the accused, over the removal of such claims to tort or administrative tribunals.

The use of intervention orders to direct the offender to therapy, or to an act of contrition seeking to restore the victim emotionally or materially, characterises the innovative use of the intervention order in local courts or magistrates' courts. Such orders now comprise a more specific sentencing process in NSW in the form of forum sentencing. Such practices are also widely used amongst circle sentencing courts.

These practices run against the adversarial model in that they seek participation from a variety of agents of justice traditionally excluded from the sentencing process, including victim, police, community representatives, lawyers, and support agencies. The exclusion of victim impact statements in NSW homicide cases draws from increasing concerns over the normative positioning of the interests of the victim against those of the defendant that tend to be seen as primary, and indeed constitutive, of the adversarial trial process. The English situation is compared to that of NSW. The increased use of compensation and restitution as part of an offender's sentence, however, rather than as an ancillary administrative or civil order, presents similar issues for discussion. Practices such as those adopted in South Australia and England suggest how new and innovative orders may be considered in sentencing to include acts of compensation, or reparation moving from offender to victim, to make the sentencing process more inclusive of the interests of the victim. The tendency toward the inclusion of victim and community perspectives may well be beneficial to the offender, victim and community alike. At the very least, the broader use of intervention programs, victim impact statements and compensation in sentencing shows that courts need not adhere to the tenets of adversarialism as an exclusive discussion as to liability and seriousness between Crown and accused. The sentencing process, as a reflective exercise of the weighting of various competing factors in a proportionate way, increasingly provides room for participation for a number of agents of justice.

Intervention programs, forum and circle sentencing

As a result of the need for certainty, most sentencing courts only deal with restorative justice as a factor relevant to sentencing when such programs are offered as an intervention program. In NSW, intervention programs may be offered under s11 of the *Crimes (Sentencing Procedure) Act 1999* (NSW). Section 11 allows a court to adjourn sentencing proceedings for up to 12 months while the offender attends an intervention program, such as alcoholics anonymous, road safety classes, or anger management, to provide the offender the opportunity to show the court, upon final sentencing, that the offender is indeed committed to their rehabilitation and is making progress toward that ideal. These types of programs, depending on their scope and context, may or may not fit the general definition of restorative justice.

Innovative sentencing programs, such as circle or forum sentencing (see Attorney-General's Department, 2008), also encourage the participation of victims. Such forms of sentencing replace the traditional sentencing hearing. Rather, offenders are invited to participate in a sentencing 'conference' inclusive of the police, victim and other relevant members of the community. In the case of circle sentencing, this also involves Aboriginal elders. The sentencing process is thus extended to include a conference of relevant participants such that the sentencing process itself may aid the restoration of offender and victim, but would otherwise provide for a sentence that includes the input of the offender personally, rather than a removed adversarial process prescribing an appropriate punishment.

Circle or forum sentencing is predicated on the basis of encouraging a dialogue between victims and offender, allowing the court to make more definitive judgements as to the state of the offender's contrition, rehabilitation and likely level of recidivism as a result of their willingness to discuss their offence openly. These types of assessments fit well with the requirements of proportionality, even the more restrictive version of ordinal proportionally put forward by von Hirsch and Ashworth (2005). Many of these types of intervention programs, however, do not engage a dialogue between victim and offender that is ongoing unless a separate act of reparation bringing offender and victim together is agreed to, and approved by the magistrate. This is in no way seen to be a limitation of such a program, which contributes significantly toward establishing a dialogue between victim and offender compared to traditional processes of sentencing before a judicial officer sitting alone. At the very least, such modes of sentencing encourage participation from a variety of sources, the victim included, and encourage the participation of the victim as an active agent of justice able to participate on their own motion. The requirement in *R v P* (1992) 64 A Crim R 381, that the victim act through a prosecutor appearing in the public interest, is overcome. The therapeutic benefits of appearing before a circle or forum are generally assumed as benefiting the victim. It should be noted, however, that just as the capacity to draft and read aloud an impact statement has at least some recognised therapeutic benefits for victims (see Erez, 2004), the participation of the victim in these alternative modes of sentencing may also encourage therapeutic results. The issue remains, however, as to the extent to which the potentially subjective content of victim input may be deemed relevant to sentence and further still, the extent to which the forum, or intervention plan arising out of the forum, actually constitutes the sentence of the offender.

The operating procedure on forum sentencing provided by the Attorney-General's Department (2008: 29) indicates that the 'intervention plan' agreed to by participants at the forum (specifically between offender and victim) may constitute the sentence of the offender once it is approved or affirmed by a magistrate. Following successful negotiation before the forum, a magistrate may approve an intervention plan and formally sentence an offender using the following sentencing options available under the *Crimes (Sentencing Procedure) Act 1999* (NSW):

> When the Magistrate has considered and approved the draft intervention plan, he or she makes an 'intervention plan Order'.
> The Court (via the Court Officer) is to notify the Program Administrator of the terms of any intervention plan Order, which will include the date by which the plan must be completed.
> An intervention plan Order can be any of the following Orders:
> (a) a grant of bail that is subject to a condition referred to in section 36A (20)(b) (i) on the Bail Act 1978
> (b) an Order referred to in section 10 (1) (c) of the Crimes (Sentencing Procedure) Act 1999
> (c) an Order referred to in section 11 (1) (b2) of the Crimes (Sentencing Procedure) Act 1999 or
> (d) an Order providing for an offender to enter into a good behaviour bond that contains a condition referred to in section 95A (1) of the Crimes (Sentencing Procedure) Act 1999
> In other words, the intervention plan Order may be an actual sentence (such as a bond) or a further deferral of sentencing.

Little guidance is given in terms of the proportionality requirements of such interventions, other than that the victim, offender or magistrate may not be willing to agree to an intervention plan that is disproportionate to the harm occasioned as a result of the offence. Otherwise, given that repeat offenders or serious offences are excluded from the program in the first instance,[8] most intervention programs agreed to would not be responding to offences of a high level of seriousness or recidivist offenders. Offences including acts of violence, serious drug offences and homicide are excluded from the program. This means that the interventions agreed to may not need to be strictly proportionate given that it is more likely that an offender will over-commit if willing to participate, given that they would otherwise be facing a term of imprisonment, and that the final order of a dismissal of charges with a bond restriction or a twelve month intervention program would generally be unavailable.

Forum sentencing will generally only be considered as a relevant option where the offender is likely to be sentenced to a term of imprisonment. Following the negotiation of a reasonable intervention plan, an offender may be sentenced to a dismissal of charges with a bond or intervention order, indicative of the fact that the offender's capacity to respond to discourses of restorative justice is relevant to their proportionate sentence. Forum sentencing thus seeks to connect the discourses of restorative justice and proportionality. Forum sentencing demonstrates how such disparate measurements of punishment, restoration and proportionality, can be seen as an appropriate response for lower level offences where a term of imprisonment may have been originally contemplated.

Victim impact statements

Since their inception into NSW law under the *Victim Rights Act 1996* (NSW), victim impact statements have provided victims of crime increased opportunity to participate in the sentencing process. Prescribed under s28 of the *Crimes (Sentencing Procedure) Act 1999* (NSW), both primary and family victims have the ability to tender an impact statement following conviction.[9] Family statements may be tendered where the primary victim dies following an offence. A sentencing judge will generally consider the impacts of an offence through the information tendered in evidence, usually at trial. Recognition of the impacts of an offence upon the victim is a long serving rationale of punishment that is specifically relevant to the formation of an appropriate sentence. It is out of the need to constitute such impacts objectively, however, that victim impact statements have tended to be poorly received by sentencing courts. This is because such statements are not always seen to be consistent with the established doctrines of punishment that require a sentence to be objectively proportionate to all circumstances of the offence and offender (Walters, 2006; Kirchengast, 2005; Booth, 2000, 2004, 2007; Edwards, 2002, 2003, 2004, 2009).

Due to the principle that punishment be objectively proportionate to the assessment of the harm occasioned, *R v Previtera* (1997) 94 A Crim R 76 rules that sentencing courts must exclude any consideration of family impact statements where the primary victim dies. This is because, as Hunt CJ at CL (Chief Judge at Common Law) states, death is the ultimate harm, such that a sentencing court must not, by reference to a family victim impact statement, value one life as greater than another (*R v Previtera* (1997) 94 A Crim R 76 at 86). This, as indicated below, emphasises the need to consider the death of the primary victim in terms of the immediate circumstances of the offence. It is thus reasoned that no opinion on the victim, from family members or others, be allowed to influence the assessment of harm unless that opinion is specifically relevant to the immediate circumstances of an offence. Considering such perspectives on the loss of the victim would, under *Previtera*, entertain the possibility that the primary victim was more valued than another. *Previtera* thus supports the sentencing principle that all life is of equal value. Hunt CJ at CL indicates this in the following terms (at 86):

> A problem arises, however, in those cases – such as the present – where the crime involves the death of the victim. The consequences of the crime upon the victim (death) has already been proved (or admitted) by the time the offender comes to be sentenced...
>
> The law already recognises, without specific evidence, the value which the community places upon human life...

Hunt CJ at CL indicates that victim interests can be more suitably administered as a matter of victim's compensation than in the context of a sentencing hearing, which requires an objective assessment as to offence seriousness and offender culpability.[10] In terms of this objective assessment, Hunt CJ at CL argues against the notion that the views of family victims not directly injured in the homicide may be able to contribute to the assessment of the offence without diminishing the principle of the universality of the value of human life.[11] Harm, arguably, needs to be limited to the immediate circumstances of the death of the victim out of respect for this principle.

The New South Wales Court of Criminal Appeal (NSWCCA) has, however, indicated that the *Previtera* rule may now need to be revisited in the context of s3A of the *Crimes (Sentencing Procedure) Act 1999* (NSW). Section 3A(g) prescribes that a court may impose a sentence on an offender to recognise the harm done to the victim and the community. Considering this new section, Spigelman CJ indicates in *R v Berg* [2004] NSWCCA 300 at par 43–44, that family impact statements may be able to influence sentence where the content of the statement may appropriately inform the court as to the harm done to the community.

This argument for reform was again addressed in *R v Tzanis* [2005] NSWCCA 274. In this instance, the NSWCCA was convened as a panel of five judges to determine the issue of the admissibility of family statements. Though declining to consider the issue on that occasion, the court did indicate the gravity of the issue by suggesting that 'no suitable vehicle has emerged for the purposes of the grant of special leave by the High Court' per *R v Tzanis* [2005] NSWCCA 274 at par 16.

Although the recent cases of *Berg* and *Tzanis* indicate some possibility that the utility of family victim impact statements be reconsidered in the future, the arguments in favour of the continued exclusion of such statements accord, arguably, with the view that such statements may well prejudice the interests of justice by including perspectives inconsistent with sentencing principles that assess seriousness and culpability from the perspective of the offender. Booth (2000, 2004, 2007) has written extensively on this topic and has recommended the continued exclusion of family statements from homicide sentencing decisions, despite recognising narrow scope for the legitimate use of such statements in terms of indicating general rather than specific harms, occasioned as a result of the offence. This perspective, arguably, is supported by normative perspectives that reduce the trial to the discrete interests of defendant and state, in that the views of victims are excludable on the basis that they prejudice a process otherwise deemed fair to the defendant.

However, in *SBF v R* [2009] NSWCCA 231, Johnson J determines that, despite the authoritative value of *Previtera*, a court may include significant reference to a victim impact statement as a reflection of the harm caused to the families of the victim (at par 88, 91):

> The sentencing Judge set out, in some detail, the content of the victim impact statements made by the mother of MA and the mother of DF (prepared on behalf of herself and the stepfather and siblings of DF), together with a victim impact statement of the surviving victim, KL. To the extent that complaint is made, under this ground of appeal, to the fact that extensive reference was made to the victim impact statements by the sentencing Judge, I observe that there is no statutory or other restriction upon the extent to which a sentencing Judge may set out the contents of such statements. There is no requirement for victim impact statements to be referred to in some shorthand way. It is understandable, in the present case, that his Honour set out the contents in some detail, a course which was open to the Court under s28 of the Act. The victim impact statements outlined the devastating consequences upon the families of the deceased young men and

also the profound effects upon the young woman who survived the collision.

...

It has not been demonstrated that his Honour misused the victim impact material on sentence in this case.

In England and Wales, victim personal statements may now be used as an indication of the general harm caused by homicide. However, courts may also draw upon them as indication of the more specific harm caused to family members, albeit harm of an expected nature. In *R v Pitchfolk* [2009] EWCA Crim 963 the appellant, serving a life sentence, appeals against the setting of his minimum term, following *inter alia* his conviction on the rape and murder of two young girls. The court directly acknowledges the impact statements presented by the families (at par 4):

> We have read a number of statements which have made us acutely aware of the continuing lifelong grief of the families of the two victims of murder. Their suffering is heartrending.

However, the courts are also willing to draw finer conclusions from personal statements as to the specific harms caused to individual family members. In *R v Akbar* [2004] EWHC 1819 (QB), the appellant stabbed Simon Henderson four times in the neck, killing him. Eighteen at the time of the offence, the appellant was sentenced to life imprisonment. The appellant, in this particular application, was seeking review of an already specified minimum term of 14 years. Reviewing the facts, Mr Justice Openshaw states (at par 5):

> I have read the Victim Personal Statement made by Katie O'Neil, who now cares for Simon Henderson's mother. That she needs a carer is not surprising. On hearing of his son's murder, his father (Mrs Henderson's husband) had a heart attack from shock; within a few days he had another heart attack from which he died. Simon's Henderson's girlfriend was so shocked that she miscarried. Some time later, his brother Stephen, grieving at the murder of his brother and the death of his father, committed suicide. If the effect of crimes upon victims are to have any effect on sentencers – and

indeed on sentences – it is obvious to my mind that they are a highly relevant factor in this case.

On the basis of his youth, the court further reduced the appellant's minimum term notwithstanding the specific harms caused by the killing. *R v Akbar* indicates, however, that the courts take note of victim statements prepared by family members with a view to specific harms that may, at least anecdotally, be connected to the killing. In this particular case, the passing of the father, suicide of the brother and miscarriage experienced by the girlfriend of the victim were seen to be connected to the killing of the deceased for the purpose of indicating the seriousness of the offence.

Victim's compensation, proportionality and the sentencing process

The sovereignty of the state has been increasingly asserted over the regulation of crime since the thirteenth century. In doing so, crime has generally been reserved for the criminal jurisdiction, with 'private' causes being reserved for civil law or tort. Victim compensation, being a statutory entitlement, remains distinct from common law proceedings. This is evidenced in the common law of victim's compensation, which considers the entitlement to compensation as a matter of state administration than criminal or civil law. Victim's compensation, then, is also distinguished from traditional private remedies available in the civil jurisdiction, and can be most likened to worker's compensation as an expedient means by which relevant parties may be compensated without the added stress of initiating court proceedings. Victim compensation therefore excludes the victim from the common law, removing them to an administrative jurisdiction that in some instances has been wholly transferred to government assessors or a tribunal (see Department of Justice (Vic), 2009: 50).

Victim compensation tends, therefore, to complement the removal of the victim from the criminal law by confining the victim to a jurisdiction constituted by statute, and administered as an adjunct to criminal law and procedure. This if affirmed in *R v Bowen* (1969) 90 WN 82 at 84, where Reynolds J suggests 'it [s437] is a provision of a very summary nature of doing some measure of justice to the victim of a crime without the delay, expense and formality of a civil action for, for example, assault, trespass or conversion'. *R v Cheppell* (1985) 80 Cr App R 31 furthers this argument by indicating that compensation orders are not a means of enforcing civil liability, holding that it is not necessary to establish civil liability in an application for compensation.

However, criminal injuries compensation can be likened to a civil proceeding at common law. Although it is an administrative jurisdiction distinct from the orthodox common law trial, authority suggests that it presents certain similarities providing the victim a 'trial experience'. For example, *Re Applications for Foster* [1982] 2 NSWLR 481 and *R v Field* [1982] 1 NSWLR 488 considered s4 of the *Criminal Injuries Compensation Act 1967* (NSW) affirming that compensation may be awarded even where the accused had been acquitted, or the charges dismissed. These cases support the proposition that where the quantum of compensation is assessed in accordance with civil law principles, the applicable onus of proof for facts going to quantum is the balance of probabilities, and not the criminal burden of proof, beyond reasonable doubt. Further, *R v McDonald* [1979] 1 NSWLR 451 and *R v C* [1982] 2 NSWLR 674 established that the offender be given a reasonable opportunity to be heard with respect to the application in order to contest the application as though it were a civil proceeding for an award of damages. The only exception to this rule per *R v Babic* [1980] 2 NSWLR 743 is where the offender waives their right to notice of the application, such as when an offender escapes from lawful custody or absconds whilst on parole. When assessing compensation the judge should proceed by reference to the same principles as those that apply in a civil action for damages for personal injury subject to any restrictions imposed by legislation per *McClintock v Jones* (1995) 79 A Crim R 238.

As such, victim compensation potentially mirrors orthodox common law processes, though being held apart from them. Punishment is thus left for the criminal jurisdiction under the control of the Crown and state. *R v Forsythe* [1972] 2 NSWLR 951 at 953 held that with respect to s437 of the *Crimes Act 1900* (NSW), that 'the amount determined is in no way a punishment for the convicted person. It is, as the section says, a compensation to the aggrieved person for the injury that the convicted person has done by reason of the felony'. Conventionally, the order for compensation is not to be seen as punishment, and may not be regarded as part of an offender's sentence. It is now universally accepted that where heard as part of sentencing proceedings, such awards are legitimated not out of any connection to the punishment of the offender, but out of the desirability of avoiding the burden of separate civil proceedings.[12] An earlier decision, *R v Daley* [1970] QWN 33 held that compensation is not a civil award as it is intended to be an additional punishment to the accused. *R v Braham* [1977] VR 104, however, holds that a compensation order does not form part of the penalty, and could not be used for the purposes of determining whether or not a penalty was manifestly excessive. With the exception of South Australia and in England and Wales, the gravity of authority now rests with the former assumption that compensation is a mode of administrative relief designed to hasten the receipt of damages to victims.

The law of South Australia differs from that of the other states and territories of Australia by virtue of s53(1) of the *Criminal Law (Sentencing) Act 1988* (SA). The English position is captured under s130 of the *Powers of Criminal Courts (Sentencing) Act 2000* (UK), granting the court the power to make a compensation order, or reparation to make payments for funeral expenses or bereavement, where the offence results in a death. The courts in South Australia have grappled with the extent to which an order for compensation ought to be taken into account as part of an offender's sentence. In *Brooks v Police* [2000] SASC 66, Bleby J regards the offender's willingness to pay compensation or perform an act of restitution as an important indication of contrition, something long considered relevant to sentence (at par 43):

> It can be seen that the Sentencing Act gives some prominence to the question of compensation to victims. It is not something to be left merely to action taken under the Criminal Injuries Compensation Act. Where a defendant has the means to pay compensation or make restitution, he or she should be expected to make the payment in any event. This is so especially in the case of fraudulent or like conduct where the defendant has enjoyed the benefits of that crime. But where a defendant exhibits genuine contrition borne out of a desire to pay compensation, but does not have the means to pay it (usually because the defendant never has had the means), and where it can be seen that some payment, periodic or otherwise, which the defendant can afford, may well have some therapeutic benefit in the rehabilitation of the offender, it can become a useful sentencing tool. This is so particularly where the alternative of imprisonment will mean loss of a job, a negation of any ability to pay compensation or to reimburse the Attorney-General, and a denial of any opportunity to the offender to become a useful member of the community. The impact of a custodial sentence on a person's ability to make restitution is a matter properly to be taken into account: *Ruggiero v R* (Unreported, Court of Criminal Appeal

(Cox, Prior and Olsson JJ) 1 December 1998, Judgment No S6989) at [42]–[43].

Bleby's J dicta has been affirmed in *Mile v Police* [2007] SASC 156, where Sulan J states (at par 24–25):

> During the course of the appeal, a question arose whether the order for compensation, which was a condition of the bond imposed by the Magistrate, was required to be taken into account in determining the final penalty. Whether payment of compensation or the court ordering a defendant to pay compensation is to be taken into account as part of the sentence was discussed by Bleby J in Brooks v Police. He referred to s53 of the Act and observed that the section imposes a requirement upon the court to give reasons for not awarding compensation where an application has been made by the prosecutor, or it is in the court's opinion that compensation should be awarded for loss and damage resulting from an offence. The offence of causing damage is one which an order for compensation will be considered almost as a matter of course.

Under South Australian law, victim's compensation forms part of the offender's sentence. However, it less clear whether the conflation of compensation and punishment brings the victim into consideration in new ways. The jurisprudence that has emerged from the introduction of s53(1) reinforces the need to consider sentencing from the position of the offender and victim. However, as a sentencing court needs to primarily consider the culpability of the offender and the seriousness of the offence, the private interests of the victim may be excluded as less relevant to sentence. It does bring into question, however, the extent to which the victim may be included by virtue of s53(1), and the extent that this section challenges sentencing doctrine by conflating victim interests with those of the offender. The Victorian Department of Justice has recently review the availability of compensation and has emphasised the significance of organising such services around a model of therapeutic justice that benefits the needs of all parties. The Department of Justice (Vic) (2009: 50) indicates:

> Recent reforms within the Victorian criminal justice system have emphasised the positive and beneficial nature of a therapeutic model of justice for all parties. It may be argued that a victim's experience of the criminal justice process will be enhanced if the offender's

punishment incorporates a formal recognition of the damage or injury done to the victim.

Principles of restorative justice highlight the need for the justice system to heal the injury, repair the harm, compensate the loss and prevent further victimisation. Restorative justice may have a role within the victim compensation system as either:

- a complementary process to the formal hearing of a victim compensation claim, with non-financial issues such as emotional harm or the issuing of an apology occurring
- a process by which the victim and offender negotiate the details of a compensation claim with any resulting agreement ratified and enforced by a court or tribunal.

By factoring compensation as part of an offender's sentence the criticisms of punishment as being an exclusive discourse between state and offender is overcome. Compensation as a means of remedying a wrong to the victim is not held apart from the criminal trial, addressing Christie's (1977) concern as to the restorative value of the criminal trial, and further challenges the notion that the modern criminal trial represents a process that traverses the public/private dichotomy maintaining the exclusivity of its form.

5
The Criminal Trial as Social Discourse

The trial has taken many forms over the course of the history of the common law. The form the trial has taken directly relates to the needs being satisfied by the trial at any given time. This argues against the notion that the trial, much like the broader criminal law, is shaped by general principles that have existed as part of the common law from time immemorial. To the contrary, the determination of the means and processes by which accusations of wrongdoing are heard and determined are largely the product of customary, social and political relations and it is not possible to exclude certain persons, parties, institutions or groups as bearing influence on the form that the trial ought to take. To this end, the trial as the manifestation of the means by which accusations of guilt are heard and determined, are not exclusive to the interests of select parties, but are inclusive of many voices and perspectives relevant to criminal law and justice. These voices are personal as well as institutional, and include victims, defendants, prosecutors, the Crown, the state, statutory authorities and the public at large. While it is not possible to give voice to each of these participants at each point in the process for the determination of criminal liability, we should guard against any attempt to exclude any one 'voice' as irrelevant or detrimental to justice. The controversy, rather, is in the balance of these voices and perspectives.

The previous chapters have shown that the criminal trial has not taken a particular or prescribed form the since its inception as a customary practice for the resolution of local disputes. Today, several trends present which suggest that the trial is continuing to transform. These trends, informed by various discourses of criminal justice policy, see the adversarial criminal trial become less adversarial and more inquisitorial, and more decentralised, in its organisation and operation. This trend is evidenced through the genesis of the criminal trial as a transgressive institution of social justice, seen through the rise of new approaches to justice such as therapeutic and problem-solving courts, the integration of human rights discourse, and the inclusion of victims into processes from which they would be otherwise excluded. The decentralised nature of the trial is also evidenced through the proliferation of a range of courts that specialise in particularised justice by meeting the discrete needs of classes of defendants and victims, and is further demonstrated by the move toward expedient modes of justice that dislocate the criminal trial from 'judge and jury' trials for local or magistrates' courts, which also adopt a range of inquisitorial processes that depart from the strict requirements of adversarialism.

This chapter focuses on the identification of the criminal trial as a site of discourse and power. Foucault's (1969, 1982, 1984, 1994) notion of disciplinary power as constitutive of social relations and the institutions which govern them assist our understanding of the transformative and decentralised nature of the modern criminal trial. This perspective also realises that the 'adversarial model', as it may be termed, is but one manifestation of a system of justice. Adversarialism comes with its own normative assumptions and prescriptions. Attached to these assumptions are commonly accepted ways of the 'conduct of conduct', to borrow Foucault's (see Gordon, 1991: 1–51; Dean, 1999: 10) notion. These normative assumptions define the accepted ways of regulating the behaviour of persons, offices, and institutions, each of which come together in an organised way to constitute the very institution of the adversarial criminal trial. The adversarial model, then, identifies who is relevant and who is not; who may speak and who may be silenced. Furthermore, as the dominant model of justice that emerged into the twentieth century, adversarialism comes to assume certain things about justice in such particularised ways that they constitute an ideology that is defendable within a normative framework as based on prescribed ways of 'conducting conduct'.

Foucault's (1969, 1982) work is pertinent here as it reminds us that such ideology, and the normative universe that rationalises its form and function, is constituted as an object of power and, most importantly, as 'truth'. Power, knowledge and truth are related to the extent that they may come together to perpetuate certain forms of knowledge as fact or truth; as unquestionable. Such truths may be constituted and supported by discursive formations that manifest out of the power of the statement and the archive. That the adversarial trial is the best guarantee of a defendant's right to a fair trial is one such truth that dominates common law systems of justice. Some deem it to be a truth that is beyond question, or indeed, significant reform. As a starting point, adversarialism may be identified as the path to a fair trial in common law jurisdictions. In a Foucauldian sense, this is a truth that manifests in the statements and discourses that advocate the superiority of adversarialism over alternative pathways to justice.

Discourse defined

A discourse may be taken to be a formalised way of articulating a given topic. In its most basic way, this articulation is manifested in language, which may be further broken down into linguistic units – vocabulary, grammar, and accepted modes of expression – or a series of signs which make up an enunciative field. Discourse thus describes a series of relatable statements that define a particular field of existence. Through discourse we refer to groups of statements that carry particular rules that make sense of things in particular ways. These rules, or 'archive', govern the interpretation of groups of statements as historical events (see Flynn, 1994). The term archaeology is concerned with the rules and principles that define the specificity of the discursive formation. Archaeology, for Foucault (1969: 147), defines the relevant territory of a discourse by articulating the outer limits of what different statements may say about a particular discourse. Archeology thus refers to the description of a discursive formation not only in terms of what may be justifiably said about a given topic, but treats that process as one that promotes that discourse as fact or truth. Archeology will being a level of homogeneity between statements that order a discursive formation. Discourses allow certain statements to be made as fact or truth, which as a corollary deny or suppress other facts or statements as false.

A simplistic example is as follows: at one point scientific discourse may have supported the notion that criminals are born, while at another may point sociological discourse supported the notion that criminals are bred. Alternatively, one can argue that the criminal trial is an institution of social power that is transformative and inclusive, while another discourse may suggest that the criminal trial is constituted within the limits of strict adversarialism – the rights of defendants to procedural justice *a priori*. Different discursive formations may thus define a different reality; a reality to which some may subscribe, and others not. What is so significant about this approach, however, is that it leads to a critical revisioning of the assumption that there is only one correct or best perspective, or archeology of thought. Perspectives abound, as do rationalising discourses, and the criminal trial is no exception to this. Field (2009: 37; reviewing Summers, 2007) provides that this tension is central to the different approaches taken to adversarial and inquisitorial processes. Searching for accepted definitions of each term proves elusive, let alone the extent to which one system may be seen to be compatible with the other:

> The problem is that this appears to leave us in a fluid world of competing discourses where there are no settled meanings for terms like 'adversarial' or 'inquisitorial'. But academics, either individually or as a group, cannot settle or stabilize the meanings of such concepts within wider legal and social discourses. All that they can do is to seek to make clear their own use of disputed terms by specifying the particular interpretations they are giving to them and to be alive to the variety of alternative uses.

In the *Archaeology of Knowledge*, Foucault (1969) analyses the notion of a 'statement' as an act of discourse that brings meaning to individual or specific acts. In a literary sense, statements may be defined by the rules that apply to basic parts of language or communication, such as words or syntax or grammar, to afford particular statements meaning or sentiment. This method may be extrapolated here, where networks of rules, procedures and perspectives define what is meaningful within a given legal order. Statements, as something meaningful to a body of rules and procedures, will largely depend on the rules of discursive formation. Understanding the practices that give groups of statements prescribed meaning enables one to interrogate the conditions that provide for the production of fact or truth. In order to demonstrate the principles of meaning and truth production in various discursive formations, Foucault (1969) focuses on the particular way 'truth claims' have emerge historically, during various epochs of rule, on the basis of examining what was actually written and said throughout these periods. For Foucault (1969, 1971, 1982), truth and meaning are dependent upon specific historical accounts that define a territory of discourse, an archive, whilst providing a practical means of truth production. Foucault (1969: 128) indicates:

> The domain of statements thus articulated in accordance with historical *a prioris*, thus characterized by different types of positivity, and divided up by distinct discursive formations, no longer has that appearance of a monotonous, endless plain that I attributed to it at the outset when I spoke of 'the surface of discourse'; it also ceases to appear as the

inert, smooth, neutral element in which there arise, each according to its own movement, or driven by some obscure dynamic, themes, ideas, concepts, knowledge. We are now dealing with a complex volume, in which heterogeneous regions are differentiated or deployed, in accordance with specific rules and practices that cannot be superposed. Instead of seeing, on the great mythical book of history, lines of words that translate in visible characters thoughts that were formed in some other time and place, we have in the density of discursive practices, systems that establish statements as events (with their own conditions and domain of appearance) and things (with their own possibility and field of use). They are all these systems of statements (whether events or things) that I propose to call *archive*.

Foucault (1969) uses the term archive to refer to a system of statements as historical events. The meaning of a statement therefore depends on the rules, methods and procedures that shape the discursive formation as they have emerged over time. Rather than lock us into a fixed or given system of rules, this method allows us to critically examine the notion that the criminal trial is exclusively interested in particular sites of meaning, or agents of justice, as a matter of given or unchallengeable fact. In *Truth and Power*, in an interview between Alessandro Fontana and Pasquale Pasquino, Foucault (1971: 131) says:

The important thing here, I believe, is that truth isn't outside power, or lacking in power: contrary to a myth whose history and functions would repay further study, truth isn't the reward of free spirits, the child of protracted solitude, nor the privilege of those who have succeeded in liberating themselves. Truth is a thing of this world: it is produced only by virtue of multiple forms of constraint. And it induces regular effects of power. Each society has its régime of truth, its 'general politics' of truth: that is, the types of discourse which it accepts and makes function as true; the mechanisms and instances which enable one to distinguish true and false statements, the means by which each is sanctioned; the techniques and procedures accorded value in the acquisition of truth; the status of those who are charged with saying what counts as true.

Foucault's (1971: 130–131) account of truth is relative to the mechanisms of power that define discourse as truthful or not, relevant or irrelevant, and explains how certain approaches to justice may be likewise identified as correct or incorrect, compatible or incompatible, or justified or not. Much of the legal change canvassed herein speaks to the variability of empowering discourses. Certain approaches to justice will be consistent with the system of statements, or archive, of the adversarial criminal trial in that they fit neatly within its rubric of adversarialism. Others may be inconsistent with the archive of adversarialism to the extent that they fundamentally challenge the very concept of the adversarial criminal trial that has emerged into the latter part of the twentieth century. As the following section demonstrates, the inclusion of out of court evidence as inconsistent with the strict requirements of adversarialism is largely dependent on the rationalising discourse adopted by the judges in each case. Of significance here is the extent to which each court relies on enabling legislation (including the Constitution of the United States), precedent or even ideas of public policy, culture or logic. Such sources will invariably guide the court as to the particular view that one interpretation is acceptable, or preferable, while another is not. These cases show that the archeology Foucault (1969: 147–148) speaks of may bring context to the growth and development of the criminal trial as indicating an adversarial tradition, rather than an inquisitorial approach, or at least an openness to its form. This realisation enables the consideration of a broader and perhaps interconnected discursive process that allows for the 'bourgening of discoveries', or the inclusion of new pathways to justice, that may relate to but be established apart from a main or more dominant rationalising process, *a priori*:

> Archaeology – and this is one of its principal themes – may thus constitute the tree of derivation of a discourse. That of Natural History, for example. It will place as the root, as *governing statements*, those that concern the definition of observable structures and the field of possible objects, those that prescribe the forms of description and the perceptual codes that it can use, those that reveal the most general possibilities of characterization, and thus open up a whole domain of concepts to be constructed, and, lastly, those that, while constituting a strategic choice, leave room for the greatest number of subsequent opinions. And it will find, at the ends of the branches, or at various places in the whole, a bourgeoning of 'discoveries' (like that of fossil series), conceptual transformations (like the new definition of the genus), the emergence of new notions (like that of mammals or organism), technical improvements (principles for organizing collections, methods of classification and nomenclature)… One can thus describe the archaeological derivations of

Natural History without beginning with its undemonstrable axioms or its fundamental themes...

On the other hand, the archaeology of the criminal trial at common law may be seen to be so prescribed that alternative methods and forms of trial, such as problem-solving justice, may be so distinct that they belong to another 'tree of discourse', or archaeology. Whether any one approach is within the archaeology of the common law trial depends, arguably, on the extent to which is it seen as a departure from the orthodoxy of the criminal trial in the first instance. This may not be an easy perspective to resolve, given that all discourses of justice, even those that significantly depart from the adversarial criminal trial, may be relatable to a common core of principles and perspectives that nonetheless connect those departures to the broad ambit of the criminal trial as an institution of law and society. It may therefore be best to proceed on the footing that such discourses, even those of therapeutic or problem-solving justice that significantly depart from the adversarial criminal trial, may derive from a common 'tree of derivation' on the possibilities of the criminal trial.

Power, knowledge and the adversarial criminal trial

> No knowledge is formed without a system of communication, registration, accumulation, and displacement that is in itself a form of power, linked in its existence and its functioning to other forms of power. No power, on the other hand, is exercised without the extraction, appropriation, distribution, or restraint of a knowledge.
> Michel Foucault (1994) 'Penal Theories and Institutions' in *Ethics: Subjectivity and Truth*, p. 17.

Making sense of the adversarial criminal trial requires one to 'think like a lawyer'. As Hayne J indicates in *Gately v The Queen* (2007) 232 CLR 208, below, the criminal trial is accusatorial and adversarial. On the contrary, to escape the inextricable logic of adversarialism one must realise that the adversarial criminal trial is premised on a discursive formation that prescribes a model of justice in strict terms. These terms do seem to prescribe a model form for the adversarial trial. Any 'trial' which goes against this model confronts the tenets of adversarialism in such as way that it risks changing the criminal trial into some other, perhaps less acceptable, form. Thus, where the criminal trial is modified to accommodate nuanced perspectives on therapeutic justice, such as the emergence of drug courts, sex offences courts, or community prosecution, the dominant notion of 'the criminal trial' may be fundamentally confronted.

However, in order to grasp the capacity of the adversarial trial to adapt to change, the internal rules and modalities that prescribe certain acts relevant, and others irrelevant or excludable, must be understood. These rules emerge in the current form through a detailed law of evidence and trial procedure that is largely predicated on notions of fairness, due process, or in the ECHR context, an 'equity of arms'. The notion of equity of arms refers to the right of the accused to be provided a reasonable opportunity to present his or her case to the court under conditions that are not a substantial disadvantage. The right to a fair trial has been described variably, and may be inclusive of the ability to understand the proceedings generally, to have access to counsel, to receive a copy of the charge or indictment and the content of the prosecution against the accused, and to be prosecuted before an independent magistrate or judge who publishes reasons justifying their decision. The right to a fair trial is contained under art. 6 of the ECHR and has been interpreted, in the Bulger case in *V v United Kingdom* (2000) 30 EHRR 121, in the context of two 11 year old children tried in a Crown Court for the murder of a two year old child, thus (at 125):

> The Court notes that the applicant's trial took place over three weeks in public in the Crown Court. Special measures were taken in view of the applicant's young age and to promote his understanding of the proceedings: for example, he had the trial procedure explained to him and was taken to see the courtroom in advance, and the hearing times were shortened so as not to tire the defendants excessively. Nonetheless, the formality and ritual of the Crown Court must at times have seemed incomprehensible and intimidating for a child of eleven, and there is evidence that certain of the modifications to the courtroom, in particular the raised dock which was designed to enable the defendants to see what was going on, had the effect of increasing the applicant's sense of discomfort during the trial, since he felt exposed to the scrutiny of the press and public. The trial generated extremely high levels of press and public interest, both inside and outside the courtroom, to the extent that the judge in his summing-up referred to the problems

caused to witnesses by the blaze of publicity and asked the jury to take this into account when assessing their evidence....

Tantamount to a fair trial is thus the ability to participate in proceedings by understanding the basic processes of the court. It also requires that the accused be able to examine the case against them. In *Windisch v Austria* (1990) 13 EHRR 281, the applicant was convicted on the basis of anonymous testimony from witnesses that were not called to give evidence. The Court's task was to ascertain whether the proceedings, when examined as a whole, including the way in which evidence was taken, was fair. The general principle provides that all evidence should be tendered before the accused in a public hearing with a view to adversarial argument. Statements obtained at a pre-trial hearing may be used so long as the rights of the defence are taken into account and a process is formed that affords the accused some chance to examine those making the statements. Despite witness anonymity, the accused must, at some point, have an adequate and proper opportunity to challenge and question a witness making accusations against them.

The recent movement amongst several common law jurisdictions to provide a mechanism for the receipt of the testimony of child or other vulnerable or intimidated witnesses, particularly in sexual assault matters, challenges the traditional framework of the adversarial criminal trial. The basis upon which adversarialism is predicated provides that the accused ought to have full and complete access to the prosecution case against them. There should be no tricks or surprises. The accused ought to be afforded every opportunity to contest and challenge the case against them. This requirement is no mere rule. It is a fundamental requirement to common law justice and is particularly important in the criminal trial context given that the liberty of the accused is at stake. These fundamental requirements are therefore not to be impeded lightly.

In this context, *R v Camberwell Green Youth Court* [2005] 1 All ER 999 raises some interesting points as to the transcendental nature of the criminal law. Of interest here is the extent to which criminal procedure is open to influence by factors considered to be external to the tenets of adversarialism. The plight of the victim, and the interests of child witnesses, would generally stand against the processes of fairness that are held out as paramount. A long list of cases provides that it is within the power of the court or tribunal to ensure that the accused receives a fair trial.[1] Tantamount to this requirement is the ability for the accused to receive certain information, in particular, the charge or indictment against them, the prosecution evidence, to face their accuser, and to cross-examine all witnesses called by the prosecution. *R v Camberwell Green Youth Court* makes a case for departing from some of these standards on the basis of the needs of a particular class of witness that are particularly vulnerable in the context of the adversarial court environment. Child witnesses of sexual assault would be one of the most vulnerable types of victim that could be called to court to give evidence. Nonetheless, tensions exist as to the ability to afford such vulnerable witnesses necessary protections while ensuring that the requirements of a fair trial are maintained. Several courts have now dealt with the issues raised in *R v Camberwell Green Youth Court* in comparatively different ways.

This section will consider the use of 'out of court' or hearsay evidence, such as that provided by statement, video tape or via video link, to examine the various discourses that impact on the shaping of this area of criminal jurisprudence. Three cases will be considered in this regard: *R v Camberwell Green Youth Court* [2005] 1 All ER 999; *Gately v The Queen* (2007) 232 CLR 208; and *Crawford v Washington* (2004) 541 US 36. Though sourced from different jurisdictions, each case demonstrates how the adversarial criminal trial is able to respond to dynamic and challenging circumstances, specifically the call for a modified procedure to accommodate victim or other interests deemed subordinate to the requirement that the accused receive full access to the prosecution case, and witnesses in particular.

R v Camberwell Green Youth Court [2005] 1 All ER 999

In *R v Camberwell Green Youth Court* [2005] 1 All ER 999, Baroness Hale of Richmond refers to the submission of counsel on behalf of D (a minor). This submission sought to persuade the House of Lords that art. 6(3)(d) of the ECHR provides the accused with the right to confront his accusers, 'to look them in the eye', while they are testifying (at 1016):

> Mr Starmer stressed that the Strasbourg case law should be seen in the light of the traditions of our domestic legal system. The nature of criminal proceedings in each contracting State affects the European Court's approach to the basic principle that 'all the evidence must be produced in the presence of the accused at a public hearing with a view to adversarial argument.' In our system the starting point is that all the evidence is given literally in the court room in front of the accused. Thus any departure should be shown to be necessary.

However, this cannot mean that the Strasbourg Court would regard our domestic legal system as so set in stone that Parliament is not entitled to modify or adapt it to meet modern conditions, provided that those adaptations comply with the essential requirements of article 6. In this case, the modification is simply the use of modern equipment to put the best evidence before the court while preserving the essential rights of the accused to know and to challenge all the evidence against him. There are excellent policy reasons for doing this. Parliament having decided that this is justified, the domestic legal system is entitled to adopt the general practice without the need to show special justification in every case.

R v Camberwell Green Youth Court has been extracted elsewhere throughout this book and, collectively, these citations show that the House of Lords is not bound by any particular interpretation of adversarialism other than to allow for equity of arms between defendant and victim. Doak (2005b: 294–295) examines the holding of *R v Camberwell Green Youth Court* in the context of the long held tradition of orality in the English criminal trial. Courts and policy makers seem comfortable using technology to present testimony in non-direct ways. However, the departure from traditional adversarial processes in *R v Camberwell Green Youth Court* provides for the significance of the case. This significance is provided in Lord Rodger of Earlsferry's dicta, '[s]ince the forms of trial have evolved in this way over the centuries, there is no reason to suppose that today's norm represents the ultimate state of perfection', extracted in full at the start of Chapter 4. There are several points raised here. The first is that the current trial process is identified as a 'norm', and that, secondly, this 'norm' is not the 'ultimate state of perfection'. These statements combined suggest that the adversarial criminal trial occupies an unquestioned, fixed status that may be held out, arguably, as the pinnacle of the development of the common law. Lord Rodger of Earlsferry's judgement traverses the dominance of the adversarial paradigm for something more enlightened, the realisation that the trial will continue to transform to meet new needs (see Schwikkard, 2008: 8).

Gately v The Queen (2007) 232 CLR 208

Gately v The Queen (2007) 232 CLR 208 determined that a pre-recorded video of the testimony of a child witness in a sexual assault matter may be presented to the jury during deliberations, without causing a substantial miscarriage of justice. The accused was prosecuted for the indecent treatment of a girl under 16, with one count of incest. A prerecorded video of the victim testifying and being cross-examined was shown to the jury as part of the trial, pursuant to s21A[M] of the *Evidence Act 1977* (Qld). During deliberations, the jury asked to see the video again. Counsel for both the prosecution and defence agreed that the jury could watch the video in the courtroom, supervised by the bailiff. Following an unsuccessful appeal to the Court of Appeal of Queensland, the appellant further appealed to the High Court of Australia on the basis that there had been a miscarriage of justice as the trial judge allowed the jury to watch the video twice, treating it as a physical exhibit entered into evidence. The appellant further alleged that the trial judge failed to direct the jury not to give undue weight to the victim's evidence, and that his Honour further erred by allowing the prosecutor to tender the girl's written statement to police when she had already given full pre-recorded evidence.

The High Court of Australia, by majority, dismissed the appeal and held that the means by which the video was replayed in an out of court session was irregular, but that in the circumstances of the case, this had not caused a miscarriage of justice. The majority rejected the submission that the trial judge ought to have warned the jury not to give the video evidence undue weight. Further, the court dismissed the submission that the police statement was incorrectly received in evidence, being admitted under s 93A of the *Evidence Act 1977* (Qld), which provides that written statements by children or intellectually impaired persons be admitted into evidence at trial.

Hayne J, with whom Gleeson CJ, Heydon and Crennan JJ agreed, Kirby J dissenting, ruled that (at 235–236):

> First, there are some fundamental characteristics of Australian trial processes, particularly at a criminal trial, that must be borne at the forefront of consideration. Subject to whatever statutory modifications may have been made to applicable rules of procedure, a criminal trial in Australia is an accusatorial and adversarial process. It is essentially an oral process. Subject to exceptions, the hearsay rule excludes evidence of out-of-court assertions when tendered as evidence of the truth of the assertions. As a result, the focus of the trial falls chiefly upon what is said in the evidence given in the courtroom. As three members of this Court said in *Butera v Director of Public Prosecutions* (Vict):
>
>> 'The adducing of oral evidence from witnesses in criminal trials underlies the rules of procedure which the law ordains for their

conduct. A witness who gives evidence orally demonstrates, for good or ill, more about his or her credibility than a witness whose evidence is given in documentary form. Oral evidence is public; written evidence may not be. Oral evidence gives to the trial the atmosphere which, though intangible, is often critical to the jury's estimate of the witnesses. By generally restricting the jury to consideration of testimonial evidence in its oral form, it is thought that the jury's discussion of the case in the jury room will be more open, the exchange of views among jurors will be easier, and the legitimate merging of opinions will more easily occur than if the evidence were given in writing or the jurors were each armed with a written transcript of the evidence.'

The whole of the oral evidence of an affected child, adduced by the prosecution at a relevant proceeding, is pre-recorded. (In this and in other important respects the Evidence Act differs from some generally similar provisions made in other jurisdictions.) The record is then played before the jury and the jury both hear and observe the child giving evidence. The evidence that the affected child gives, although given at a 'preliminary hearing', is given subject to all applicable rules governing relevance and admissibility. It is pre-recorded in accordance with, and for the achievement of the purposes described in, s21AA – to preserve the integrity of the evidence and to limit the distress and trauma that the child might otherwise experience when giving evidence. None of those considerations suggests that the record itself is to be treated as an item of real evidence. All point only to the conclusions that the evidence is what the child says, and that the record itself is not evidence. Those conclusions are reinforced by the fundamental characteristics of a criminal trial that have been mentioned earlier.

Hayne J comes to understand the pre-recorded evidence through the lens of the adversarial trial. The departure that the *Evidence Act 1977* (Qld) affords child witnesses is rationalised in terms of the modification it makes to an otherwise established process. In this light, the departure is not seen to be radical nor inconsistent. The change is incremental, and not gross, in that the departure is explained through the conventional adversarial model. The out of court testimony is made 'subject to all applicable rules' such that the standards set down in *Butera v Director of Public Prosecutions (Vic)* (1987) 164 CLR 180 are still able to be maintained. The video is thus not physical evidence – it is to be treated as though the child witness is testifying in court.

What makes this a legitimate application of the facts to the law is the way the rules of adversarialism are extended to cover the otherwise anomalous process of pre-recording oral evidence. Although the trial court treated the (pre-recorded) oral evidence of the child irregularly, as though it was physical evidence that could be shown to the jury over again, the majority dismiss the appeal on the basis that, in the whole of the circumstances of the case, there had been no substantial miscarriage of justice. This was rationalised in terms of the rules of adversarial engagement. Had Gately's counsel contested the second viewing, the majority may have come to a different decision. What is so significant about this decision, therefore, is the way the language of adversarial justice is employed to condition the anomalous evidence as compatible with the tenets of oral adversarial process per *Butera*. The dismissing of the appeal on the basis of the proviso is also justified in terms of the rationalising of the action (or inaction) of Gately's counsel as part of the gambit of adversarial interaction.

Kirby J provides a dissenting judgment that places emphasis on the lack of supervision or guidance given by the trial judge, either in terms of supervising the second viewing, or by giving appropriate warnings as to the weight to be given to the replayed testimony (at 222):

> The trial judge gave no warning or direction to the jury, then or later, about the way they should approach such evidence. On the contrary, the jury were permitted unrestricted and unsupervised access to the recorded evidence, otherwise than in open court and after the close of the evidence. It may be inferred that they viewed the whole or parts of it at least once, and perhaps repeatedly. Effectively, it happened in secret. The judge, the accused and the public were unaware of the course that the jury took.
>
> When, the following day, the jury also requested to see the complainant's written statement to the police, the entire statement was read to them in open court. Again, no direction or warning was given by the trial judge as to the weight to be accorded to the statement in light of its repetition. The jury requested that part of the statement be read yet a third time. Once more, that request was complied with, but without any judicial warning or direction along the lines of the governing principles. Verdicts of guilty were subsequently returned by the jury, almost 24 hours after they had been

charged to consider their verdicts. The conviction of the accused and his sentencing followed.

That a conviction followed is thus of no surprise. Kirby J objects to the lack of judicial supervision to the range of general departures from standard trial procedure. For his Honour, such departures are unacceptable in light of a criminal trial process that requires some measure of judicial intervention. That counsel consented to these departures is not, in itself, a sufficient basis upon which to determine that no substantial miscarriage of justice occurred. Kirby's J thus takes a different perspective than the majority as to the appreciable parameters of the adversarial process.

Crawford v Washington (2004) 541 US 36

The United States Supreme Court ruled in *Crawford v Washington* (2004) 541 US 36 that the sixth amendment to the Constitution of the United States gives the accused the right to confront witnesses and cross-examine their testimony admitted during trial.[2] This includes statements taken by the police. The court reasoned that the framers of the constitution intended the 'confrontation clause' to prohibit out of court testimony as evidence against defendants.[3] The accused, Michael Crawford, stabbed a man he claimed was attempting to rape his wife. As part of their investigations, the police interviewed the accused's wife who gave a different account of the stabbing than that offered by the accused. At trial, the prosecution played a tape of the interview for the jury. The jury convicted the accused. The accused submitted that playing his wife's statement, with no chance for cross-examination under Washington's martial immunity rules, violated the sixth amendment guarantee that '[i]n all criminal prosecutions, the accused shall enjoy the right... to be confronted with the witnesses against him'. The Washington Supreme Court upheld the conviction, relying on the Supreme Court's decision in *Ohio v Roberts* (1980) 448 US 56, providing for the admission of out of court testimony against a defendant if that testimony was reliable (see Friedman, 2004).

The opinion of the court was delivered by Scalia J, with Rehnquist CJ, joined by O'Connor J, concurring. Scalia J refers to the history of the right of the accused to be confronted with the case against them, and, in particular, to cross-examine witnesses (at 45–46):

> One recurring question was whether the admissibility of an unavailable witness's pretrial examination depended on whether the defendant

had had an opportunity to cross-examine him. In 1696, the Court of King's Bench answered this question in the affirmative, in the widely reported misdemeanor libel case of *King v. Paine*, 5 Mod. 163, 87 Eng. Rep. 584. The court ruled that, even though a witness was dead, his examination was not admissible where 'the defendant not being present when [it was] taken before the mayor... had lost the benefit of a cross-examination.' Id., at 165, 87 Eng. Rep., at 585. The question was also debated at length during the infamous proceedings against Sir John Fenwick on a bill of attainder. Fenwick's counsel objected to admitting the examination of a witness who had been spirited away, on the ground that Fenwick had had no opportunity to cross-examine. See *Fenwick's Case*, 13 How. St. Tr. 537, 591–592 (H. C. 1696) (Powys) ('[T]hat which they would offer is something that Mr. Goodman hath sworn when he was examined... ; sir J.F. not being present or privy, and no opportunity given to cross-examine the person; and I conceive that cannot be offered as evidence ...'); id., at 592 (Shower) ('[N]o deposition of a person can be read, though beyond sea, unless in cases where the party it is to be read against was privy to the examination, and might have cross-examined him.... [O]ur constitution is, that the person shall see his accuser'). The examination was nonetheless admitted on a closely divided vote after several of those present opined that the common-law rules of procedure did not apply to parliamentary attainder proceedings – one speaker even admitting that the evidence would normally be inadmissible. See id., at 603–604 (Williamson); id., at 604–605 (Chancellor of the Exchequer); id., at 607; 3 Wigmore s1364, at 22–23, n. 54. Fenwick was condemned, but the proceedings 'must have burned into the general consciousness the vital importance of the rule securing the right of cross-examination.' Id., s1364, at 22; cf. *Carmell v. Texas*, 529 US 513, 526–530 (2000).

The history of the lack of rights afforded to the accused and the development of a law of evidence that sought to address this weakness, supports his Honors final ruling (at 65–66):

> Sylvia Crawford made her statement while in police custody, herself a potential suspect in the case. Indeed, she had been told that whether she would be released 'depend[ed] on how the investigation continues.' App. 81. In response to often leading questions from police detectives, she implicated her husband in Lee's stabbing and at least arguably undermined his self-defense claim. Despite all this,

the trial court admitted her statement, listing several reasons why it was reliable. In its opinion reversing, the Court of Appeals listed several *other* reasons why the statement was *not* reliable. Finally, the State Supreme Court relied exclusively on the interlocking character of the statement and disregarded every other factor the lower courts had considered. The case is thus a self-contained demonstration of Roberts' unpredictable and inconsistent application.

Justice Rehnquist, joined by O'Connor J, concurred, but opposed overruling *Ohio v Roberts* (at 74–75):

Indeed, cross-examination is a tool used to flesh out the truth, not an empty procedure. See *Kentucky v. Stincer*, 482 US 730, 737 (1987) ('The right to cross-examination, protected by the Confrontation Clause, thus is essentially a "functional" right designed to promote reliability in the truth-finding functions of a criminal trial'); see also *Maryland v. Craig*, 497 US 836, 845 (1990) ('The central concern of the Confrontation Clause is to ensure the reliability of the evidence against a criminal defendant by subjecting it to rigorous testing in the context of an adversary proceeding before the trier of fact'). '[I]n a given instance [cross-examination may] be superfluous; it may be sufficiently clear, in that instance, that the statement offered is free enough from the risk of inaccuracy and untrustworthiness, so that the test of cross-examination would be a work of supererogation.' 5 Wigmore s1420, at 251. In such a case, as we noted over 100 years ago, 'The law in its wisdom declares that the rights of the public shall not be wholly sacrificed in order that an incidental benefit may be preserved to the accused.' *Mattox*, 156 US, at 243; see also *Salinger v. United States*, 272 US 542, 548 (1926). By creating an immutable category of excluded evidence, the Court adds little to a trial's truth-finding function and ignores this longstanding guidance.

Friedman (2004: 5) suggests that the confrontation clause provides that the accused access the evidence against them in a direct way. The hearsay exceptions to the confrontation clause are permitted out of recognition that there may be reliable exceptions to the general rule. *Ohio v Roberts* thus provides grounds for these exceptions if a statement is supported by a guarantee as to its trustworthiness. Friedman (2004: 6) goes on to suggest that reliability as a criterion upon which trustworthiness is to be judged deflects the fact that not all evidence before the jury is meant to be reliable. It is for the jury to sift the reliable evidence from the unreliable, and much evidence permitted under a hearsay exception may indeed by of 'dubious trustworthiness'. The problem of child testimony is flagged here as raising some difficult issues under *Crawford v Washington*.

Mosteller (2005: 513) has suggested that *Crawford v Washington* has now limited the once common practice of video recording victim statements for use at trial:

> For example, the practices in some jurisdictions of having victims make statements to investigating officers on videotape shortly after the crime *were* once very useful to the prosecution, but now produce inadmissible testimonial statements. Police and prosecutors are certain to develop alternative investigative methods in an attempt to avoid *Crawford's* impact.

King-Ries (2005: 303–308; also see Lininger, 2005) has suggested that the prosecution of abusive partners will now be more protracted and complicated under *Crawford v Washington*. Domestic violence interventions raise a point of concern where there is a state decision to prosecute but where the victim refuses to charge their partner. Previously, victims of domestic violence did not have to present as witnesses as the combination of exceptions to the hearsay rule in the form of 'excited utterances' and the careful gathering of police evidence at the time of the initial investigation meant that a prosecution case could be nonetheless formed. However, the confrontation requirement under *Crawford v Washington* provides that testimonial statements, the specific definition of which is not given, must be tested through cross-examination in court. Statements must now be classified into testimonial or non-testimonial. An 'excited utterance' may still found the basis of a charge for certain accusations of wrongdoing, because an utterance may be considered 'non-testimonial'. Domestic violence situations would, however, be unlikely to fit a 'non-testimonial exception' as the violence that founds such a charge may occur over lengthy periods, and not 'under the influence of a startling event' (King-Ries, 2005: 318).

The United States Supreme Court in *Crawford v Washington* combines an originalist interpretation of the sixth amendment in the context of the history of the adversarial processes to justify the narrowing of the out of court and hearsay exceptions in *Ohio v Roberts*. The significance of this approach is that the history referred to is reactonist to the extent that it was developed at a time when the accused had few rights to challenge the prosecution case, at least by today's standards of due process and procedural fairness. Scalia J's opinion is strongly founded upon the history of the right to confront your accuser. The ability to cross-examine a prosecution witness is thus fundamental to the 'truth finding function' of the criminal trial, as supported by a long line of cases that flow back into English jurisprudence. It is a functional process that is key to the requirements of adversarialism as it is concerned with the discovery of 'truth' through a contested version of events. This provides for a significant point of analysis in terms of the constitutive discourses of adversarialism drawn upon and explains the significant divergence between approaches to vulnerable victims, child witnesses, and domestic violence prosecutions that would now result across the three jurisdictions traced in this section.

The criminal trial, disciplinary power and the periphery of justice

Cotterrell (1995, 1992: 298–299) has suggested that the end of the twentieth century is witness to the breakdown of the legal autonomy of law as a distinct form of regulation. Referring to Foucault's (1976: 93) notion of power, Cotterrell (1992) suggests that state power as a centralised force is being displaced by a variety of disciplinary powers founded upon technical or scientific knowledge. This may certainly be the case, at least in terms of the proliferation of new tribunals, such as problem-solving courts. Such courts seek to manage specific offences, offenders and victims under a rubric of specialty knowledge, treatment and practice to best meet the particularised needs of those before the court. Kamenka and Tay (1978) suggest that common law systems are becoming less autonomous because the distinctions between formal legal concepts and procedures that would otherwise separate courts from tribunals, and justice from administration, is becoming less clear. Nonet and Selznick (1978: 89, 110) further suggest that law is becoming more 'open-textured', such that the sources of law are broadened to include contexts, concepts and subject matter otherwise deemed unimportant or irrelevant (or even prejudicial) to its processes. As a result, the law becomes more purposive or responsive, and the 'cognitive competence' of law is increased. Nonet and Selznick (1978) argue that this 'opening up' of law to otherwise outside sources of information evidences the historical development and growth of law. Purposive law thus sees a decline in artificial distinctions and processes of reason, and provides for the reintegration of legal and political participation. The significance of Nonet and Selznick (1978) perspective, moreover, lies in the discursive basis for the development of law beyond a single discourse.

It has been argued that the law, as a discipline of rules, principles and approaches that predicate what discourses may be relevant and which may be not, is constituted in terms of the statement and the archive, or Foucault's (1969) 'archaeology of knowledge'. The differential treatment of out of court evidence as shown above, suggests that law, and the criminal trial in particular, functions in terms of the statement and archive. Law is essentially discursive to the extent that it is flexible and open to change. Historically, this can be said to be a constitutive basis for the continued evolution of the common law. It is certainly true of the growth of criminal law to the extent that agents and approaches once deemed irrelevant or prejudicial to 'fairness', such as victims and victim's interests, are now relevant to the proportionality requirements of a fair trial. Nonet and Selznick (1978: 106–107) suggest this in their account of the rise of responsive law:

> Procedural justice is only one obligation among others and one resource among others. It does not follow that fairness and individual justice are valued any less. On the contrary, purposive law encourages a fuller realization that individual justice, in the long run and not only in the case at hand, depends on supportive institutional conditions. Legal energies should be devoted to diagnosing institutional problems and redesigning institutional arrangements. New modes of supervision, new ways of increasing the visibility of decisions, new organizational units, new structures of authority, new incentives – these are the characteristic remedies of purposive law.

Purposive law is thus constituted as a discursive process. It ceases to play by the rules of adversarialism to move beyond convention and 'artificial reason' for a blurring of powers and institutional boundaries. The extent to which the criminal trial may be capable of change, however, depends on the degree to which society entertains the capacity to 'face its problems'. Nonet and Selznick (1978: 113) see this as the condition prerequisite of responsive law, in short, '[r]esponsive law presupposes a society that has the political capacity to face its problems...'.

The concept of law as autonomous is central to any inquiry that seeks to understand the extent to which the criminal trial is able to adapt to social change. Clune (1989: 189) suggests that concepts of core and periphery are central to a lawyer's understanding of the evolution and growth of the legal system. The 'core' of legal thought thus predicates content that is consistent with the accepted mode of legal analysis. Such content may go unchallenged because it fits naturally with existing norms and tests, on a substantive and procedural basis. No inconsistencies will therefore arise where content can be explained by the paradigms and rationales prescribed by a 'core' analytics. The consideration of evidence of the defendant that seeks to mitigate the culpability of the offence, for instance, fits comfortably with traditional legal analysis. The sentencing phase of the criminal trial is largely directed toward the consideration of such evidence. On the other hand, the 'periphery' of legal thought is much more uncertain. This is where information fits uncomfortably with traditional legal analysis, on either a substantive or procedural level. Victim input as to the range of harms that have resulted following an offence, for instance, does not fit with a traditional sentencing process. Such processes are focussed on objective sources, and the victim is not deemed to be a trustworthy source of information on such reasoning. Innovations at the periphery of legal analysis, such as the use of victim impact statements in sentencing, challenge conventional legal processes in a way that renders such processes ambiguous (see Edwards, 2004). Such evidence may sit at the margins, such that the courts may diminish the use of such evidence against the 'core' content prescribed by the dominant mode of analysis.

Clune (1989) argues, however, that it is at the periphery where law appears more modern and relevant, substantive and powerful. In the context of sentencing, inroads have been made in many jurisdictions, but most courts continue to grapple with the notion that victims ought to be able to play a substantive role in proceedings. It does little to convince the public that the legal process is open to new and innovative movements in social thought. Alternatively, law, and criminal trial in particular, must develop in a principled way that identifies the sources of law from which it draws. Furthermore, the extent to which 'core' legal analysis is influenced by outside thought, and most importantly, which thoughts are principled to the extent that they ought to be factored into a legal analysis, remain a controversy that is debated throughout common law systems. This is a vexed issue; and one that confronts all lawyers, judges and policymakers. Furthermore, it takes form through discourses that are deemed to be central and authoritative to the exclusion of other perspectives that sit at the fringes, or even outside, normative legal analysis.

Cotterrell (1992) argues that law has a perceived identity crisis, manifest in the blurring of the public/private dichotomy.[4] The distinction between legal principle and public policy are seen to undermine the autonomy of law and in particular the integrity of the legal process. As Cotterrell (1992: 300) indicates, this goes as far as to undermine the law's 'specific competencies'. The modification of the criminal trial to accommodate new perspectives and agents of justice provides a key study here. Whether the criminal trial is open to new discourses that seek to integrate victim and other interests as significant to the trial process is dependent on the extent to which decision makers are open to new approaches to justice that may challenge the competencies of a traditional or orthodox analytics of rule.

Decentralised justice

The discursive formations relevant to individual judgements are clearly different. Different discourses are drawn upon by each judge in the consideration of the adversarial trial, and the extent to which such a trial is flexible enough to accommodate new and different approaches to justice. The acceptability of any departure to the adversarial trial will thus largely depend upon the discursive formation the judge adheres to in constituting their worldview or perspective on how the adversarial trial ought to manifest in practice and procedure. This is arguably a point of distinction between the three cases above. Although each court is being asked to respond to different questions on the use or acceptability of out of court evidence, different discourses present. The number of discourses that guide each judge to their respective decision are numerous and cannot be reduced to a mere list. However, agreed perspectives do emerge that show that departures from the adversarial model, in terms of the acceptable use of out of court evidence, are more or less justifiable depending on the type of discursive formation referred to. The discursive formation and the archive have the ability to empower those who speak to its rules and practices. Flynn (1994: 30) indicates that the archive:

> ... is the locus of the rules and prior practices forming the conditions of inclusion or exclusion that enable certain practices and prevent others from being accepted...

Discursive formation has a particular meaning in Foucault's (1969) work. Arguably, a range of discourses, each of which with a historical specificity and preference for 'truth', may be drawn upon to constitute an acceptable notion of the adversarial trial. The judgements extracted thus draw from statements that support particular discourses on the appreciable outer limits of adversarial justice. Arguably, the result of the extent to which out of court evidence is acceptable will largely depend on the discursive formation, or archaeology of knowledge, to which each judge refers. As can be seen in *Gately v The Queen*, clear differences emerge between the acceptable limits of adversarial processes between the majority decision of Hayne J and the dissenting decision of Kirby J. Similarly, the United States Supreme Court and House of Lords refer to a particular discursive formation when considering the extent to which out of court evidence is an acceptable departure from adversarial process in their respective decisions. This is supported by a particular reading of the rights of the accused to cross-examine prosecution witnesses per *Crawford v Washington*, or the need to work within the confines of a legislative framework that purposefully departs from aspects of the adversarial process but in a limited and discrete way per *Gately v The Queen*. Foucault (1969: 130) refers to the operative limits of the discursive formation, thus:

> Between the *language* (*langue*) that defines the system of constructing possible sentences, and the *corpus* that passively collects the words that are spoken, the *archive* defines a particular level: that of a practice that causes a multiplicity of statements to emerge as so many regular events, as so many things to be dealt with and manipulated. It does not have the weight of tradition; and it does not constitute the library of all libraries, outside time and place; nor is it the welcoming oblivion that opens up to all new speech the operational field of its freedom; between tradition and oblivion, it reveals the rules of a practice that enables statements both to survive and to undergo regular modification. It is *the general system of the formation and transformation of statements*. (original emphasis)

Discursive formation thus provides for a particular interpretation and truth that is not reflective of all knowledge but contained to a series of rules and practices that allow certain statements to make sense, and to be seen as fact. That different discursive formations may be relevant to the same process of adversarial justice leads to the argument that adversarialism, as a particular epoch of criminal justice, is an inherently decentralised and fragmented field. This is significant realisation and point of justification for the various movements in criminal justice policy that seek to challenge the dominant paradigm by the introduction of new modalities of rule. What may be perceived by some to be a doctrine founded upon principles of general application, principles that constitute the trial as a prescribed adversarial process, can be critiqued and displaced for the realisation that the trial is constituted as a discursive institution of social justice. As such, the criminal trial as discursive leads to the suggestion that the criminal trial is decentralised to the extent that no one discourse ought to dominate the constitution of the trial to the displacement of all others perspectives. The criminal trial is revealed as a disciplinary institution in that it is constituted of social power and operated to the extent permitted by the discourses used to justify its cause.

6
The Trial as Hermeneutic: A Critical Review

The idea that the criminal trial is not constituted around normative approaches that prescribe its form and scope remains controversial. Normative approaches not only indicate what the trial ought to 'look' like, but will prescribe those individuals who are protected by the criminal trial, and the nominal rights afforded to them. These rights might be protected in an agreed or common process summarised in terms that prescribe the limits of the normative process. The right to a 'fair trial', due process or procedural fairness each ascribe a framework of rules and principles that operate within and constitute the given normative context, specifically the adversarial criminal trial. The problem is that such perspectives omit several agents relevant to justice, including victims and the community, and does not account for the genealogy of the trial as transformative or discursive. Today, there is increasing concern over the varying scope of the criminal trial, seen in the emergence of problem-solving courts, courts of therapeutic justice, summary process, pre-trial process and agreements, out of court processes, applications for control orders,[1] and the modification of conventional adversarial processes, including the role of the jury, the law of evidence, and the introduction of victims into trial and sentencing proceedings. As the proceeding chapters have shown, the criminal trial is not bound by one determinative model. However, the criminal trial continues to be identified as an accusatory and adversarial process that emerged into the eighteenth and nineteenth centuries with the exclusive function of testing the truth of the accusation of wrongdoing. It is at this point where, as a historical archive, the criminal trial came to be associated with the dominant discourse of adversarialism to the exclusion of all other possibilities.

Those fortunate enough to warrant protection under the adversarial model, or be empowered as an agent of standing within its processes, may be highly critical of any modification of such processes. This would nominally include defendants whose rights may be protected under such a model, but would also include lawyers and the judiciary versed in the art of adversarialism. The public may well support the contested trial as an artefact of liberal society, despite emerging criticisms as to its exclusivity, limited scope, or need for reform.

In *R v Cook* [1997] 1 SCR 1113, the Supreme Court of Canada considered the extent to which the Crown ought to be required to call a witness. The court ruled that the duty to call prosecution witnesses ought to be left to the Crown as a matter of discretion, save in exceptional circumstances. Where the trial judge thinks a witness ought to be called then they possess the power to do so. The prosecution is not compelled to call any particular witness, including the victim of the offence. The prosecution's ability to 'ambush' the defence with a surprise case is limited by its duty to disclose the prosecution case to the defence. It is thus for the defence to call a witness where not previously called by the prosecution. The trial judge would only call a witness on his or her own motion in extraordinary circumstances, such as if there is a 'gap' left in the prosecution case or where a witness's testimony may give the defendant a real change of acquittal. With regard to the exercise of that discretion, L'Heureux-Dubé J makes the following remarks on the adversarial process (at par 39):

> The adversarial process functions on the premise that it is the obligation of the Crown to establish a case beyond a reasonable doubt against the accused. Once this threshold has been surpassed, however, it is up to the accused to call evidence or face conviction: *R. v. Noble*, 1997 CanLII 388 (S.C.C.), [1997] 1 S.C.R. 874. The adversarial nature of the trial process has been recognized as a principle of fundamental justice (*R. v. Swain*, 1991 CanLII 104 (S.C.C.), [1991] 1 S.C.R. 933). As such it should be construed in a way that strikes a fair balance between the interests of the accused and those of society: *R. v. Levogiannis*, 1993 CanLII 47 (S.C.C.), [1993] 4 S.C.R. 475; *Cunningham v. Canada*, 1993 CanLII 139 (S.C.C.), [1993] 2 S.C.R. 143, at p. 148; *Re B.C. Motor Vehicle Act*, 1985 CanLII 81 (S.C.C.), [1985] 2 S.C.R. 486. In my view, placing an obligation upon the Crown to call all witnesses with information bearing on the case would disrupt the inherent balance of our adversary system. I note, however, that the accused is also not obliged to call the witness. As I propose to expand upon, there are other options which are available to the accused in an appropriate case including, but not limited to, asking the trial judge to call the witness,

commenting in closing on the witness' absence, or asking the trial judge to comment.

The adversarial process that the Supreme Court of Canada defends in *R v Cook* is neither prescriptive nor exclusive.[2] The court holds open the possibility that a trial judge may intervene beyond any motion put by the litigants. The notion that the trial judge remains neutral, independent and, to the extent he or she is called upon to rule on matters of law submitted by either party, passive, is open to challenge. Clarifying the obligations of the prosecution against the oversight of the trial judge, the Supreme Court of Canada refers to the Privy Council decision of *Seneviratne v R* [1936] 3 All ER 36. In this case, the Privy Council provides a much broader role for the prosecution than that envisaged in *Cook*. The duty of the prosecution may well require the calling of all relevant witnesses, whether or not these may be destructive to the Crown case. The ruling is clarified to the extent that such a power, where relevant, may be exercised by the trial judge. The Privy Council nevertheless provides a model of adversarial justice that departs from the accepted duties of the prosecution as commonly agreed today (at 48–49):

> Their Lordships do not desire to lay down any rules to fetter discretion on a matter such as this which is so dependent on the particular circumstances of each case. Still less do they desire to discourage the utmost candour and fairness on the part of those conducting prosecutions; but at the same time they cannot, speaking generally, approve of an idea that a prosecution must call witnesses irrespective of considerations of number and of reliability, or that a prosecution ought to discharge the functions both of prosecution and defence. If it does so confusion is very apt to result, and never is it more likely to result than if the prosecution calls witnesses and then proceeds almost automatically to discredit them by cross-examination. *Witnesses essential to the unfolding of the narratives on which the prosecution is based, must, of course, be called by the prosecution, whether in the result the effect of their testimony is for or against the case for the prosecution.* (emphasis added)

Seneviratne v R is significant to the extent that it suggests that approaches to justice, and indeed the adversarial criminal trial, are not determinate nor given. The Privy Council, writing their decision in the first half of the twentieth century well after the adversarial trial had emerged as the dominant mode of trial, show that while the adversarial process delineates the role of prosecution and defence on one hand, it obscures it on the other. This obfuscation does not detract from the ambit of the trial to the extent that the role of the litigants is confused. Rather, it leaves enough room so that special duties are placed on the prosecution to call all witnesses so as to offer a complete narrative of the case, perhaps even to the demise of the prosecution case. To the extent that such a narrative is required in order to secure a conviction, the duty to ensure cohesion in the prosecution case has not been removed under *Cook*, but displaced to the trial judge.

The cases of *R v Cook* and *Seneviratne v R* demonstrate the point that the criminal trial is not entering a new phase or era in which the criminal trial has reach some crisis point. Rather, the trial is acting in exactly the same manner as it has since antiquity. It is true that the rigidities of adversarialism that prescribe the trial as a closed institution of limited access to Crown and defendant are increasingly displaced for alternative pathways to justice. The rise of problem-solving courts and other movements toward therapeutic justice suggest this is the case. However, these movements do not spell the end of adversarialism nor do they suggest the beginning of something new. Rather, the development of the criminal trial as traced herein suggests that the trial is a transformative institution of justice. As such, the trial may be seen as a hermeneutic of traditional adversarial doctrine and text. Chapters 3 and 4 considered the rise of the transformative criminal trial as something familiar to the history of criminal law and justice. As such, the criminal trial as a transformative institution of justice is not something that has recently emerged, in a most controversial way. Rather, the transformative trial is hermeneutic in that it is always discursive, and is more than the adversarial trial struggling in the modern age. The transformative criminal trial is not based on any normative or prescribed account of what the trial ought to be. A normative model of the criminal trial, as a representation of a particular time and place, ought to be rejected for a model that understands the trial as a disciplinary institution of competing discourses and approaches to justice.

Adversarial, inquisitorial and integrative approaches

The notion that the criminal trial is constituted through the interplay of various discourses as to accusation and participation that traverse the adversarial and inquisitorial approaches to justice is controversial. Central to this context is the extent to which these discourses may be constituted as a more truthful or authoritative account of how the trial should be constituted. The scope, function, procedures and rules by which the institutional presence of the trial is constructed is thus largely determined by the discourses that are entertained as significant and determinative. The cases of *R v Camberwell Green Youth Court* [2005] 1 All ER 999, *Gately v The Queen* (2007) 232 CLR 208, and *Crawford v Washington* (2004) 541 US 36 show how discourses of adversarial justice may be divergent as based on particular perspectives or archives of knowledge. Each may be taken to be a true or accurate account of the state of the criminal trial. As Chapter 5 indicates, there may be common points between the discourses, but there are also significant differences.

These differences notwithstanding, perspectives emerge that suggest that the criminal trial is 'under attack' due to the introduction of victim rights, the pursuit of local and national security, the decline of the contested trial, and out of a general critique of the values of adversarialism, that is, the trial is under a normative attack by those seeking a different kind of trial experience such as one that seeks to include the aims of reconciliation and restoration (see Duff et al., 2007: 1–10). However, as indicated in *R v Cook*, the adversarial process, in so far as it defines the modern criminal trial, is not as ridged as one may think. The decline of the contested trial and the influence of the politics of national and domestic security, law and order, and victim rights, may well challenge aspects of the criminal process, but it is arguable whether any of these fronts do anything to the trial that history and discourse does not already provide. This is because the model of adversarial justice that is emerging into the twenty-first century could already be found in the various (and competing) discourses of justice that have shaped the trial over the last century or more.

In *R v Cook*, the Supreme Court of Canada indicates the outer limits of the adversarial process as noted in the extract. These limits help the court establish the ambit of the prosecution's discretion to call witnesses, including the victim or complainant. However, L'Heureux-Dubé J makes clear the fact that the trial judge may still exercise that discretion where a witnesses' testimony is materially relevant to the indictment or where it is necessary to call a witness in the interests of justice, to prevent an unjust conviction. The adversarial process thus endorsed by the Supreme Court of Canada is far from an antiquated trial by battle, where each party engages the other with the slightest of judicial oversight. Rather, a modern adversarialism, although guiding to the extent that it defines the roles afforded to each presenting party, does not limit the court in its duty to ensure that justice is done. Much like the inquisitorial courts of continental Europe, judicial intervention is a significant aspect of the adversarial tradition. As *Jago v District Court of NSW* (1989) 168 CLR 23 reminds us, once the case is brought before a court it is for the judge to exercise a measure of judicial oversight to ensure that a fair trial ensues. This means that despite the tenets of adversarialism that limit each party in a procedural and substantive way to ensure that a contested version of the facts emerge, the court is still able to exercise a measure of supervision restoring the scope of the trial to that recognised in obiter in *Seneviratne v R*. This point is significant and challenges the assumption that the adversarial trial is opposed to, or incompatible with, inquisitorial approaches. Inquisitorial approaches allow the court to go beyond a supervisory role to call witnesses of its own motion. Counsel in such jurisdictions will assist the court rather than contest a version of evidence as adduced by each party. Issues raised in *R v Cook* and *Seneviratne v R* would thus be familiar to an inquisitorial court of criminal justice.

Discursive tensions: Re-asserting the adversarial model

Chapter 5 covered three cases that dealt with the admissibility of out of court or hearsay evidence in criminal trials across three common law jurisdictions. Although different points of appeal were at stake, the courts each drew from different discourses to justify their departure or confirmation of common law doctrine. Out of the cases of *R v Camberwell Green Youth Court*, *Gately v The Queen*, and *Crawford v Washington*, it is *Crawford v Washington* that stands out as the decision seeking to re-affirm the adversarial approach to the potential use of out of court evidence. This section deals with this departure by examining this decision as an affirmation of the dominant discourse of adversarialism. This discourse is wholly legitimate and authoritative and so *Crawford v Washington* stands as a judgment consistent with the development of the American criminal trial and common law more generally. As far as a strict legalism is concerned, *Crawford v Washington* presents a more palatable argument for the legal conservative than either *R v Camberwell Green Youth Court* or *Gately v The Queen*.

In the context of these different approaches, each of which entertain processes that diverge from the requirement that testimony is required to be presented orally, arguments have emerged suggesting that we are seeing the re-assertion of the adversarial model. Sklansky (2009) suggests that the United Stated Supreme Court has recently moved away from its earlier tolerance of inquisitorial approaches to justice. He argues that 'anti-inquisitorialism' has influenced the development of American criminal jurisprudence to the extent that the small inroads made toward inquisitorial approaches have now been rejected. Examples of this reassertion of the incompatibility of inquisitorial approaches to justice in an otherwise adversarial system are evidenced through the Supreme Court's recent rulings. These include the restricted interpretation of the confrontation clause in *Crawford v Washington*, the court's invalidation of mandatory sentencing schemes, the rejection of procedural default rules set by the International Court of Justice (ICJ), and the invocation of inquisitorial processes in the law of interrogations and confessions. Three reasons are explored for the rejection of the inquisitorial approach. These include the originalist argument, that the inquisitorial approach was the 'chief set of evils' that the criminal procedure provisions of the Constitution sought to restrain; the holistic account, that the organic integrity of the adversarial system cannot incorporate inquisitorial ideals and processes; and the functionalist argument, that the inquisitorial system 'simply is worse than ours', especially at uncovering the truth of a criminal accusation, protecting rights and limiting abuses of government authority. Sklansky (2009) is not convinced that these arguments amount to fundamentally undermine the uses of the inquisitorial approach and further asserts that it is unlikely that the organic character of American adversarial justice is so fragile that it is unable to withstand the integration of inquisitorial methods, where relevant.

In *McNeil v Wisconsin* (1991) 501 US 171, a case determining that the sixth amendment right to counsel does not constitute the invocation of the fifth amendment right to counsel pursuant to *Miranda v Arizona* (1966) 384 US 436 following arrest, Scalia J observes (at 181, note 2):

What makes a system adversarial, rather than inquisitorial, is not the presence of counsel, much less the presence of counsel where the defendant has not requested it, but rather the presence of a judge who does not (as an inquisitor does) conduct the factual and legal investigation himself, but instead decides on the basis of facts and arguments pro and con adduced by the parties. In the inquisitorial criminal process of the civil law, the defendant ordinarily has counsel; and in the adversarial criminal process of the common law, he sometimes does not. Our system of justice is, and has always been, an inquisitorial one at the investigatory stage (even the grand jury is an inquisitorial body), and no other disposition is conceivable. Even if detectives were to bring impartial magistrates around with them to all interrogations, there would be no decision for the impartial magistrate to umpire. If all the dissent means by a 'preference for an inquisitorial system' is a preference not to require the presence of counsel during an investigatory interview where the interviewee has not requested it – that is a strange way to put it, but we are guilty.

In *McNeil v Wisconsin*, Scalia J finds points of connection between the adversarial and inquisitorial approaches. These are connections that were expressly rejected in *Crawford v Washington*, where Scalia J indicates that the inquisitorial process is 'the principal evil at which the Confrontation Clause was directed' (at 50). Sklansky (2009: 1638–1639), however, questions the Supreme Court's dismissal of the usefulness of the inquisitorial process, in particular, the notion that evidence gathered under an inquisitorial process is somehow less trustworthy than evidence presented in person:

> Whether the consensus is warranted is another question. Take *Crawford* and *Davis*, for example. Construing the Confrontation Clause as a bulwark against Continental forms of criminal adjudication led the Court to some odd conclusions, including that the formality of the setting in which a statement was made – meaning, for the most part, the steps the government took to keep an accurate record of the statement or to assure its reliability – should count heavily against admissibility of the statement in a later trial. More fundamentally, in relying on 'the civil-law mode of criminal procedure' as a contrast-model, the Court never made clear what, precisely, was wrong with that mode of procedure, or how it threatened values that warranted constitutional protection. Sometimes the Court said that inquisitorial process was bad because it relied on untrustworthy evidence. At other times the Court suggested the real concern was that Continental criminal procedure lent itself too easily to authoritarian abuse. And sometimes it seemed as if the chief sin of Continental criminal procedure was simply that it was Continental – 'wholly foreign' to our way of doing things.

The inquisitorial process is rejected out of recognition that it may distract from an adversarial process. *Blakely v Washington* (2004) 542 US 296 firmly indicates the Supreme Court's rejection of an inquisitorial approach. This decision further indicates that the adversarial approach, as far as it is based on processes of accusation of fact to be determined by a jury, is incompatible with inquisitorial, or judge centered, approaches. *Blakely v Washington* concerns the extent to which a judge may be arbiter of facts relevant to sentencing. In this case, Blakely was sentenced to

90 months in prison after pleading guilty to second-degree kidnapping involving domestic violence and the use of a firearm. Washington State prescribed a sentencing guideline whereby the standard range of sentences should be between 49 and 53 months, unless substantial and compelling reasons existed to sentence the offender outside that range. The sentencing judge found that such reasons did exist, specifically, that Blakely had acted with deliberate cruelty. Blakely appealed, arguing that the decision that he had acted with 'deliberate cruelty' was an additional determination on the judge's part, violating his sixth amendment right under *Apprendi v New Jersey* (2000) 530 US 466, to have the jury determine the facts necessary for sentence, beyond reasonable doubt. Scalia J delivered the majority opinion, in which Stevens, Souter, Thomas, and Ginsburg JJ, joined. In *Blakely v Washington* (2004) 542 US 296, Scalia J ruled (at 313):

> Ultimately, our decision cannot turn on whether or to what degree trial by jury impairs the efficiency or fairness of criminal justice. One can certainly argue that both these values would be better served by leaving justice entirely in the hands of professionals; many nations of the world, particularly those following civil-law traditions, take just that course. There is not one shred of doubt, however, about the Framers' paradigm for criminal justice: not the civil-law ideal of administrative perfection, but the common-law ideal of limited state power accomplished by strict division of authority between judge and jury. As *Apprendi* held, every defendant has the *right* to insist that the prosecutor prove to a jury all facts legally essential to the punishment.

The 'inquisitorial approach' rejected by the majority include those procedures, such as sentencing guidelines, that call for a judge to arbitrate facts in question. As *Apprendi v New Jersey* indicates, such facts are reserved for jury determination under the sixth amendment.

Sanchez-Llamas v Oregon (2006) 548 US 331 ruled that foreign nationals not made aware of their right to consular notification following an arrest cannot use the Vienna Convention on Consular Relations ('the Vienna Convention') to suppress evidence obtained by the police.[3] Roberts CJ, delivering the opinion of the court, held *inter alia* that exclusionary rules of evidence are peculiar to common law systems and do not characterise the approach taken by the other member states. The ICJ has barred procedural default rules, the requirement that submissions on federal law are made to the state courts in compliance with state procedural rules, under the Vienna Convention. Roberts CJ held that a defendant could not be protected by the process, as this departure is borne out of key differences in the adversarial and inquisitorial approaches to justice (at 356–357):

> Procedural default rules are designed to encourage parties to raise their claims promptly and to vindicate 'the law's important interest in the finality of judgments.' *Massaro*, 538 US, at 504. The consequence of failing to raise a claim for adjudication at the proper time is generally forfeiture of that claim. As a result, rules such as procedural default routinely deny 'legal significance' – in the Avena and LaGrand sense – to otherwise viable legal claims.
>
> Procedural default rules generally take on greater importance in an adversary system such as ours than in the sort of magistrate-directed, inquisitorial legal system characteristic of many of the other countries that are signatories to the Vienna Convention. 'What makes a system adversarial rather than inquisitorial is… the presence of a judge who does not (as an inquisitor does) conduct the factual and legal investigation himself, but instead decides on the basis of facts and arguments pro and con adduced by the parties.' *McNeil v. Wisconsin*, 501 US 171, n. 2 (1991). In an inquisitorial system, the failure to raise a legal error can in part be attributed to the magistrate, and thus to the state itself. In our system, however, the responsibility for failing to raise an issue generally rests with the parties themselves.

Other inquisitorial procedures rejected by the court include the ability to lead evidence through *ex parte* examination of the accused, or the reliance on confessional evidence (Sklansky, 2009: 1639). A long line of cases indicates the Supreme Court's attitude to the continental approach to confessional evidence, especially as an artefact of inquisitorial justice, and the association between state tyranny, torture and the denial of defendant rights to justice (see *Brown v Walker* (1896) 161 US 591).

Of the three approaches that resist the adaptation of inquisitorial approaches in American criminal procedure, originalist, holistic or organic, or instrumental or functionalist, Sklansky (2009: 1680), notes that the basis for an 'organic' incompatibility proves to be most elusive:

> Protecting the organic integrity of our legal system by guarding against inquisitorialism makes sense only if the key characteristics

of inquisitorialism can be identified. And that proves surprisingly difficult.

The issue then for the integration of inquisitorial and adversarial approaches is the extent to which we can agree on the qualities and characteristics of inquisitorial methods. In this sense, certain characteristics are readily apparent, such as the initial investigation into an offence being conducted by, or with the oversight, of a magistrate rather than a police officer. On the other hand, the provision of counsel as indicative of an adversarial or inquisitorial approach has divided the Supreme Court (see Sklansky 2009: 1668; *McNeil v Wisconsin* (1991) 501 US 171 at 189 per Stevens J; *McNeil v Wisconsin* (1991) 501 US 171 at 181 per Scalia J; *Watts v Indiana* (1949) 338 US 49 at 55 per Frankfurter J). Originalist accounts have also been criticised as a substantive basis for anti-inquisitorial argument. The originalist argument entails that the Constitution of the United States envisages an adversarial criminal procedure. Sklansky (2009: 1674) suggests that the argument in favour of an anti-inquisitorial approach generally 'exaggerates the importance of Continental criminal procedure to the Founding generation', and the 'importance of the Founding generation'. The functionalist perspective, which assumes that the common law approach is simply 'better' than inquisitorial procedures, may also be open to criticism. In Sklansky's (2009: 1687) view, the functionalist perspective is largely founded on assumptions that are untested or rhetorical:

> The problem with overblown rhetoric about the advantages of the adversary system is not just that it lumps together questions best considered separately. It can also mix together myth and reality, papering over the notorious gaps between an idealized version of the American adversary system and the system's actual, day-to-day operation.

Discourses that support adversarial argument over inquisitorial, or for that mater, alternative approaches that may incorporate the two, may be defined in terms of Sklansky's (2009) originalist, organic and functionalist perspectives. What has emerged through this analysis, however, is the need to be wary of 'truth claims' that find their legitimacy in specific accounts of history and interpretation. The usefulness of any one approach in the interpretation of the Constitution, statute or common law, must thus be considered in terms of the significance of discourse as discussed in Chapter 5. The argument of this chapter rests on the claim that the trial is discursive, and as such key interpretations as to the flexibility of adversarial justice reside in the discourses that best make sense to the judgements that comprise each case. Structural contexts and documentary sources, such as the enabling legislation or Constitution upon which an action is based, or the basic framework of the justice system in each jurisdiction, will impact on the dimensions of the final decision. However, within these variables lies an enormous field of discourse that may found and make legitimate a decision in any particular case. The significance of this approach resides in those works that identify the inquisitorial approach as having something to offer adversarialism. Those that champion the discursive basis of law and justice will find inquisitorial method in adversarial doctrine. The different approaches to the use of counsel, mentioned above, provides a case in point.

History, discourse and genealogy: Displacing truth claims

Blackstone (1783, 9: 343) praises the laws of England and the trial processes established therein as the safest and most trusted mechanism by which arbitrary power may be restrained, and the liberties of the English best protected:

> Our law has therefore wifely placed this strong and two-fold barrier, of a presentment and a trial by jury, between the liberties of the people, and the prerogative of the crown. It was necessary, for preserving the admirable balance of our constitution, to vest the executive power of the laws in the prince: and yet this power might be dangerous and destructive to that very constitution, if exerted without check or control, by justices of oyer and terminer occasionally named by the crown; who might then, as in France or Turkey, imprison, dispatch, or exile any man that was obnoxious to the government, by an instant declaration, that such is their will and pleasure. But the founders of the English laws have with excellent forecast contrived, that no man should be called to answer to the king for any capital crime, unless upon the preparatory accusation of twelve or more of his fellow subjects, the grand jury: and that the truth of every accusation, whether preferred in the shape of indictment, information, or appeal, should afterwards be confirmed by the unanimous suffrage of twelve of his equals and neighbours, indifferently chosen, and superior to all suspicion. So that the liberties of England cannot but subsist, so long as this palladium remains

sacred and inviolate, not only from all open attacks (which none will be so hardy as to make), but also from all secret machinations, which may sap and undermine it; by introducing new and arbitrary methods of trial....

Holdsworth (1903–38, 5: 177) suggested that '[i]n the course of the fourteenth and fifteenth centuries the humanity of the English system began to stand out in striking contrast to the continental system; and the records of Parliament show that Englishmen appreciated its advantages at their true value'. Stephen (1883, 1: 431) also wrote of the qualities of the adversarial process against the continental system, being '[t]he examination-in-chief is followed by the cross-examination. Cross-examination is a highly characteristic part of an English trial, whether criminal or civil, and hardly any of the contrasts between the English and Continental systems strikes an English lawyer so forcibly as its absence in the Continental system'.

Sklansky (2009: 1686) outlines the characteristics of the adversarial trial that are often cited as preferable or superior to inquisitorial systems:

> Arguments for the superiority of common law criminal trials vary along two dimensions: the particular features singled out for praise and the nature of the advantage those features are said to offer. As to the first, at various times defenders and admirers of Anglo-American criminal procedure have focused on each of the following characteristics of common law trials: (1) the use of lay jurors; (2) the public nature of the proceedings; (3) the reliance on oral testimony rather than a written dossier; (4) the detachment and institutional independence of the judge; (5) the regard for the defendant's autonomy, both in gathering evidence and with respect to procedural choices; and (6) the vigorous, partisan advocacy provided by defense counsel. Four different kinds of advantages have been claimed for these procedural features: (1) improved accuracy in fact finding; (2) more meaningful participation by the defendant and the public; (3) stronger checks against abuse of power; and (4) greater respect for human dignity. At one time or another, each of these four advantages has been claimed for each of the common law trial's celebrated features – with a few minor exceptions.

These assumptions as to the superiority of adversarial process hold significant weight in advancing the cause of adversarial justice. However, such assumptions are largely powered by the discursive function and archive of adversarial justice as the better restraint to power than proffered by any alternative system. Further, such discourses also suggest why adversarialism does not (at least openly) condone a mixed or comparative method that allows for the sharing of processes and ideals between the models. Adversarial justice is thus closed to outside processes and the opening up of the adversarial criminal trial to such processes may well be to unacceptably weaken the criminal trial. Such discourses are found in the originalist method of constitutional interpretation, discussed above.

On this point, however, Summers (2007: 9; also see Schwikkard, 2008, 2007) recognises the fluid and dialogic basis of adversarial and inquisitorial approaches as demonstrated in the jurisprudence of the ECtHR. Central to her argument, Summers (2007: 3–7) eschews the terms adversarial and inquisitorial, which are seen to be dichotomous, for a focus on the emergence of an internationalised criminal procedure. This clarification allows Summers (2007) to move away from debates within the comparative scholarship that have tended to focus on the classification of systems of justice rather than the substantive and principled content of their form. Many for these assumptions are rarely tested but are adopted out of an unquestioned method of comparative analysis such that lawyers automatically refer to one system of justice in terms of points of disconnection to the other. A concerted nationalism also positions most as against one system and in favour of another, such that the use of each term is 'loaded' (Summers, 2007: 9, 11–13). A new approach for the analysis of European procedural law may be found in several perspectives already canvassed in the existing literature. One such perspective, that of Packer's (1968) crime control model, re-focuses the debate around the need to balance the control of crime on one hand, and rights of due process that protect against abuses of power, on the other. Damaška's (1986: 10) work is also significant in its focus on the organisation of state authority between common and civil law jurisdictions. Similarities rather than differences define the qualities of state authorities between common and civil law jurisdictions such that it is possible to argue for important connections between the jurisdictions.

The significance of discourse to the development of systems of procedural justice is discussed in terms of the development of the 'accusatorial trinity'; the role of prosecution, defence and judge (Summers, 2007: 27). This 'trinity' allows for points of connection between the two systems of justice that provide for the movement of ideas and approaches that may be rooted to the structural framework of the legal system of each state. Summers (2007: 99–103) argues that this 'accusatorial trinity', and the balancing of interests therein, became the accepted basis upon which the jurisprudence of the ECtHR is considered as successfully mapping a coherent notion of the 'fair trial'. This cohesion is mete out through the adversarial procedural requirement and doctrine of equity of arms that has emerged in the ECtHRs jurisprudence (see *Doorson v The Netherlands* (1996) 22 EHRR 330). However, the process as it applies to criminal proceedings is defined in terms of a 'balancing' of rights and is not exacting. This approach appears to focus on the fundamental characteristics common to each jurisdiction, as Summers (2007: 180) explains:

> Although inconsistencies in the Court's notion of fairness are particularly evident in relation to the case law on the right to question witnesses, they are also reflected in the failure to address serious institutional flaws in various European criminal procedural systems. There can be little doubt that the coherence and consistency of procedural fairness could be improved through an acknowledgement of the reliance of its adversarial proceedings and equality of arms doctrines on the accusatorial trinity. A more sound approach to the regulation of fairness in European criminal trials requires recognition both of the European procedural tradition and of the common institutional values which it implies.

Field (2009), critically reviewing and ultimately rejecting Summers (2007) thesis, suggests that this discursive approach strongly supports the genesis of local practices as apparently distinctive and, arguably, incompatible.[4] Local or jurisdictional practices are therefore not bound by any particular approach to justice, despite appealing to the rigidities of a certain system or process as superior, or as prescribed or given. In this sense, local practices draw from an archive of discourses that are localised around a certain approach or perspective, which carries its own claim to truth. A significant part of these truth claims lies in their denial of the legitimacy of what is taken to be a foreign system of justice. Field (2009: 370) remarks:

> This dialogic and fluid notion of tradition suggests we should expect 'traditions' of criminal procedure to bear only a contingent relationship with procedural practice in any particular modern European jurisdiction. This is in part because each modern jurisdiction will

have, over time, developed its own local interpretation of how criminal law should be implemented, applied and enforced. Characteristically, given the fluidity of legal ideas across Europe, this will not just be a local interpretation of one procedural tradition, but a local interpretation that is likely to draw, to a lesser or greater extent, on both major traditions in Europe. Furthermore, this is a process that evolves over time: inherited attitudes and practices are mediated by subsequent histories.

It is worth noting however that there are dissimilarities between the adversarial and inquisitorial traditions that do not appear to be directly compatible, as Hodgson (2006: 237) notes:

> To the common lawyer, this direct judicial questioning of the accused may seem overbearing. In England and Wales, the defendant is protected from such interrogation and is not questioned directly unless she chooses to take the stand to give evidence. However, questioning of the accused in an adversarial process is very different from judicial questioning in France. It is not conducted by a neutral party, designed to clarify matters or to give the accused the opportunity to explain herself, but rather, by a partisan player whose concern is not with the truth, but with the construction of a case that undercuts that of the accused.
> However, it is important to remember that the judge's questioning of the accused in France is based upon the case dossier.

For better or worse, therefore, European civil law places a different focus on the accused and their requirement to directly participate in proceedings. The 'right to silence' in the common law tradition, or at least the right to put the prosecution case to proof (see *Woolmington v DPP* [1935] AC 462), unless displaced by statutory modification, may be a significant point of departure between inquisitorial and common law systems. On the other hand, this apparent disconnect may not be borne out in practice, given that in most instances matters will be disposed of in the lower courts constituted by a summary process. In inquisitorial and adversarial courts, this will largely involve the participation of the accused in one form or another, with significant oversight by the court, rather than direct input from defence counsel.[5] This point is exacerbated where litigants appear in person, as a great many do in courts of summary justice. There may, however, be points of significant departure around notions of 'truth' as they are constructed from the facts in evidence or case dossier in each tradition. Hodgson (2006: 240) suggests this in terms of the fundamental differences between the agreed function of prosecution, defence and state:

> Whilst the functions of prosecution, defence and trial exist in both jurisdictions, the ways in which these tasks are defined and understood by, and distributed between, legal actors is not the same in inquisitorial and adversarial procedure. Much depends upon the relationship between trial and pre-trial, the nature of the 'truth' that is sought through the process of investigation and trial, and who is responsible for the establishment of that 'truth'.

Although we must proceed carefully to group the various ways in which inquisitorial and adversarial process may present consistently in terms of a common trial process, the focus on discourse as a justification takes us beyond procedural limitations in a technical sense to focus on enabling statements that are defined in accordance with a given archive. This means that certain assumptions may be taken as given although they may be plainly arguable in practice. The example of summary justice once again challenges the normative assumption that suggests the version of truth is judge focused in one jurisdiction, and counsel led in the other. For those reasons, summary justice breaks so many of the rules that constitutes the adversarial process. Normative thinking draws so significantly from rhetoric that it blinds one to what is already conceived.

A note on normative thinking

Summers (2007) argues that the divergent approaches to adversarial and inquisitorial justice have tended to manifest in the development of normative assumptions as to the description and function of each system of justice. Such approaches arguably mask the utility of a comparative approach and the realisation that each system of justice may be no more preferable as a means of determining liability for wrongdoing. Normative assumptions as to the standing of the adversarial criminal trial as the only means by which a contested version of the truth may be arrived at in common law systems masks the diverse procedures that comprise the pre-trial, trial and sentencing phase of common law systems. The assumption that the adversarial criminal trial is an exclusive institution of justice incompatible with alternative modes of inquiry resides in the archive of the criminal trial as responding to the paucity of defendant rights and abuses of state power toward the latter part of the seventeenth century. Scalia J's majority opinion in *Crawford v Washington* shows how determinative such discourses are as an affirmation of an originalist reading of the confrontation clause and the incompatibility of an inquisitorial model. As demonstrated in Chapter 2, the criminal trial does not ascribe to one model of justice. The criminal trial is transgressive, and has always performed a number of functions across a number of forms. Summers (2007) argues that the tendency to bifurcate the trial process into either adversarial or inquisitorial has limited rather than developed our capacity to act inventively and creatively in order to secure fundamental human rights to all agents of justice.

Rather than promote an idealised vision of justice in terms of a criminal process of universal application, normative theorising has instead limited our realisation of the development of adversarialism as it has blinded us for concerted nationalism over a discussion of the nature and scope of procedural rights generally. As Summers (2007: 11–12) indicates:

> Evidence of legal nationalism pervades much of the work on comparative criminal procedure, but it would be wrong to imagine that this is a novel phenomenon in the European legal forum. Disparaging the criminal justice system of other countries, and by extension the other countries themselves, seems to be a pastime with a considerable heritage. Sometimes the language is direct and absurd, a combination which occasionally achieves an almost comical tone. At other times, the nationalist sentiment is subtly concealed by the rationality of legal argument.

The tendency toward normative theorising out of the preserve of a strict adversarialism has significant implications. These manifest in terms of the limited scope for change and inclusion against inquisitorial processes that allow for fuller and more direct participation by a number of parties to the criminal offence. Victims of crime have much to gain, as do defendants, if this allows for nuanced procedures that call for the actual participation of the accused in an appropriate way. Therapeutic and problem-solving courts provides one example. The notion of problem-solving justice, currently emerging across the common law world, would prove less of a departure from adversarial procedure if it were not bound by normative assumptions as to who should, and who should not, actively participate. The realisation in Summers (2007) work that normative assumptions significantly stifle our jurisprudential development against a range of desirable measures is, in itself, a significant development. There exits, however, a strong argument in favour of dismantling the normative assumptions around adversarial and inquisitorial processes not only out of the appreciation that the criminal trial does not have to be constituted through normative theory, but also through the realisation that the criminal trial has never been normative.

The criminal trial is a discursive institution of justice. Against this approach, the criminal trial cannot be constituted, controlled or corralled by normative assumptions because it has never been constituted as such. Such normative assumptions notwithstanding, common law systems in England, the United States and Australia each evidence the growth and genesis of new procedures and courts that integrate principles of adversarial and inquisitorial justice. Historically this has also been the case. Discourse and archive have produced certain perceptions of what a criminal trial ought to be. This includes rules as to who is to speak, who is to listen, and who is to be excluded. The issue is not that there are discourses which constitute various aspects of the criminal trial, but that there are competing visions as to what discourses ought to dominate, and be seen as constitutive, of common law justice. We see this in any appeals court where judges learned in the law compose their reasons by following entirely different streams of reason and logic, sometimes even coming to the same set of orders, but by substantively different paths.

Law and social systems

Identifying criminal law and justice as a site of communication provides a basis upon which we may challenge the assumption that law is a normative system. Systems of communication are understood in the autopoietic perspective as self-referential and interconnected. Teubner (1993: 22) identifies the characteristics of autopoiesis as based on the work of Maturana (1982: 158), as a unit which has a 'recursive effect on the network of the production of constituents which also produces these constituents', and 'which realize the network of production as a unit in the same space in which the constituents are located'. Applied to the field of law, Teubner (1993) suggests that law maintains its own system of self-referential rules that create its own meaning as a process internal to the operation of law. Law is therefore perpetuated through self-referential processes that do not need to connect to or communicate with sources 'outside' the law. The development of the common law out of reference to previous court decisions may be one example. Luhmann (1993) argues for a concept of social autopoiesis, in that law provides a system of communication along with other social systems of communication. Applied to the field of criminal justice, Nobles and Schiff (2001) argue that autopoiesis provides particular insights into criminal justice that allow for the development of a more complex concept of law and legality. Central to Nobles and Schiff's (2001) conceptualisation is the idea that criminal justice calls upon different disciplines of knowledge and modes of thought that 'breathes life' into an otherwise sterile domain of substantive and procedural justice, distinctions in a rule-bound, positivist tradition. Referring to this dynamic notion of 'criminal justice', Nobles and Schiff (2001: 197) indicate:

> That phrase is used to refer to numerous unifying themes about matters pertaining to criminal law and its operation. Sometimes it is used to situate or contextualize substantive criminal law ... sometimes to compare, contrast and draw attention to the relationship between criminal law in the books, and law in action.

Autopoiesis provides a framework through which we can account for the interpretive flexibility of criminal law and justice. By realising that the substantive and procedural aspects of criminal law may be informed by alternative discourses and fields of knowledge the normative positioning of law, and the adversarial criminal trial in particular, may be challenged. Instead, Nobles and Schiff (2001: 200) offer an alternative perspective based on two interrelated assumptions. The first, that autopoiesis provides a conceptualisation that explains the coexistence of multiple interpretations of law, and second, that 'criminal justice' is a site occupied by various discourses, each with their own processes of communication that reflex back onto themselves. Criminal justice thus emerges as an interdisciplinary arena that is constituted by the interrelationship between different systems of communication each of which may contain processes and rules that, self-referentially, constitute the terrain of that discipline. What is significant about Nobles and Schiff (2001) perspective is that criminal law constituted solely in terms of a substantive area of law, positivist in character, is removed from outside perspectives. Criminal law constituted in terms of criminal justice provides the opportunity for the continued development and interpretation of substantive criminal law by connecting the self-referential content of criminal law with other disciplinary arenas and contexts. As Nobles and Schiff (2001: 198) suggest, the 'latter approach invites one to look outside of or beyond statutes and cases to find meanings'.

An autopoiesis of the criminal justice system thus explains the interdependency between substantive criminal law doctrine and disciplinary processes that connect criminal law to the wider social world. Various disciplines communicate with the content of criminal law in this way: mental health, social welfare, police practice, national security, and human rights, just a few disciplines that have a significant impact on the growth and development of the substantive criminal law. For Nobles and Schiff (2001), this is a significant realisation of the communicative potential of criminal law and explains why problems arise when criminal law is challenged as a normative system. The coexistence of multiple systems of communication, each of which provide an interpretation of what criminal law ought to be, challenges the dominant interpretations of criminal law and call for the defending of criminal law along normative lines, as something prescriptive in form and content. Nobles and Schiff (2001: 215–216) remark that this is inconsistent with the discursive and disciplinary nature of the criminal justice system:

> Autopoietic insights coalesce into the simple conclusion that the ubiquitous use of the phrase the criminal justice system can be highly misleading. Such use encourages the political desire to integrate and co-ordinate the various institutions, actors, and practices of criminal justice. But in doing so, and trying to achieve a working interdependence, what is under-represented are the consequences of separate systems of communication. The counter offered by autopoiesis is that it is instructive to analyse criminal justice as a common site of many systems of communication.

Cotterrell (1992) sees this normative tension or rather, fight over normative supremacy, in terms of the hegemony of the professional knowledge of lawyers. The self-referentiality of law may thus be held out as integral to the internal operation of the law and ultimately, the rule of law. As purely self-referential and self-constitutive, law may be defendable from a professional perspective but, as Cotterrel (1992: 300–301) reminds us, from another perspective law appears highly vulnerable. This vulnerability may cause law and lawyers to act defensively to the great number of disciplines that legitimately seek to influence the scope and content of law. Criminal law and procedure is no exception here, and the dominance of certain models of criminal justice, the adversarial criminal trial in particular, may come to be significantly defended against the perception that its boundaries are being compromised by disciplines, politics or movements that are incompatible with its substance and form.

7
Implications for Criminal Justice Policy

The modern criminal trial does significantly more than sit in judgement of the normative theory of the trial. It provides the basis for understanding, evaluating and integrating criminal justice policy, agents of justice, and the community more generally, into criminal justice policy. The conceptualisation of the trial as discursive advances our understanding of the criminal trial by acknowledging that the trial is shaped by social values, as an institution of social power. The criminal trial, as a significant institution of criminal justice policy, may be constituted around legitimating principles of the fair trial. These principles, however, are neither exclusive nor isolated but constituted through a process of discursive formation and archive. This provides for the dynamic basis of the institution of the criminal trial in society, and indicates why it continues as an institution of significant social power over time.

By critically evaluating the criminal trial as hermeneutic, the trial is identified as transgressive, and open to a broad number of discourses once excluded as irrelevant. This had led to the examination of alternatives to the adversarial criminal trial, namely, doctrines of inquisitorial justice and human rights frameworks under the ECHR. Such perspectives challenge the normative positioning of adversarialism in common law systems, by arguing for the balancing of defendant rights with those of other stakeholders, including victims and the community. The transformative criminal trial thus emerges as much more than the critique of the assumed hegemony of the adversarial criminal trial. It provides a means for the integration of criminal justice policy by allowing for the questioning of normative arrangements that exclude various voices, positions and agendas. Such perspectives may be now taken into account – those of the defendant, victim and state – in a way that balances the needs of these various proponents of justice leaving behind the assumption that any particular agent or institutional arrangement is fundamentally unacceptable, detrimental or inapplicable to the interests of justice. This is a challenging perspective that seeks to debunk the very significant role of normative thinking in the world of the jurist and lawyer. It may lead to the assumption that such thinking is dangerous as it encourages the modification of processes deemed fundamental to the very idea of a fair trial and due process.

The modern criminal trial is a legal hermeneutic to the extent that it is more than a new model of justice. It invites the re-conceptualisation of the adversarial criminal trial as archive, history and dominant discourse. It does away with taken for granted assumptions and normative worldviews that corral our vision of justice. This new way of conceptualising the criminal trial is vital to the continued development of criminal law and justice in common law jurisdictions as it allows for the principled development of the trial in a way that leaves behind the restraints of the common law for a more inclusive procedure that focuses on the substantive and procedural rights of all relevant parties.

Substantive and procedural justice

The trial is a balancing ground for the substantive and procedural rights of parties that exercise agency within a dispute. Rather than focus on whose rights are recognised by a particular model or under an accepted approach, a focus on substantive and procedural rights asks us to question to scope, content, application and outcome of the rights afforded by legal processes. This approach does not assume that certain agents or stakeholders, as discussed in Chapter 1, are irrelevant or prejudicial to the interests of justice. Rather, a substantive and procedural justice perspective invites new perspectives and participants but only to the extent that they may be relevant to the resolution of the dispute. It is in the balancing of the interests of various, at times competing, parties, that we are able to break away from normative approaches to embrace nuance and innovation. The rise of problem-solving courts provides a key example. Victims and the community are not deemed irrelevant or prejudicial within such perspectives. However, in order to establish problem-solving justice as an inclusive court of law one must challenge the normative perspective that constitutes the trial as an exercise between prosecution and defence, within common law jurisdictions. Interestingly, it is those jurisdictions that have seen the re-assertion of the adversarial model (see Sklansky, 2009; Summers, 2007), which have led the charge in establishing these nuanced and innovative programs as viable alternatives to adversarial justice.

In *R (on the application of McCann and others) v Crown Court at Manchester; Clingham v Kensington and Chelsea Royal London Borough Council* [2002] 4 All ER 593, Lord Hutton remarks that the standard of proof applicable to ASBOs needs to be read in the context of the balancing of competing interests (at 631):

> The submissions of counsel on behalf of the defendants and on behalf of Liberty have laid stress on the human rights of the defendants. However the European Court has frequently affirmed the principle stated in *Sporrong and Lönnroth v Sweden* (1982) 5 EHRR 35, 52, para 69, that the search for the striking of a fair balance 'between the demands of the general interest of the community and the requirements of the protection of the individual's fundamental rights' is inherent in the whole of the Convention. In these cases which your Lordships have held are not criminal cases under the Convention and therefore do not attract the specific protection given by Article 6(3)(d) (though even in criminal cases the European Court has recognised that 'principles of fair trial also require that in appropriate cases the interests of the defence are balanced against those of witnesses or victims called upon to testify': see *Doorson v Netherlands* (1996) 22 EHRR 330, 358, para 70), and having regard to the safeguards contained in section 4 of the 1995 Act, I consider that the striking of a fair balance between the demands of the general interest of the community (the community in this case being represented by weak and vulnerable people who claim that they are the victims of anti-social behaviour which violates their rights) and the requirements of the protection of the defendants' rights requires the scales to come down in favour of the protection of the community and of permitting the use of hearsay evidence in applications for anti-social behaviour orders.

The rise of new and innovate court proceedings for the determination, control and punishment of wrongdoing has been most controversial, especially from a human rights perspective (Ashworth, 2004, 2009; also see Matthews, Easton, Briggs and Pease, 2007: 55–62). Criticisms abound as to the extent to which new procedures may impact on the liberty of individuals without the safeguards of full procedural fairness or due process. The movement away from criminal law for civil proceedings, seen through the development of alternative frameworks for the regulation of conduct in ASBOs and control orders, may point toward the unsatisfactory degradation of the criminal trial by usurping the criminal jurisdiction for the novel use of civil law. This has certainly generated a heated response (see Duff et al., 2007; Ashworth, 2004, 2009; Doak, 2008; Wolhunter et al., 2009) out of concern that the rights of defendants are being diminished for a popular reactionist politics that may well be driven by popular media, than well thought-out and principled criminal justice policy. Such policies have been identified in terms of a re-direction of criminalisation that is largely a response to the dramatic events of the beginning of the twenty-first century, specifically 9/11 and the destruction of the World Trade Centre (Tadros, 2007: 664). These various changes to criminal justice policy, in particular, the development and proliferation of the control order and associated processes for the detention of persons suspected of terrorist activity, are now well familiar within domestic law and order, with the use of control orders or ASBOs for the regulation of specific 'risky' groups. The use of control orders in NSW and South Australia restricting the association of members of organised motorcycle clubs indicates how, for instance, such orders have wider appeal than suspected terrorists. The increase in alternative modes of 'trial', whether characterised as civil or criminal, is of concern if such alternatives lack the specific safeguards of procedural justice and a right to a fair trial that are affiliated with the adversarial criminal trial. Ashworth (2009: 96) deems such alternatives to be a 'carefully designed hybrid' to the extent that they traverse the civil and criminal jurisdictions. ASBOs, for example, may be a civil order until a controlled individual is in breach of an order. Once breached, the individual is brought within the criminal law, and exposed to a term of imprisonment, whether the breach is disposed of summarily or on indictment.

As the House of Lords accepts in *Clingham*, however, there are various interests to be balanced by the introduction of new frameworks for the control of civil unrest. The 'balancing act' that is requisite of the fair trial as indicated in *Doorson v The Netherlands* is treated as a constitutive principle of justice that extends beyond the appreciable limits of the adversarial criminal trial. It is held out as a transformative principle to the extent that it reinforces the expectation that human rights discourse provides for an inclusive doctrine of justice that speaks for all individual liberties, including those of victims, witnesses or as considered in *Clingham*, vulnerable communities and individuals that suffer under the threat of anti-social behavior. The rights of the 'weak and the vulnerable' are thus as constitutive of the fair trial, as are the individuals to whom such orders are directed.

Given these changes, and the fact that departures from the adversarial criminal trial as a model of justice are increasingly prevalent, our focus must shift to the protection of substantive rights within a procedural model of justice. The normative positioning of the criminal trial as the method by which wrongdoers will be held to account for their conduct has shifted and a range of alternative processes have been supplemented. These alternatives constitute a new apparatus of holding to account to the extent that they break some of the rules of criminal procedure, while holding onto others. Ashworth's (2009: 96) 'hybrid' perspective illustrates the fact that we are long removed from coherent, jurisdictionally based, justice that is constituted by a set of principles of general application. The acceptability of nuanced modes of calling to account, whether classed as civil or criminal, must therefore be assessed from the perspective of a procedural model of justice that emphasises the rights of all persons in a fair and transparent way. Depravations of liberty may need to stand separately from restrictions of liberty, per *Witold Litwa v Poland* (2001) 33 EHRR 1267 and *Enhorn v Sweden* (2005) 41 EHRR 643. These cases outline a set of procedures that indicate that deprivation of liberty ought to be implemented in extreme situations where no other viable alternatives are available. Ashworth (2009: 102) indicates this approach as one of procedural justice, as guided by three founding principles:

> The importance of these two Strasbourg judgments is that they approach the difficult task of devising appropriate limits on liberty by a procedural route, requiring consideration to be given to certain criteria. Three familiar Strasbourg principles are put to work here – the principle of necessity, that it must be clear that the restrictions are necessary to prevent the harm; the principle of subsidiary, that less intrusive measures must have been considered and adjudged to be insufficient; and the principle of proportionality, that the measures taken must not be out of proportion to the danger apprehended.

These founding principles of necessity, subsidiary and proportionality present a guiding framework that operate to impose some constraints upon the imposition of a preventative order. These constraints, however, do more than provide a measure of procedural justice by requiring that certain conditions be met, or alternatives considered, before an order is imposed. These constraints impose procedural standards that require a measure of substantive judgment, as provided for in an organised set of principles that traverse the normative divide between civil and criminal law.

Summers' (2007) focus on procedural justice over any normative or nationalised perspective is a powerful reminder that justice need not be organised in a prescribed or determinant way. Under the ECHR, the content of the substantive criminal law is generally left to the individual state, with the ECtHR focusing on matters of process and procedure that may deprive an accused of a fair trial. The significant differences between state authorities have been cited as limiting a common conception of procedural rights. Adversarial and inquisitorial justice, for example, has been deemed incompatible to the extent that each model of justice values processes that are denied by the other. The re-assertion of the parameters of adversarialism by the United States Supreme Court, under the new restricted interpretation of the confrontation clause as discussed in Chapters 5 and 6, demonstrates how an adversarial processes may be phrased in terms of an anti-inquisitorial process (see Sklansky, 2009). What belies such approaches is the assumption that adversarialism operates according to a set of normative constraints that render it incompatible with other, perhaps foreign, perspectives. Such assumptions seek to protect and constrain the operation and development of a jurisdiction in accordance with certain preconceived notions as to what it means to be adversarial. This defines a set of institutional arrangements that provides voice and representation to some but not to others.

Summers (2007: 17) overcomes this assumptions in her analysis of the ECtHR by steering away from the comparative perspective that seeks to rate the extent to which adversarial procedure may be compatible with inquisitorial processes. Such methods continue the assumptions that Summers (2007) seeks to critique, or at the very least, argues should be left behind. Summers (2007: 17) argues that the ECtHR offers us something more, 'for its existence hints at the possibility of pre-existing common, underlying values in the field of criminal procedure law'. Chapter 4 referred to the Swedish criminal trial as a hybrid model of adversarial and inquisitorial processes. Schwikkard's (2007, 2008) work on the convergence of criminal procedure between adversarial and inquisitorial systems is, for instance, founded upon the strength of shared values between common and civil law traditions. The development of an adversarial approach out of an inquisitorial process demonstrates that neither system ought to be restrained by the other but can benefit greatly by moving beyond normative assumptions that limit the development of the trial in one direction. By moving away from the language of adversarial and inquisitorial justice, Summers (2007) seeks to raise the prominence of a fair criminal procedure. This is a result, arguably, that manifests in the current Swedish practice of integrating both 'models' of justice into the one process for the determination of liability and punishment.

On discourse and power

Discourse, as a sociological process, is one that allows for the development of 'rituals of truth'. Discourse constructs the topic. It defines and produces the objects of our knowledge. It governs the way a topic can be meaningfully talked about and reasoned about. This book has argued that the criminal trial is a transformative institution of social justice and discursive power. It is constituted as a socially significant institution by discourses that are variable, and often competing. This means that on any one issue, say the extent to which rules against the use of out of court or hearsay evidence may be modified to accommodate the needs of vulnerable victims within the bounds of adversarial justice, the statement, history and archive adopted in each case will help determine how, and the extent to which, such change is indeed possible. As Foucault (1969: 26) indicates, 'once the immediate forms of continuity are suspended, an entire field is set free'. Close examination will suggest degrees of symmetry, convergence and divergence exist between judgments depending *inter alia* on the statement, history and archive referred to. As Chapter 5 demonstrates, discourses may share intermingled roots, be read as consistent with other discourses, or be constructed as opposed to a particular perspective so as to render the 'other' discourse irrelevant, inconsistent, invalid or illegitimate.

The criminal trial as a linear construct was challenged at the outset, given the bifurcated process of summary and indictable disposal. Historically, the trial has taken various forms, from inquisitorial to altercation proceedings, to the emergence of the adversarial model in the form of the 'accusatorial trinity' and under an 'equity or arms'. Trial process and the law of evidence continue to transform with regard to various perspectives – human rights, law and order, the interests of the victim, the defendant's right to a fair trial, and the modification of the public/private dichotomy – being notable sources. It is not only the institutional form that the trial takes which is transforming. The very processes that constitute the criminal trial, including forms of evidence and the manner in which it may be presented and adduced, has been negotiated with regard to a new set of discursive constraints presented in the forms of an international human rights law. As preventative law continues to expand, taking the form of control orders and ASBOs, the centrality of the criminal trial as the chief means by which common law systems determine liability and mete out censure for wrongdoing is increasingly dislocated. The trial process is thus shown to be fragmented across various institutional fronts – some identified as mostly adversarial within the criminal jurisdiction, while others are more firmly placed within civil law, or a hybrid of the two.

The rise of therapeutic jurisprudence and problem-solving courts, following the rise of drug courts diverting drug addicted offenders from conventional court processes, indicates a significant departure from the adversarial paradigm. The rise of new problem-solving courts concerned with the welfare of all agents to justice, including victim, community and offender, is evidenced through the array of problem-solving courts in the State of New York, specifically sexual offences, domestic violence and community prosecution courts. Such models are now being piloted in England. The rise of a human rights discourse and the modification of trial process to accommodate a 'fair trial' experience for both victim and defendant suggest how due process rights are not normative but disciplined by the intersection of various and often competing interests in the criminal justice process.

Foucault's (1969, 1982, 1984, 1994) hermeneutics and discourse of power provides for the questioning of the normative positioning and dominance of the adversarial criminal trial. His method suggests that the criminal trial is a discursive, decentralised institution that is increasingly focused on innovative modes of substantive and procedural justice, consistent with the history and genealogy of the trial from antiquity. This means that the criminal trial is transforming in a way that is consistent with broader changes in law and justice that see the continued negotiation of the boundaries of criminal law and procedure. That the criminal trial is fixed to a set of prescribed assumptions as to its form and scope may be challenged by reference to the discursive processes that support one position while denying another. Such perspectives were encountered through this book, demonstrated through the numerous changes to criminal justice policy, the emergence of a transformative criminal trial, and through the comparison of approaches to the use of out of court evidence. That each court comes to a different position on the appreciable parameters of the criminal trial is of no surprise, at least for Foucault (1969), who would suggest that discourses have a specificity of existence to the extent that they determine which discourses may be included, and importantly, which types of discourses ought to be excluded. That the different courts consider the use of out of court evidence, for instance, an affront to the principles of adversarial justice is consistent with the way in which each court phrases its case by drawing on different discourses that are constituted around different fields of acceptable and unacceptable statements. Foucault (1969: 28) suggests that this is manifested in the production of a 'specific existence' that transpires from the empowering discourse alone:

> The analysis of the discursive field is orientated in a quite different way; we must grasp the statement in the exact specificity of its occurrence; determine its conditions of existence, fix at least its limits, establish its correlations with other statements that may be connected with it, and show what other forms of statement it excludes. We do not seek below what is manifest the half silent murmur of another discourse; we must show why it could not be other than what it was, in what respect it is exclusive of any other, how it assumes, in the midst of others and in relation to them, a place that no other could occupy. The question proper to such an analysis might be formulated in this way: what is this specific existence that emerges from what is said and nowhere else?

The specificity of the discursive formation is such that it occupies its own territory to the exclusion of the other. This is true to the extent that in criminal law, certain discourses are open to a new criminal procedure, while other discourses limit this possibility as antithetical to the interests of justice as conceived within the ambit of the more dominant discourse. The rise of adversarialism into the twentieth-century presents constraints as to what is relevant to the field of law. The law of evidence as a discursive field or archeology of its own is an elaboration of the principles of adversarial justice that maintain that exclusivity. As Doak and McGourlay (2009: 22) have indicated, however, radical suggestions for the transformation of the law of evidence provide that adversarial processes may be amenable to inquisitorial methods, at least in the pre-trial phase. The erosion of exclusionary rules of evidence and the rise of protective mechanisms for victims of crime suggest that the criminal trial is being transformed out of the internationalisation of trial procedure, through the ECtHR, the ICC, and other international tribunals. This evidences how dominant paradigms may change, over time, for the realisation of other discourses of justice that provide an alternative means to justice. The destabilising of the dominant approach for an appreciation of alternatives suggests that the criminal trial will continue to be amenable to new approaches and innovations that provide new roles for participants formerly excluded from the justice system. Furthermore, this provides an analytic through which to argue for future developments in criminal law and justice without being bound by arguments that are constrained by normative terms and assumptions.

Revolutionising criminal law and justice

As we move from an era characterised by the fear of state power to one in which various interests, including those of the state, defendants and victims, are seen as integral to justice, the nature of the criminal trial must also transform to provide an arena for the balancing of these competing interests. In this context, the criminal trial is much more than a static tribunal bound by immovable rules for the testing of evidence against an accused. The trial emerges as a dynamic institution reflective of the changing interests of society, which, in the recent past, has been significantly determined by the fear of the arbitrary exercise of state power against the interests of the individual. Debate as to the scope, content and form of the trial is a healthy sign of a society concerned with one of its most crucial institutions. Lawyers, lawmakers and scholars need to be mindful that an argument favouring a normative perspective of the trial may be to prescribe the trial's form and function in a way that is inconsistent with its dynamic function as an institution of social power. Normative assumptions have the potential to silence voices relevant to the broader interests of justice and may stifle the growth and development of the law.

The criminal trial performs a significant function important to society as a whole. The way in which we go about restraining individual liberty out of an accusation of wrongdoing is not to be dealt with lightly. The movement toward normative theorising indicates that the trial is seen to be shifting from its accepted praxis for the development and modification of its institutional, procedural and substantive character to meet needs and interests formerly excluded as irrelevant. On a normative account, such interests reside outside the relevant boundaries of the trial. In a Foucauldian (1971, 1982) sense, the trial can be understood as being constituted as an object of power that is inclusive rather than exclusive. The criminal trial is thus more than the medium through which defendant rights come to be protected. This, arguably, is central to its capacity to transform to meet new social needs and explains its position as an institution of justice of significant longevity.

Cotterrell (1992: 300) observes that:

> ... law in modern conditions retains not only autonomy but also the capacity to reproduce endlessly its own discourse without subversion from other discourses. It transforms all signals from its environment – economic, scientific, technological, cultural or political events, developments and demands – into its own specific terms. In this way law must never be undermined nor fragmented. But its autonomy must be understood in new ways.

Against the history of the criminal trial as an institution of transformative justice, the modern trial is increasingly understood as performing a limited function. It is the limits of the criminal trial that are said to be increasingly vulnerable to attack from political, social, and global movements. These movements seek to displace the institutional structure of the criminal trial for alternative forms, and in doing so, risk displacing the focus of the trial from the vulnerable defendant. In the context of a strict adversarialism, this is dangerous and unacceptable because it accedes to certain claims that fundamentally undermine common law systems of justice. The hallmarks of adversarialism are at stake: the independence of the judge, use of lay juries, the protective law of evidence, and the role of counsel that seek to establish the 'truth' of an accusation via a contested version of events. The history of the criminal trial, and the proliferation of its modern form, provides for the critical review of the notion that the trial is now emerging as something foreign to its given form. Chapter 3 canvassed various movements within criminal law and justice that seek to challenge the notion of the centrality of the judge and jury trial as the representation of adversarial justice. Chapter 4 expanded upon this broad assessment by examining particular ways in which the modern adversarial trial is transforming. Chapter 5 examined the significance of discourse to this process, and concluded that the trial may be constituted in practice and in substance as a discursive process *a priori*.

Critical of the essentialism that argues that the character of law as autonomous, fixed and given, Nonet and Selznick (1978) argue for the rise of a responsive legal order through the convergence of law, policy and institution. Legal institutions, such as the criminal trial, are connected to the criminal justice system and the changes therein. What emerges, Nonet and Selznick (1978: 110) suggest, is a view of the law that is open, inclusive and disciplinary:

> A corollary of the blending of powers is a further attenuation of 'distinctively legal' institutions, ideas, and modes of reasoning. We have already pointed to several aspects of this evolution: With purposive law there is a decline in artificial reason, a convergence of legal and policy analysis, a reintegration of legal and moral judgement and of legal and political participation. Another facet of that transformation is the absorption of law into the larger realm of administration.

The various means by which wrongdoers are held to account in modern society suggests that the criminal trial is a transformative institution. The transformative criminal trial emerges, however, as significantly more than the re-conceptualisation or critique of the assumed autonomy of the adversarial criminal trial. This process provides a vehicle for the integration of criminal justice policy by providing an analytics for the integration of views and perspectives relevant to the trial process – those of the defendant, victim and state – in a way that balances the needs of these various agents of justice. The transformative criminal trial thus emerges as a disciplinary arena of criminal justice. A focus on substantive and procedural justice emerges that does away with the normative limitations upon which so much of our discussion of criminal justice is founded. A fair process that takes account of the needs of those relevant to the trial process, at a standard that seeks to challenge accusations of wrongdoing to a high standard of liability or proof, indicates how this transformation is taking shape (see Summers, 2007: 169–178). Such standards must reside with the individual and institution, in that they become an individual right to justice that takes an institutional form. The higher standard of proof endorsed by the House of Lords in *Clingham* provides an example of this process. Whether one agrees with the general tenor of ASBOs or not, the alternative (non criminal) process that is deemed to apply to s1 of the *Crime and Disorder Act 1998* (UK) is safeguarded by an appropriately higher standard of proof than would otherwise apply in civil proceedings. On this basis the framework for control orders available in South Australia and in NSW may be questionable, each currently endorsing the lower standard of the balance of probabilities.[1]

This book has focussed on the development of an intellectual method for the analysis of history and discourse, based on a focussed and disciplined interrogation of various sources, as a reflection of social and intellectual practices that lead to the acceptance and implementation of certain approaches to justice, or discourses, over others. The interplay between these discourses has revealed a power structure that assesses the legitimacy of arguments for change through the lens of adversarialism. Rather than affirm one perspective as the true means to justice, this book has established that the criminal trial is transformative to the extent that it is a construct of competing relationships of power and resistance, over time.

History presents various perspectives on the development of the criminal trial, but in the English and American legal traditions this emerges as a reflection of the autonomy of the criminal law and trial process. This history presents the trial as the assemblage of practices that brought us to the point of the hegemony of the adversarial criminal trial, removed from society to the extent that it is constituted through a range of procedures that process accusations of wrongdoing according to a model of procedural fairness and due process. Such processes may do little to serve the interests of all parties relevant to the trial (*cf.* Christie, 1977). This book tells a different story of the criminal trial. It focuses on the criminal trial as a contested institution of the criminal justice system that is discursive to the extent that the criminal trial is a combination of discourses that attempt to mete out and administer justice in particular ways. Certain modalities of justice are seen as authoritative or true while others are seen, by reference to the authoritative discourses, as less valuable, removed or even incompetent. Considering the utility of inquisitorial justice from the self-referentiality of the common law will likely lead to the questioning of the merits of such an approach. To first question the centrality of the adversarial model one must remove themselves from it, at least epistemically, to realise that there is more than one way of doing justice to the satisfaction of the stakeholders of justice. On the other hand, this book has sought to develop a more complex picture of what constitutes the criminal trial by examining a selection of discourses that contest the boundaries of the adversarial trial as a transgressive institution of justice. Chapter 5 examined how the use of out of court evidence varies significantly between the jurisdictions depending on extent to which the different courts were willing to depart from preconceived notions of adversarial and trial process. Such perspectives, and the willingness to modify the boundaries of the trial, were seen to be deeply rooted to notions of procedural fairness and due process as based on various discourses and traditions.

That the criminal trial is a manifestation of competing discourses is borne out of the realisation that the criminal trial is a process of social accusation and dispute resolution that is an essential part of our social fabric. The qualities that allow the criminal trial to be a transformative institution are found in its history as a vehicle of social change and government. This does not mean that the trial can be whatever we say it to be, or be used as a means of control as though we do not live in a society constituted by a separation of powers. It is true that the criminal trial is under constant pressure from individuals or groups advocating a sectarian politics. The trial may be taken to be failing or succeeding depending on an individual's perspective or experience within the system. Victims, for instance, when provided with state funded lawyers, access to the sentencing phase through the ability to tender victim impact evidence, and with support mechanisms such as compensation and reparation, may still be dissatisfied should their case end with the acquittal of the accused, or a lower sentence than might have been deemed personally proportionate (*cf.* Findlay and Henham, 2010: 43–44).

The criminal trial, while being discursive, is not fragile to the extent that it becomes whatever it is claimed to be. This is the resolving function of the integration of competing discourses. Foucault's (1969) focus on statements and language, broken down into linguistic units, such as vocabulary, grammar, and accepted modes of expression, provides a mechanism by which statements relate to other statements. These linguistic units make up an enunciative field which constitutes the statement of discourse. The elemental nature of the enunciative field determines what may rightfully be said on a given topic. This is not a process of random definition and allocation of meaning. Statements connect with other statements. Ideas link to other ideas. The realisation is that some statements do not fit with others, and ideas cannot be simply forced together. However, the focus on discourse does indicate that our imagination must be open to new possibilities of liability and penalty for wrongdoing. Just as we must continue to revise old ideas from our law, decriminalise acts that we no longer deem to be so offensive they warrant the attention of the criminal law, we must consider the institutions which apportion liability and punishment as evolving. The criminal trial is a living institution. The corollary position is that the criminal trial is no more adversarial than it needs to be to effect a full measure of justice to all agents seeking to participate in the criminal process.

The modern criminal trial is thus decentralised and fragmented according to the numerous discourses that seek to constitute its form.

It emerges as much more than a simple re-conceptualisation or critique of the assumed autonomy of the adversarial criminal trial. The modern criminal trial is a discursive entity to the extent that new and innovative modes of trial are evolving to meet new and pressing social circumstances. Some of these forms will be controversial, such as the rise of control orders and preventative law, while others celebrated, such as problem-solving courts, as providing new solutions to old problems. The criminal trial as discursive provides a vehicle for the integration of criminal justice policy by providing a model that allows various perspectives to be taken into account – those of the defendant, victim and state – in a way that balances the needs of these various stakeholders of justice. This allows for the development of the criminal trial beyond those discourses taken as truth. Such discourses currently form the rhetoric of criminal justice to give criminal law, and the trial in particular, its public appearance in the form of a trial before judge and jury. We need to move away from this rhetoric to realise its place as part of the rich field of statements as to the possible form and shape of the modern criminal trial as a transformative institution of justice. Once we do this our discursive field is set free, and we can move toward the realisation of a dynamic criminal procedure that responds to the needs of various sites of criminological concern.

Notes

Chapter 1   Criminal Trials, Foucault, Discourse

1 For a detailed discussion of the Foucauldian approach as it is applied to the discourses of adversarial justice, see Chapter 5, *Discourse Defined*.
2 See Chapter 6, *History, Discourse and Genealogy: Displacing Truth Claims*.
3 For an extended discussion of the issues, see Chapter 1, *Courts of Therapeutic Justice*, and Chapter 4, *Therapeutic Jurisprudence and Problem Solving Courts*.
4 See Chapter 3 for an extended discussion of control orders for domestic law and order.
5 The European Court of Justice (ECJ) is the highest court of the European Union (EU) on issues of community law. National law is left for the domestic courts. The national courts may refer issues of EU law to the ECJ. The national court will then apply the decision of the ECJ within its own domestic framework, including other cases that may share similar facts or points of law than that decided by the ECJ. This process enables all courts within a national hierarchy to refer questions of EU law. The ECJ is bound to apply EU law similarly throughout the EU, in the attempt to bring a measure of consistency between national courts.
6 The European Court of Human Rights (ECtHR) is an international court bound to interpret the European Convention on Human Rights and Fundamental Freedoms (ECHR). Litigants will complain to the ECtHR where they feel that their rights under the ECHR have been violated. However, a decision of the ECtHR does not become part of domestic law unless it is ratified by the government of the member state. In England and Wales, for instance, the courts may take the jurisprudence of the ECtHR into account when formulating future decisions pursuant to s2 of the *Human Rights Act 1998* (UK).
7 For an extended discussion of the cases flowing from art. 6 of the ECHR, see Chapter 4, *Human Rights under the ECHR*.
8 Horwitz (1981: 1058) considers such modes of analysis as anti-historical, regarding them with a fervent cynicism, thus 'History came to be subversive at just the moment when, for reasons that are difficult and obscure, the analytic tradition committed itself to the suppression of contradiction to the basic attempt to reconcile the irreconcilable by showing that X and not X can exist at the same time, which is essential to demonstrating that an unjust social order is capable of being rational. The interesting and difficult question, the really complicated question of historical explanation, is: Why did this particular form of rationalizing analytic scholarship come, by 1900, to represent the dominant apologetic mode of thought? Why, in turn, was history given up as a mode of apology?'.
9 See Chapter 4, *Intervention Programs, Forum and Circle Sentencing*.
10 Other issues which have been cited as significantly modifying the criminal trial include the law and order debate and the need for greater expediency in criminal justice. Each of these issues is discussed in detail in Chapter 3.

11 Criminal law is used as a key reference here, however, whether the reforms introducing control orders or the establishing of alternative mechanisms for the hearing of evidence is seen to be a development in criminal law, or civil law, or the common law more generally, is open to debate. This issue is canvassed in Chapter 1 but is referred to throughout this book. Also see Chapter 3, *Control Orders – A Criminal Charge?*.
12 Indeed, this has led some to argue for a normative theory of the criminal trial. See Duff et al. (2007).
13 See Chapter 3, *Non-derogating Control Orders and the ECHR*, for an extended discussion of the relevant cases in English law. The House of Lords have addressed the use of preventative detention in *A v Secretary of State for the Home Department* [2005] 2 AC 68. In this case, the House of Lords declared s23 of the *Anti-Terrorism, Crime and Security Act 2001* (UK) is incompatible with articles 5 and 14 of the ECHR. The discussion in the book tends to focus on control orders, however, given that such orders have been said to usurp the criminal trial for an alternative means to justice and punishment (Fairall and Lacey, 2007: 1075).
14 The English authorities are discussed in Chapter 3.
15 See Chapter 3 for an extended discussion as to the extent to which non-derogative control orders under the English legislation may be considered a criminal charge.
16 For a further discussion of ASBOs and control orders for the restraint of domestic order see Chapter 3, *Control Orders, ASBOs and Domestic Order*.
17 See Chapter 4 for an extended discussion of victim rights under the ECHR.
18 The Act of Settlement 1701 (12 and 13 Will 3 c 2) provided for judicial tenure *quamdiu se bene gesserint*, or during good behaviour. Such standards reflect judicial tenure today, which requires a vote of both houses of parliament on the proven incapacity or misbehaviour of a judge.

Chapter 2   A Genealogy of the Trial in Criminal Law

1 See the discussion of the Assize of Clarendon of 1166 and local governance, below.
2 Warren (1973: 283) describes the ordeal by water as a process whereby the hands of the accused were bound under their bent knees, who was then bound around the loins with a strong rope, such that the rope formed a knot at the distance of the length of his hair. The accused was then let down into the water without a splash. If the accused sank he was pulled up and saved, otherwise the accused would be adjudged a guilty man by the spectators.

Chapter 3   Shifting Boundaries: Recent Changes to Criminal Justice Policy

1 See Chapter 2, *The Trial in Customary Law*.
2 As to other innovations involving the use of the jury, see Spigelman CJ's suggestion as to the expansion of the jury into the sentencing process, by

228 Notes

allowing the jury to make recommendations to the sentencing judge on the appropriate sentence that the offender should serve. This proposal was considered but ultimately rejected by the NSWLRC (2007) as inappropriate, as confidence in the justice system ought to be encouraged by further public education rather than direct participation. See Spigelman CJ, *A New Way to Sentence for Serious Crime,* Address for the Annual Opening of Law Term Dinner for the Law Society of New South Wales (31 January 2005).

3 Section 80 of the Australian Constitution 1900 provides that 'The trial on indictment of any offence against any law of the Commonwealth shall be by jury, and every such trial shall be held in the State where the offence was committed, and if the offence was not committed within any State the trial shall be held at such place or places as the Parliament prescribes.'

4 See Chapter 3, *Infringements and Penalty Notices.*

5 See Chapter 7, *Substantive and Procedural Justice,* for a discussion of the rise of ASBOs in the context of human rights.

6 See *Gouriet v Union of Post Office Workers* [1978] AC 438 at 487, discussed in Chapter 3, *Charge Bargaining.*

7 See the discussion of *Thomas v Mowbray* (2007) 233 CLR 307 in Chapter 1.

8 Also see *Chu Kheng Lim v Minister for Immigration Local Government and Ethnic Affairs* (1992) 176 CLR 1 as to the power of the executive to detain without charge. In this case, it was held that the executive power to detain persons who arrive in Australia without an entry permit is a valid exercise of executive power. Brennan, Deane and Dawson JJ note, however, (at 27–28): 'In exclusively entrusting to the courts designated by Ch. III the function of the adjudgement and punishment of criminal guilt under a law of the Commonwealth, the Constitution's concern is with substance and not mere form. It would, for example, be beyond the legislative power of the Parliament to invest the Executive with an arbitrary power to detain citizens in custody notwithstanding that the power was conferred in terms which sought to divorce such detention in custody from both punishment and criminal guilt. The reason why that is so is that, putting to one side the exceptional cases to which reference is made below, the involuntary detention of a citizen in custody by the State is penal or punitive in character and, under our system of government, exists only as an incident of the exclusively judicial function of adjudging and punishing criminal guilt. Every citizen is "ruled by the law, and by the law alone" and may with us be punished for a breach of law, but he can be punished for nothing else'.

9 See Chapter 7, *Substantive and Procedural Justice.*

Chapter 4 The Transformative Criminal Trial Emerges

1 See Chapter 1 for a discussion of the protective mechanism in place for rape victims in international law.

2 For an extended discussion of the statutory modification of victim rights in sexual assault and rape trials, see Chapter 4 *Human Rights and Statutory Reform.*

3 Art. 2 of the ECHR provides: (1) Everyone's right to life shall be protected by law. No one shall be deprived of his life intentionally save in the execu-

tion of a sentence of a court following his conviction of a crime for which this penalty is provided by law. (2) Deprivation of life shall not be regarded as inflicted in contravention of this article when it results from the use of force which is no more than absolutely necessary: (a) in defence of any person from unlawful violence; (b) in order to effect a lawful arrest or to prevent the escape of a person lawfully detained; (c) in action lawfully taken for the purpose of quelling a riot or insurrection.

4 Art. 6 of the ECHR provides: (1) In the determination of his civil rights and obligations or of any criminal charge against him, everyone is entitled to a fair and public hearing within a reasonable time by an independent and impartial tribunal established by law. Judgment shall be pronounced publicly but the press and public may be excluded from all or part of the trial in the interests of morals, public order or national security in a democratic society, where the interests of juveniles or the protection of the private life of the parties so require, or to the extent strictly necessary in the opinion of the court in special circumstances where publicity would prejudice the interests of justice. (2) Everyone charged with a criminal offence shall be presumed innocent until proved guilty according to law. (3) Everyone charged with a criminal offence has the following minimum rights: (a) to be informed promptly, in a language which he understands and in detail, of the nature and cause of the accusation against him; (b) to have adequate time and facilities for the preparation of his defence; (c) to defend himself in person or through legal assistance of his own choosing or, if he has not sufficient means to pay for legal assistance, to be given it free when the interests of justice so require; (d) to examine or have examined witnesses against him and to obtain the attendance and examination of witnesses on his behalf under the same conditions as witnesses against him; (e) to have the free assistance of an interpreter if he cannot understand or speak the language used in court.

5 Art. 8 of the ECHR provides: (1) Everyone has the right to respect for his private and family life, his home and his correspondence. (2) There shall be no interference by a public authority with the exercise of this right except such as is in accordance with the law and is necessary in a democratic society in the interests of national security, public safety or the economic well-being of the country, for the prevention of disorder or crime, for the protection of health or morals, or for the protection of the rights and freedoms of others.

6 Also see the discussion of *Doorson v The Netherlands* (1996) 22 EHRR 330 in Chapter 1.

7 See Summers (2007) argument for the emergence of a criminal procedure that overcomes the normative boundaries of adversarial and inquisitorial processes, as discussed in Chapters 6 and 7.

8 Criminal Procedure Regulation 2005 (NSW) Sch 5, cl 7. For al list of offences for which intervention programs are appropriate, see *Criminal Procedure Act 1986* (NSW) s348.

9 Primary victims include persons or witnesses to an offence that have suffered personal injury as a result of an offence. Family victims include members of the primary victim's immediate family. See *Crimes (Sentencing Procedure) Act 1999* (NSW) s26.

230   Notes

10   Also see recommendation 3 of the New South Wales Law Reform Commission, *Sentencing*, Report No 79 (1996). Hunt J advocates the treatment of family impact statements in homicide cases along similar lines to those proposed by the NSWLRC.
11   The one exception recognised by Hunt CJ at CL may be where the primary victim dies a slow, lingering death. The circumstances of the offence would thus come to encompass family victims, who may come to care for the primary victim before death. See *R v Previtera* (1997) 94 A Crim R 76, 86.
12   Also see *Re Gangemi* [1971] QWN 19, *R v Allsop* [1972] QWN 34, *R v Johnson; Ex parte McLeod* [1973] Qd R 208.

Chapter 5   The Criminal Trial as Social Discourse

1   See *Barton v The Queen* (1980) 147 CLR 75; *Dietrich v The Queen* (1992) 177 CLR 292 at 299–300. As to art. 6 of the ECHR, see *Khan v United Kingdom* (2001) 31 EHRR 45; *Rowe and Davis v United Kingdom* (2000) 30 EHRR 1; *Fitt v United Kingdom* (2000) 30 EHRR 480; *Windisch v Austria* (1990) (1990) 13 EHRR 281.
2   The Sixth Amendment to the Constitution of the United States reads: 'In all criminal prosecutions, the accused shall enjoy the right to a speedy and public trial, by an impartial jury of the state and district wherein the crime shall have been committed, which district shall have been previously ascertained by law, and to be informed of the nature and cause of the accusation; to be confronted with the witnesses against him; to have compulsory process for obtaining witnesses in his favor, and to have the assistance of counsel for his defense.'
3   Also see *Davis v Washington* (2006) 547 US 813. In *Davis v Washington*, the United States Supreme Court ruled that the transcript of an emergency 911 call was not testimony and so the sixth amendment did not require the caller to appear at trial and be cross-examined.
4   The blurring of the public/private dichotomy may be taken to the extent that one can question whether it is fair to conceptualise clear public and private spheres. The focus on discourse attempts to debunk such concepts as taken for granted assumptions, at least in criminal law. What is offered instead is an interrelated concept of public and private that seeks to problematise the legal convention that separates life into spheres, constituting the terrain of certain jurisdictions such as criminal law and civil law.

Chapter 6   The Trial as Hermeneutic: A Critical Review

1   See Chapter 4. Non-derogating control orders have been characterised as non-criminal but this point is, arguably, debatable.
2   As to the centrality of the adversarial tradition in Canadian criminal law, see *R v Swain* [1991] 1 SCR 933.
3   Also see *Medellín v Texas* (2008) 552 US 491.
4   See Chapter 5, *Discourse Defined*.

5 Compare the *tribunal correctionnel* or *tribunal de police* in France and local or magistrates' court in common law jurisdictions in terms of the degree to which cases are dealt with by direction of the judicial officer over party representing the accused. See Hodgson (2006) and McBarnett (1981a, 1981b).

Chapter 7   Implications for Criminal Justice Policy

1 See *Crimes (Criminal Organisation Control) Act 2009* (NSW) s32(1); *Serious and Organised Crime (Control) Act 2008* (SA) s5(1).

References

Ashworth, A. (2004) 'Social Control and Antisocial Behaviour: The Subversion of Human Rights', *Law Quarterly Review*, 120, 263–291.
Ashworth, A. (2009) 'Criminal Law, Human Rights and Preventative Justice', in McSherry, B., Norrie, A. and Bronitt, S. (eds) *Regulating Deviance: The Redirection of Criminalisation and the Futures of Criminal Law*, Hart Publishing: Oxford, pp. 87–108.
Attorney-General's Department (2008) *Forum Sentencing: Facing up to Crime*, NSW Government.
Baker, J.H. (1990) *An Introduction to English Legal History*, Butterworths: London.
Berman, G. (2000) 'What is a Traditional Judge Anyway? Problem Solving in the State Courts', *Judicature*, 84, 2, 78–85.
Berman, G. and Feinblatt, J. (2001) 'Problem-Solving Courts: A Brief Primer', *Law and Policy*, 23, 2, 125–140.
Berman, G. and Feinblatt, J. (2005) *Good Courts: The Case for Problem-Solving Justice*, The New Press: New York.
Berman, G. and Fox, A. (2001) 'From the Margins to the Mainstream: Community Justice at the Crossroads', *Justice System Journal*, 22, 2, 189–207.
Blackstone, W. (1783) *Commentaries on the Laws of England*, Strahan, W. and Cadell (eds) (1978), Oxford: London.
Bloch, M. (1961) *Feudal Society*, Routledge: London.
BOCSAR (2008) *New South Wales Criminal Courts Statistics 2007*, Bureau of Crime Statistics and Research, Attorney-General's Department: NSW.
Booth, T. (2000) 'The Dead Victim, the Family Victim and Victim Impact Statements in New South Wales', *Current Issues in Criminal Justice*, 11, 3, 292–307.
Booth, T. (2004) 'Homicide, Family Victims and Sentencing: Continuing the Debate about Victim Impact Statements', *Current Issues in Criminal Justice*, 15, 3, 253–257.
Booth, T. (2007) 'Penalty, Harm and the Community: What Role Now for Victim Impact Statements in Sentencing Homicide Offenders in NSW?', *University of New South Wales Law Journal*, 30, 3, 664–685.
Brienen, M.E.I. and Hoegen, E.H. (2000) *Victims of Crime in 22 European Criminal Justice Systems*, Wolf Legal Publishers: The Netherlands.
Brown, H. (1999) 'Provocation as a Defence to Murder: To Abolish or Reform?', *Australian Feminist Law Journal*, 12, 137–141.
Cam, H. (1960) *Hundred and the Hundred Rolls: An Outline of Local Government in Medieval England*, Burt Franklin.
Carlen, P. (1976) 'The Staging of Magistrates' Justice', *British Journal of Criminology*, 16, 1, 48–55.
Casey, L. (2008) *Engaging Communities in Fighting Crime*, Crime and Community Review, Prime Ministers Cabinet Office: United Kingdom.
Christie, N. (1977) 'Conflicts as Property', *British Journal of Criminology*, 17, 1, 1–15.

Clune, W.H. (1989) 'Legal Disintegration and a Theory of the State', in Joerges, C. and Trubek, D.M. (eds) *Critical Legal Thought: An American-German Debate*, Oxford University Press: Oxford, pp. 127–242.

Corns, C. (2003) 'Retrial of Acquitted Persons: Time for Reform of the Double Jeopardy Rule?', *Criminal Law Journal*, 27, 2, 80–101.

Corns, C. (2004) 'Videotaped Evidence in Victoria: Some Evidentiary Issues and Appellate Court Perspectives', *Criminal Law Journal*, 28, 1, 43–51.

Cotterrell, R. (1992) *The Sociology of Law*, Butterworths: London.

Cotterrell, R. (1995) *Law's Community*, Butterworths: London.

Cross, R. (1979) *Cross on Evidence*, Butterworths: Sydney.

Crown Prosecution Service (CPS) (2007) *Victim Focus Scheme Guidance on Enhanced CPS Service for Bereaved Families*, United Kingdom.

Damaška, M.R. (1986) *The Faces of Justice and State Authority: A Comparative Approach to the Legal Process*, Yale University Press: London.

Dean, M. (1994) *Critical and Effective Histories: Foucault's Methods and Historical Sociology*, Routledge: London.

Dean, M. (1999) *Governmentality: Power and Rule in Modern Society*, Sage: London.

Department of Justice (Vic) (2009) *Reviewing Victims of Crime Compensation: Sentencing Order and State Funded Awards*, Discussion Paper, Department of Justice: Melbourne, Victoria.

Doak, J. (2005a) 'Victims' Rights in Criminal Trials: Prospects for Participation', *Journal of Law and Society*, 32, 2, 294–316.

Doak, J. (2005b) 'Child Witnesses: Do Special Measures Directions Prejudice the Accused's Right to a Fair Hearing? – R v Camberwell Green Youth Court, ex p. D; R v Camberwell Green Youth Court, ex p. G', *International Journal of Evidence and Proof*, 9, 4, 291–295.

Doak, J. (2008) *Victims' Rights, Human Rights and Criminal Justice: Reconceiving the Role of Third Parties*, Hart Publishing: Oxford.

Doak, J. and McGourlay, C. (2009) *Criminal Evidence in Context*, Routledge-Cavendish: New York.

Dreyfus, H.L. and Rabinow, P. (1982) *Michel Foucault: Beyond Structuralism and Hermeneutics*, University of Chicago Press: Chicago.

Duff, A., Farmer, L., Marshall, S. and Tadros, V. (2007) *The Trial on Trial Volume 3: Towards a Normative Theory of the Criminal Trial*, Hart Publishing: Oxford.

Duff, P. (2001) 'The Limitations on Trial by Jury', *International Review of Penal Law*, 72, 1–2, 603–609.

Dworkin, R. (1986) *Law's Empire*, Harvard University Press: Cambridge, Massachusetts.

Edwards, I. (2002) 'The Place of Victims' Preferences in the Sentencing of "Their" Offenders', *Criminal Law Review*, September, 689–702.

Edwards, I. (2003) 'Victim Participation in Sentencing: The Problems of Incoherence', *Howard Journal of Criminal Justice*, 40, 1, 39–54.

Edwards, I. (2004) 'An Ambiguous Participant: The Crime Victim and Criminal Justice Decision-Making', *British Journal of Criminology*, 44, 6, 967–982.

Edwards, I. (2009) 'The Evidential Quality of Victim Personal Statements and Family Impact Statements', *International Journal of Evidence and Proof*, 13, 4, 293–320.

Elias, N. (1982a) *The Civilizing Process Vol. 1: The History of Manners*, Pantheon: New York.

Elias, N. (1982b) *The Civilizing Process Vol. 2: Power & Civility*, Pantheon: New York.
Elias, N. (1988) 'Violence and Civilisation: The State Monopoly of Physical Violence and its Infringement', in Keane, J. (ed.) *Civil Society and the State: New European Perspectives*, Verso: London, pp. 177–198.
Ellison, L. (2002) *The Adversarial Process and the Vulnerable Witness*, Oxford University Press: Oxford.
Emsley, C. (1983) *Policing and its Context, 1750–1870*, Schocken Books: New York.
Emsley, C. (1987) *Crime and Society in England 1750–1900*, 2nd edn, Longman: London, New York.
Erez, E. (2004) 'Victim Voice, Impact Statements and Sentencing: Integrating Restorative Justice and Therapeutic Jurisprudence Principles in Adversarial Proceedings', *Criminal Law Bulletin*, 40, 5, 483–500.
Evans, E.P. (1987) *The Criminal Prosecution and Capital Punishment of Animals*, Farber and Farber: London.
Fairall, P. and Lacey, W. (2007) 'Preventative Detention and Control Orders Under Federal Law: The Case for a Bill of Rights', *Melbourne University Law Review*, 31, 3, 1072–1089.
Feld, B. (1994) 'Juvenile Justice Swedish Style: A Rose by Another Name?', *Justice Quarterly*, 11, 4, 625–650.
Feldthusen, B. (1993) 'The Civil Action for Sexual Battery: Therapeutic Jurisprudence', *Ottawa Law Review*, 25, 2, 205–234.
Field, S. (2009) 'Fair Trials and Procedural Tradition in Europe', *Oxford Journal of Legal Studies*, 29, 2, 365–387.
Findlay, M. and Henham, R. (2010) *Beyond Punishment: Achieving International Criminal Justice*, Palgrave Macmillan: Houndmills, Basingstoke, Hampshire.
Findlay, M. and Henham, R. (2005) *Transforming International Criminal Justice: Retributive and Restorative Justice in the Trial Process*, Willan Publishing: London.
Flynn, T. (1994) 'Foucault's Mapping of History', in Cutting, G. (ed.) *The Cambridge Companion to Foucault*, Cambridge University Press: Cambridge, pp. 28–46.
Foucault, M. (1969) *Archaeology of Knowledge and the Discourse on Language*, Pantheon Books: New York.
Foucault, M. (1971) 'Truth and Power', in Gordon, C. (ed.) *Power/Knowledge: Selected Interviews and Other Writings 1972–1977*, Pantheon Books: New York, pp. 109–133.
Foucault, M. (1976) *The History of Sexuality Vol 1: An Introduction*, Penguin Books: Sydney.
Foucault, M. (1982) 'The Subject and Power', in Dreufus, H.L. and Rabinow, P. (eds) *Beyond Structuralism and Hermeneutics*, University of Chicago Press: Chicago, pp. 208–226.
Foucault, M. (1984) 'Nietzsche, Genealogy, History', in Rabinow, P. (ed.) *The Foucault Reader*, Pantheon Books: New York, pp. 76–100.
Foucault, M. (1994) *Ethics: Subjectivity and Truth*, The New Press: New York.
Fox, R.G. (1994) 'The Meaning of Proportionality in Sentencing', *Melbourne University Law Review*, 19, 489–511.

Friedman, N. and Jones, M. (2005) 'Children Giving Evidence of Sexual Offences in Criminal Proceedings: Special Measures in Australian States and Territories', *Journal of Judicial Administration*, 14, 3, 157–170.

Friedman, R.D. (2004) 'Adjusting to *Crawford*: High Court Restores Confrontation Clause Protection', *Criminal Justice*, 19, 2, 4–13.

Garkawe, S. (2006) 'Victim Impact Statements and Sentencing', *Monash University Law Review*, 31, 1, 90–114.

Gil, D.G. (2008) 'Toward a "Radical" Paradigm of Restorative Justice', in Sullivan, D. and Tifft, L. (eds) *Handbook of Restorative Justice*, Routledge: London, pp. 499–511.

Girgen, J. (2003) 'The Historical and Contemporary Prosecution and Punishment of Animals', *Animal Law Review*, 9, 97–133.

Goldstein, A. (1982) 'Defining the Role of the Victim in Criminal Prosecution', *Mississippi Law Journal*, 52, 3, 515–561.

Goldstein, H. (1987) 'Toward Community-Oriented Policing: Potential, Basic Requirements, and Threshold Questions', *Crime and Delinquency*, 33, 1, 6–30.

Goodey, J. (2005) *Victims and Victimology: Research, Policy and Practice*, Pearson Education Limited: United Kingdom.

Goodrich, P. (1992) '*Ars Bablativa*: Ramism, Rhetoric, and the Genealogy of English Jurisprudence', in Leyh, G. (ed.) *Legal Hermeneutics: History, Theory and Practice*, University of California Press: California, USA, pp. 43–82.

Gordon, C. (1991) 'Governmental Rationality: An Introduction', in Burchell, G., Gordon, C. and Miller, P. (eds) *The Foucault Effect: Studies in Governmentality*, University of Chicago Press: Chicago, pp. 1–51.

Hay, D. (1975) 'Property, Authority and the Criminal Law', in Hay, D., Linebaugh, P., Rule, J.G., Thompson, E.P. and Winslow, C. (eds) *Albion's Fatal Tree: Crime and Society in Eighteenth-Century England*, Allen Lane: London, pp. 33–63.

Haydock, R. and Sonsteng, J. (1991) *Trial: Theories, Tactics, Techniques*, West Group: USA.

Herman, K. (2006) 'Sex Offence Courts: The Next Step in Community Management?', *Sexual Assault Report*, 9, 5, 65–80.

Herrmann, J. (1996) 'Models for the Reform of the Criminal Trial in Eastern Europe: A Comparative Perspective', *Saint Louis-Warsaw Transatlantic Law Journal*, 127–51.

Hodgson, J. (2006) 'Conceptions of the Trial in Inquisitorial and Adversarial Procedure', in Duff, A., Farmer, L., Marshall, S. and Tadros, V. (eds) *The Trial on Trial Volume 2: Judgement and Calling to Account*, Hart Publishing: Oxford, pp. 223–242.

Holdsworth, W. (1903–38) *A History of English Law*, Vols. 1–17, Methuen & Co.: London.

Horwitz, M.J. (1981) 'The Historical Contingency of the Role of History', *Yale Law Journal*, 90, 1057–1059.

Hoy, D.C. (1992) 'Intentions and the Law: Defining Hermeneutics', in Leyh, G. (ed.) *Legal Hermeneutics: History, Theory and Practice*, University of California Press: California, USA, pp. 173–186.

Hyams, P. (1981) 'Trial by Ordeal: The Key to Proof in Early Common Law', in Arnold, M.S., Green, T.A., Scully, S.A. and White, S.D. (eds) *On the Laws and*

Customs of England: Essays in Honor of Sameul E Thorne, University of North Carolina Press: Chapel Hill, pp. 90–126.

Jacoby, S. (1976) *Wild Justice: The Evolution of Revenge*, Harper and Row: New York.

Joutsen, M. (1987) 'Listening to the Victim: The Victim's Role in European Criminal Justice Systems', *Wayne Law Review*, 34, 95–124.

Kamenka, E. and Tay, A. (1978) 'Socialism, Anarchism and Law', in Kamenka, E., Brown, R. and Tay, A. (eds) *Law and Society: The Crisis in Legal Ideals*, Edward Arnold: London, pp. 48–80.

Kaye, J.S. (2004) 'Delivering Justice Today: A Problem-Solving Approach', *Yale Law and Policy Review*, 22, 1, 125–151.

Keyzer, P. and Blay, S. (2006) 'Double Punishment? Preventive Detention Schemes Under Australian Legislation and their Consistency with International Law: The Fardon Communication', *Melbourne Journal of International Law*, 7, 2, 407–242.

Kimball, E.G. (1978) *A Cambridgeshire Gaol Delivery Roll 1332–1334*, Cambridge Antiquarian Records Society: Cambridge.

King, M., Freiberg, A., Batagol, B. and Hyams, R. (2009) *Non-Adversarial Justice*, The Federation Press: Sydney.

King, M.S. (2006a) 'Therapeutic Jurisprudence in Australia: New Directions in Courts, Legal Practice, Research and Legal Education', *Journal of Judicial Administration*, 15, 3, 129–141.

King, M.S. (2006b) 'The Therapeutic Dimensions of Judging: The Example of Sentencing', *Journal of Judicial Administration*, 16, 2, 92–105.

King-Ries, A. (2005) '*Crawford v Washington*: The End of Victimless Prosecution?', *Seattle University Law Review*, 28, 2, 301–327.

Kiralfry, A.K.R. (1958) *Historical Introduction to the English Law and its Institutions*, Sweet and Maxwell: London.

Kirchengast, T. (2005) 'Victim Impact Statements and the *Previtera* Rule: Delimiting the Voice and Representation of Family Victims in NSW Homicide Cases', *University of Tasmania Law Review*, 24, 2, 127–154.

Kirchengast, T. (2006) *The Victim in Criminal Law and Justice*, Palgrave Macmillan: Houndmills, Basingstoke: Hampshire.

Kirchengast, T. (2009) 'Criminal Injuries Compensation, Victim Assistance and Restoration in Australian Sentencing Law', *International Journal of Punishment and Sentencing*, 5, 3, 96–119.

Klerman, D. (2001) 'Settlement and the Decline of Private Prosecution in Thirteenth Century England', *Law and History Review*, Spring, 1–66.

Knipps, S.K. and Berman, G. (2000) 'New York's Problem-Solving Courts Provide Meaningful Alternatives to Traditional Remedies', *New York State Bar Association Journal*, 72, 8–10.

Knoops, G.J. (2007) *Theory and Practice of International and Internationalized Criminal Proceedings*, Kluwer Law International: The Netherlands.

Langbein, J.H. (2003) *The Origins of the Adversary Criminal Trial*, Oxford University Press: Oxford.

Law Commission of England and Wales (LCEW) (2004) *Partial Defences to Murder: Final Report*, UK Government.

Lee, M. and Herborn, P. (2003) 'The Role of Place Management in Crime Prevention: Some Reflections on Governmentality and Government Strategy', *Current Issues in Criminal Justice*, 15, 1, 26–39.

Leyh, G. (1992) 'Legal Education and the Public Life', in Leyh, G. (ed.) *Legal Hermeneutics: History, Theory and Practice*, University of California Press: California, USA, pp. 269–294.

Lininger, T. (2005) 'Prosecuting Batterers After *Crawford*', *Virginia Law Review*, 91, 3, 747–822.

Lorenzmeier, S. (2006) 'The Legal Effect of Framework Decisions – A Case-Note on the Pupino Decision of the European Court of Justice', *Zeitschrift für Internationale Strafrechtsdogmatik*, 12, 583–588.

Luhmann, N. (1993) *Law as a Social System*, Oxford University Press: Oxford.

Matthews, K., Easton, H., Briggs, D. and Pease, K. (2007) *Assessing the Use and Impact of Anti-Social Behaviour Orders*, Policy Press: Bristol.

Maturana, H. (1982) *Erkennen: Die Organisation und Verkorperung von Wirklichkeit*, Braunschweig: Vieweg.

Mauet, T.A. (2007) *Trial Techniques*, 7th (ed.) Aspen Publishers: USA.

Mawby, R. (2007) 'Public Sector Services and the Victim of Crime', in Walklate, S. (ed.) *Handbook of Victims and Victimology*, Willan Publishing: London, pp. 209–239.

McBarnet, D. (1981a) *Conviction: Law, the State and the Construction of Justice*, Palgrave Macmillan: UK.

McBarnet, D. (1981b) 'Magistrates' Courts and the Ideology of Justice', *British Journal of Law and Society*, 8, 2, 181–197.

McConville, M. (1984) 'Prosecuting Criminal Cases in England and Wales: Reflections on an Inquisitorial Adversary', *Liverpool Law Review*, 4, 1, 15–32.

Mercado, C.C. and Ogloff, J.R.P. (2007) 'Risk and the Preventive Detention of Sex Offenders in Australia and the United States', *International Journal of Law and Psychiatry*, 30, 1, 49–59.

Ministry of Justice (2005) *Making a Difference: Taking Forward Our Priorities*, United Kingdom.

Ministry of Justice (2009) *Engaging Communities in Criminal Justice – Green Paper*, UK Government.

Mosteller, R.P. (2005) '*Crawford v Washington*: Encouraging and Ensuring the Confrontation of Witnesses', *University of Richmond Law Review*, 39, 2, 511–625.

Nerhot, P. (1992) *Law, Writing, Meaning: An Essay in Legal Hermeneutics*, Edinburgh University Press: Edinburgh.

New South Wales Law Reform Commission (NSWLRC) (1997) *Partial Defences to Murder: Provocation and Infanticide*, Report No. 83, NSW Government.

New South Wales Law Reform Commission (NSWLRC) (2007) *Role of Juries in Sentencing*, Report No. 118, NSW Government.

New Zealand Law Commission (NZLC) (2001) *Acquittal Following Perversion of the Course of Justice*, New Zealand Government.

Nobles, R. and Schiff, D. (2001) 'Criminal Justice: Autopoietic Insights', in Priban, J. and Nelken, D. (eds) *Law's New Boundaries: The Consequences of Legal Autopoiesis*, Ashgate: Aldershot, Hampshire, England, pp. 197–217.

Nonet, P. and Selznick, P. (1978) *Law and Society in Transition: Toward Responsive Law*, Transaction Publishers: London.

Norrie, A. (2001) *Crime, Reason and History: A Critical Introduction to Criminal Law*, Cambridge University Press: Cambridge.

Office for Criminal Justice Reform (2007) *Working Together to Cut Crime and Deliver Justice: A Strategic Plan for 2008–2011*, United Kingdom.

Ortwein, B.M. (2003) 'The Swedish Legal System: An Introduction', *Indiana International and Comparative Law Review*, 13, 2, 405–455.

Packer, H. (1968) *The Limits of the Criminal Sanction*, Stanford University Press: California.

Pollock, F. and Maitland, F.W. (1968) *The History of English Law before the Time of Edward I*, 2nd edn, Cambridge University Press: Cambridge.

Powell, M., Roberts, K. and Guadagno, B. (2007) 'Particularisation of Child Abuse Offences: Common Problems when Questioning Child Witnesses', *Current Issues in Criminal Justice*, 19, 1, 64–74.

Powers, E. (1966) *Crime and Punishment in Early Massachusetts 1620–1692: A Documentary History*, Beacon Press: Boston.

President of the Queen's Bench Division (2006) *A Protocol Issued by the President of the Queen's Bench Division Setting Out the Procedure to be Followed in the Victims' Advocate Pilot Areas.*

Roberts, P. (2002) 'Double Jeopardy Law Reform: A Criminal Justice Commentary', *Modern Law Review*, 65, 3, 393–424.

Roxon, N. (2005) 'Prevention or Punishment: Terrorisms Challenge to Criminal Law', *Human Rights Defender*, Special Issue, 12–14.

Sanders, A. (2002) 'Victim Participation in an Exclusionary Criminal Justice System', in Hoyle, C. and Young, R. (eds) *New Visions of Crime Control*, Hart Publishing: Oxford, pp. 197–222.

Schwikkard, P.J. (2007) 'Convergence, Appropriate Fit and Values in Criminal Process', in Roberts, P. and Redmayne, M. (eds) *Innovations in Evidence and Proof: Integrating Theory, Research and Teaching*, Hart Publishing: Oxford, pp. 331–346.

Schwikkard, P.J. (2008) *Possibilities of Convergence: An Outside Perspective on the Convergence of Criminal Procedures in Europe*, Kluwer.

Sebba, L. (2009) 'Victim-Driven Criminalisation', in McSherry, B., Norrie, A. and Bronitt, S. (eds) *Regulating Deviance: the Redirection of Criminalisation and the Futures of Criminal Law*, Hart Publishing: Oxford, pp. 59–84.

Secretary of State for Constitutional Affairs and Lord Chancellor (2006) *Hearing the Relatives of Murder and Manslaughter Victims: The Government's Plans to Give the Bereaved Relatives of Murder and Manslaughter Victims a Say in Criminal Proceeding – Summary of Responses to the Consultation Paper*, United Kingdom.

Shapiro, B.J. (1991) *Beyond Reasonable Doubt and Probable Cause: Historical Perspectives on the Anglo-American Law of Evidence*, University of California Press: California, USA.

Simon, W.H. (1978) 'Ideology of Advocacy: Procedural Justice and Professional Ethics', *Wisconsin Law Review*, 31, 1, 29–144.

Sklansky, D.A. (2009) 'Anti-Inquisitorialism', *Harvard Law Review*, 122, 1634–1704.

Smallbone, S. and Ransley, J. (2005) 'Legal and Psychological Controversies in the Preventive Incapacitation of Sexual Offenders', *University of New South Wales Law Journal*, 28, 1, 299–305.

Stephen, J.F. (1883) *History of the Criminal Law and England*, William S. Hein and Company.

Stone, J. (1991) *Evidence: Its History and Policies*, Butterworths: Sydney.

Summers, S. (2007) *Fair Trials: The European Procedural Tradition and the European Court of Human Rights*, Hart Publishing: Oxford.

Tadros, V. (2007) 'Justice and Terrorism', *New Criminal Law Review*, 10, 4, 658–689.
Tanford, J.A. (2009) *The Trial Process: Law, Tactics and Ethics*, 4th edn, LexisNexis.
Teubner, G. (1993) *Law as an Autopoietic System*, Blackwell: Oxford.
Tobias, J.J. (1979) *Crime and Police in England 1700–1900*, Gill and Macmillan: London.
Tolmie, J. (2005) 'Is the Partial Defence and Endangered Defence: Recent Proposals to Abolish Provocation', *New Zealand Law Review*, 1, 25–52.
Unger, R. (1976) *Law in Modern Society: Toward a Criticism of Social Theory*, Free Press: New York.
Victorian Law Reform Commission (VLRF) (2004) *Partial Defences to Murder: Final Report*, Victorian Government.
von Hirsch, A. and Ashworth, A. (2005) *Proportionate Sentencing: Exploring the Principles*, Oxford University Press: Oxford.
Walters, M. (2006) 'Victim Impact Statement in Homicide Cases: Should 'Recognising the Harm Done... To the Community' Signify a New Direction?', *International Journal of Punishment and Sentencing*, 2, 2, 53–71.
Walton, M. (2005) 'The Anti-Terrorism Bill (No. 2) 2005: An Overview', *Human Rights Defender*, Special Issue, 3–5.
Warner, K. (2004) 'Gang Rape in Sydney: Crime, the Media, Politics, Race and Sentencing', *Australian and New Zealand Journal of Criminology*, 37, 3, 344–362.
Warren, W.L. (1973) *Henry II*, Yale University Press: New Haven and London.
Weisstub, D. (1986) 'Crime Victims in the Criminal Justice System', in Fattah, E.A. (ed.) *From Crime Policy to Victim Policy: Reorienting the Justice System*, St Martin's Press: New York, pp. 191–209.
Wemmers, J. (2009) 'Where Do They Belong? Giving Victims a Place in the Criminal Justice System', *Criminal Law Forum*, 20, 4, 395–416.
Wexler, D.B. (1999) 'Therapeutic Jurisprudence and the Culture of Critique', *Journal of Contemporary Legal Issues*, 10, 263–277.
Wolhunter, L., Olley, N. and Denham, D. (2009) *Victimology: Victimisation and Victims' Rights*, Routledge Cavendish: Oxon.
Zedner, L. (2006) 'Neither Safe Nor Sound: The Perils and Possibilities of Risk', *Canadian Journal of Criminology and Criminal Justice*, 48, 3, 423–434.
Zedner, L. (2007) 'Pre-Crime and Post-Criminology?', *Theoretical Criminology*, 11, 2, 261–281.
Zila, J. (2006) 'The Prosecution Service within the Swedish Criminal Justice System', in Jehle, J.M. and Wade, M. (eds) *Coping with Overloaded Criminal Justice Systems: The Rise of Prosecutorial Power Across Europe*, Springer: Berlin Heidelberg, pp. 285–311.

Index

A v Secretary of State for the Home Department   26, 111, 112, 118, 227
Act of Settlement   44, 227
Adhesive Prosecution   140–141
Administration of Justice (Miscellaneous Provisions) Act 1933 (UK)   68
Adversarialism
   anti-inquisitorialism   194–200
   centrepiece of modern criminal law and justice   7, 15, 19–21
   characteristics of adversarialism   2, 6, 14, 41–42, 120, 153, 166–178, 189–194, 219, 221
   due process   17–21, 25, 118, 125, 127–128, 172, 212–213
   emergence/development of   3, 60–64
   evidence, development of   5, 15
   fair trial   6–11, 32, 63, 69, 98, 109, 125, 126, 137, 172–174, 174, 212–218
   institutional capacity of the Crown   54
   judicial independence   34, 227
   nationalism and   202, 206
   rise of counsel   3, 5–6, 8, 16–17, 63
   rise of the state   4–5, 14–15
   role of counsel   6–8, 20, 119, 178–180, 195–201
   self-representation   21, 125
   ultimate state of perfection   175
Adversarial and Inquisitorial Hybrid
   defendants and fair trial   11, 31, 133, 137–138, 165, 207, 217
   ECtHR   203, 216, 219
   European civil tradition   137–143
   hybrid process   14, 133, 168, 202–206, 213, 216–218
   Sweden   139–143
   victims and   139–143, 203, 213

Agency   24, 34, 41, 61, 212
Altercation Trial   63
Animals, Trial of
   ecclesiastical trials   48–49
   secular trials   49–51
Anonymous Witness Evidence
   Doorson v The Netherlands   32, 126, 130, 132, 203, 213–214, 229
   PS v Germany   32
   SN v Sweden   32, 133
Anti-inquisitorialism   38, 194–200, 206
Anti-Terrorism Act (No. 2) 2005 (Cth)   26, 28, 112–113
Anti-Terrorism, Crime and Security Act 2001 (UK)   113, 227
Antrobus, In re   103–107
Appeal
   EWCA   83, 111, 159
   NSWCCA   157–158
   right to   17–18
Appeal of Felony   51, 53, 73
Apprendi v New Jersey   197
Archaeology   1, 167, 170–171, 184
Archive   166–170, 184, 186, 187, 193, 202–205, 212, 217
Arrest   8, 54, 59, 68, 72, 76, 82–84, 117, 138
ASBO
   civil order   91–92
   criminal law   92
   generally   30, 36, 66, 82, 87, 91
   R (on the application of McCann and others) v Crown Court at Manchester; Clingham v Kensington and Chelsea Royal London Borough Council   91, 213–214, 222
   standard of proof   91–92
Ashford v Thornton   73–74

Assize of Clarendon   47, 51, 53–56, 66
Assize of Eyre
  appeal of felony   51, 53, 57
  gaol delivery   56, 58–62
  local governance   51–61, 62–63
  offences   53–54, 55–56
  punishment   42–48
  role of victim   40–47
  royal justice   54–56, 57, 59–60
Assize of Northampton   51, 53, 55–58
Australian Constitution
  see Constitution
Autonomy of law
  criminal justice and   207–209
  hypercycle   16
  Maturana   207
  normative perspectives   208–209
  self-referentiality   16, 209
  Teubner   16, 207
Autopoiesis   16, 208–209
Auxiliary prosecution   113, 133, 138, 139–142

Baegen v The Netherlands   128–129
Bail
  Bail Act 1978 (NSW)   85–87, 155
  changes to bail law   33, 82
  control orders and   27–29
  early committal process   68–69
  law and order   85–87
  R v Hammill   86–87
  s22A *Bail Act 1978* (NSW)   86–87
Barton v The Queen   134, 230
Battle, trial by   57, 60, 62, 72–74, 193
Becket, Thomas   57
Benefit of Clergy   57
Blackstone, Sir William   18, 28, 29, 61, 200
Blakely v Washington   196–197
Bill of Rights
  Australia, lack of   10–11, 124
  New Zealand   96
  United States   77
Bill of Rights Act 1990 (NZ)   96
Blood Feud
  see also Customary Justice

  first trial   44
  generally   40, 43–47
Bocos-Cuesta v The Netherlands   129–131
BOCSAR   20
Brooks v Police   162–163
Brown v Walker   198
Butera v Director of Public Prosecutions (Vic)   176–178

Casey Review   148
CCP   109, 150
Charge Bargaining
  district attorney   105–108
  GAS v The Queen; SJK v The Queen   79–81
  Gouriet v Union of Post Office Workers   78
  police   78–79
  R v Andrew Foster Brown   79
  sentencing and   80–81
  victims and   100–178
  Wright v McQualter   79
Cheatle v The Queen   74–76
Cheung v The Queen   134
Circle Sentencing   2, 124, 152–154
Common Law
  discourse and   184
  doctrine   194
  growth of   184
Commonwealth Criminal Code   26, 28
Community Justice   147–151
Compensation
  domestic law and   11, 97, 108, 124, 125, 151–153, 160–164, 224
  framework decisions   11
  ICC   110
  victim lawyers   97, 108
Confrontation
  confrontation and customary justice   42
  confrontation clause   118, 137, 179, 181, 182, 195, 196, 203, 216
  confrontation under the ECHR   13, 130, 132

Constitution
  see also Bill of Rights
  Australian constitution   28, 77–78, 228
  Sixth Amendment to the US Constitution   179, 182, 195, 197, 230
  United States constitution   118, 137, 170, 179, 199
Control Order
  A v Secretary of State for the Home Department   26, 28, 112–113
  Anti-Terrorism Act (No. 2) 2005 (Cth)   26, 28, 112–113
  Anti-Terrorism, Crime and Security Act 2001 (UK)   113, 227
  ASBOs   30, 36, 66, 82, 87, 91
  Australia generally   26–30, 82, 214
  contested hearings and   28, 113–118
  Crimes (Criminal Organisation Control) Act 2009 (NSW)   89–91, 231
  criminal law and   91, 110–113
  Criminal Organisations Legislation Amendment Act 2009 (NSW)   89–91
  Dangerous Prisoners (Sexual Offenders) Act 2003 (Qld)   10
  derogative and non-derogative control orders   26, 113–118, 227
  England and Wales generally   26–30, 113–118, 223
  fair hearings   117
  freedom of movement and association and   10, 26, 30, 82, 87, 214
  organised motorcycle clubs   9, 29, 214
  Prevention of Terrorism Act 2005 (UK)   26, 112–118
  proof   213–214, 26–27
  secrecy of trial   26–27, 114–118
  Secretary of State for the Home Department v AF (No. 3)   26, 116–118
  Secretary of State for the Home Department v MB and AF   26, 110, 114, 116
  sentencing options   26–27, 89–91
  Serious and Organised Crime (Control) Act 2008 (SA)   30, 87, 231
  Thomas v Mowbray   28, 111, 113, 228
  Totani and Anor. v The State of South Australia   30, 82, 87
Council of Europe   11, 139
CPS   34, 78, 99–100, 149–150
Crawford v Washington   38, 174, 179–183, 187, 193, 194–196, 206
Crime and Disorder Act 1998 (UK)   91, 222
Crime Control Model   202
Crimes (Criminal Organisation Control) Act 2009 (NSW)   89–91, 206
Crimes (Sentencing Procedure) Act 1999 (NSW)   153, 155, 156, 157, 229
Crimes Act 1900 (NSW)   68, 85, 109, 161
Criminal Code 1913 (WA)   95
Criminal Code Act 1924 (Tas)   95
Criminal Injuries Compensation Act 1967 (NSW)   161
Criminal Justice Act 1988 (UK)   135
Criminal Justice Act 2003 (UK)   96, 135, 136
Criminal Justice and Public Order Act 1994 (UK)   81, 83
Criminal Law (Sentencing) Act 1988 (SA)   162
Criminal Procedure Act 1986 (NSW)   70, 109, 125, 133–134, 229
Cross-Examination
  direct confrontation   115, 119, 125, 128, 132, 134, 136, 137, 142, 174, 176, 179, 187, 230
  rape trials   134
  statements   31–32, 102, 129–132, 135–136, 137
  truth   183
curia regis   57
Customary Justice
  appeal of felony   51, 53, 73
  blood feud   40, 43–47
  dispute settlement   42–47

familial justice   42–45
frankpledge   52, 61
hue and cry   59
local institutions and
  custom   42–60
oath of felty   52
origins   42
restoration in   43
rise of presentment   51–52
rule of law and   45
tythings   51–52
Unger, R.   42
wergild   47
CVRA   100–108

Dangerous Prisoners (Sexual Offenders) Act 2003 (Qld)   10
Dean, In re   105–107
Decentralised Justice
  discourse   1, 37, 218
  governance   61–62
  mode of trial   33, 36, 66, 92–95
  social change   119, 121
Defences
  see Provocation
Defendant Rights
  appeal   134, 157, 162
  counsel and   6, 7, 62, 179
  fair trial and   6–8
  proportionality requirement under art. 6 ECHR   31, 126, 131, 133
  Trials for Felony Act 1836 (Imp)   63
Demski v Poland   13
Dietrich v The Queen   6, 7, 8, 23, 63, 230
Director of Public Prosecution Act 1986 (NSW)   109
Discourse
  Archaeology of Knowledge   168
  communicative process   18
  competing discourses   26, 65, 168, 192, 193, 224
  decentralised justice   36–37, 61–62, 119–121, 166, 186–188, 218, 224
  Discipline and   15, 184, 208–210, 222
  enunciative field   167, 224
  Foucault and   14–17, 167–171
  genealogy and   9, 14–17, 123–124, 189, 200–205, 218
  hermeneutics and   14–17
  law and society   165–167
  rhetoric   15, 19–24, 122, 123, 199, 205, 225
  social change   220–225
  statement   38, 167–171
  truth and power   171–174, 217–220
Discretion
  courts/judicial   21, 30–31, 79
  executive   10–11, 79
  in institutions   21
  normative positioning of   79
  police   34, 36, 72
  prosecution and   41, 78–81
  subjects and   34
Discursive Formation   1, 166–169, 171, 186–188, 211, 219
Doorson v The Netherlands   32, 126, 130, 132, 203, 213, 214, 229
Double Jeopardy
  Crimes (Appeal and Review) Amendment (Double Jeopardy) Act 2006 (NSW)   96
  Criminal Justice Act 2003 (UK)   96
  Daniels v Thompson   96
  Franz Fischer v Austria   96
  The Queen v Carroll   96
Due Process
  see Fair Trial

Ecclesiastical Law   48–49, 50, 57
Effective History
  see Discourse
  see Hermeneutics
Enhorn v Sweden   215
European Convention on Human Rights
  accusatorial trinity   202–203, 217
  art. 2 ECHR   126, 228
  art. 5 ECHR   32
  art. 6 ECHR   31–32, 111, 117, 124, 126–135, 172, 174, 229
  art. 8 ECHR   11, 32, 129, 229
  art. 14 ECHR   113

European Convention on Human Rights – *continued*
  control orders   113
  equity of arms   172
  victim rights and the fair trial   31–32, 126–133
European Civil Law
  see Inquisitorial Justice
  see Sweden, Criminal Process in
  influence on ECtHR   202–206, 206–217, 222
  private prosecutions in   139, 141
European Court of Human Rights   13, 31, 116, 126, 128, 131, 133, 135, 203, 216, 219
European Court of Justice
  Pupino, Criminal Proceedings Against   12, 31
European Union   226
Evidence
  see also Procedural Justice
  anonymous witnesses   13, 31–32, 128–132, 173
  Crawford v Washington   38, 174, 179–183, 187, 193, 194–196, 206
  Doorson v The Netherlands   32, 126, 130, 132, 203, 213, 214, 229
  frightened witness   135–137
  Gately v The Queen   171, 174, 175–179, 187, 193–194
  orality, tradition of   175
  out of court or hearsay evidence   31, 37, 118, 149, 151, 170, 183, 186–188, 194, 217–223
  R v Camberwell Green Youth Court   119, 131, 135, 173–175, 193–194
  scientific evidence   64
Evidence Act 1977 (Qld)   176–177
ex officio indictment   69
Experimental Justice   36
Eyre
  see Assize of Eyre
  see also Judicial Commissions

Fair Trial
  see also Cross-Examination
  accusatorial trinity   202–203, 217
  art. 6 ECHR   31–32, 111, 117, 124, 126–135, 172, 174, 229
  art. 8 ECHR   11, 32, 129, 229
  Barton v The Queen   134, 230
  confrontation and customary justice   42
  confrontation clause   118, 137, 179, 181, 182, 195, 196, 203, 216
  confrontation under the ECHR   13, 130, 132
  control order, contested hearing   28
  cross-examination and 'truth'   183
  Dietrich v The Queen   6, 7, 8, 23, 63, 230
  direct examination of witness   125–134
  due process   17–21, 25, 118, 125, 127–128, 172, 212–213
  equity of arms   172
  Jago v District Court of NSW   94, 194
  procedural fairness   20, 25, 41, 109, 111, 116, 128, 132, 138, 183, 189, 203, 213, 223
  proportionality requirement (art. 6 ECHR)   31, 126, 133, 131
  public hearing   173, 174
  victim rights   31–32, 126–133, 133–137
Fardon v Attorney-General (Qld)   10, 82, 112
Finkensieper v The Netherlands   129
Forge v Australian Securities and Investments Commission   88
Forum Sentencing   2, 124, 152–156
Foster, Re Applications for   161
Foucault
  discipline   15, 183–186, 208
  effective history   3–4, 6, 15–17, 192–193, 200–205, 212, 217–218, 223–225
  essential fact   15
  genealogy   14–17, 123–124, 200–205
  governmentality   6
  hermeneutics   14–17, 189–200, 217–220

knowledge and power   14–17, 205–207, 217–220
statement   38, 167–171, 186–188
truth and doctrine   14–17, 200–205
Framework Decision on the Standing of Victims in Criminal Proceedings   11
Frankpledge   52

Gately v The Queen   171, 174, 175–179, 187, 193–194
Genealogy
see also Hermeneutics
discourse and   9, 14–17, 123–124, 189, 200–205, 218
Foucault and   14–17
Gouriet v Union of Post Office Workers   72, 228
Governmentality
discourse and   6
Power and   192–194
Grand Jury
see also Jury
Administration of Justice (Miscellaneous Provisions) Act 1933 (UK)   68
Grassby v The Queen   68
Guilty Plea   20–21, 22, 40, 70–71, 72, 79, 80, 102, 103, 105, 143, 144
see also R v Thomson and Houlton
Gypsy Jokers Motorcycle Club Inc v Commissioner of Police   88

H (Minors) (Sexual Abuse: Standard of Proof), In re   92
Hermeneutics
see also Genealogy
defined   16–17
discourse and   5–6, 14–17, 218
Foucault and   167–171, 218
method   14–17
Hill v Chief Constable of West Yorkshire Police   126
Holdsworth, Sir William   14, 39, 52, 201

Huff Asset Management Co., In re   104, 107
Human Rights
see Defendant Rights
see ECHR
see ECtHR
see ICC
see Fair Trial
see Victims
Human Rights Act 1998 (UK)   226
Hundred Court   51–57
Hundred Eolder   51–52

ICTR   138
ICTY   138
Indictable Offences Act 1848 (UK)   68
Indictment
appeal of felony   51, 53, 73
assize of eyre   51, 53
presentment   53–59
victim challenges to   109
Infringement
see Penalty Notice
Inquisitorial and Adversarial Hybrid
see Adversarial and Inquisitorial Hybrid
Inquisitorial Justice
see also Adversarial and Inquisitorial Hybrid
anti-inquisitorialism   194–200
European tradition   204–205
judicial independence   143, 201, 204
role of counsel   141, 204
victims and   139–143
International Criminal Court
Office of Public Counsel for Victims   110
Regulations of the ICC   110
Rome Statute   109–110
Rules of Procedure and Evidence   138
Intervention Program
see Restorative Justice
Italian Code of Criminal Procedure   12

Jago v District Court of NSW 69, 194
Judicial Commissions
  ad omnia placita 58
  gaol delivery 56, 58, 59–60, 62
  general assize 51, 57–59
  mort d'ancestor 55, 56
  nisi prius 58
  novel disseisin 55, 56
  oyer and terminer 56, 58, 59, 62, 200
Jury
  Cheatle v The Queen 74–76
  Grand jury 20, 33–34, 56, 67–69, 195, 200
  Jury Act 1977 (NSW) 74
  Kingswell v The Queen 76–78
  majority verdicts 74–76
  petit/petty jury 15, 59, 67, 75
  reforms to 68–69, 72–78
  s80 Australian Constitution 74–78
  sentencing and 227–228
Justice For All Act 2004 (US)
  see CVRA
Justice of the Peace 52, 59

K-Generation Pty Ltd v Liquor Licensing Court 88
Kable v Director of Public Prosecutions for the State of New South Wales 88
Kenna v US District Court 102, 107
Khan v United Kingdom 230
King
  see also King Henry II
  Henry I 53
  Henry II 51, 53, 56, 57, 61
  Stephen (and Empress Matilda) 53, 58
King Henry II
  Assize of Clarendon 53, 56, 61
  Assize of Northampton 56, 61
  law reform and 53
King's Bench 73, 180
Kingswell v The Queen 76–78
Kostovski v The Netherlands 131, 133

Langbein, John H. 3, 5, 8, 14, 15, 17, 35, 63

Law and Order
  ASBO 30, 36, 66, 82, 87, 91
  bail 85–87
  Criminal Justice and Public Order Act 1994 (UK) 81, 83
  Criminal Procedures and Investigation Act 1996 (UK) 82
  Cronulla riots 85
  infringement and penalty notices 36, 71–72
  Law Enforcement (Powers and Responsibilities) Act 2002 (NSW) 81–85
  Organised Motorcycle Clubs 87
  Police 82–85
  Police and Criminal Evidence Act 1984 (UK) 81–83
  pre-emptive crime control 84
Law Enforcement (Powers and Responsibilities) Act 2002 (NSW)
  see Law and Order
LCEW 93
Lippl v Haines 84
Local Court
  CPS 34, 78, 99–100, 149–150
  defendant rights and 20–21, 70–72
  guilty pleas 20–21, 70–72
  litigants in person 20–21, 70–72
  police prosecution and 20–75
  private prosecution 108–109
  rhetoric of justice and 20–21
  statistics in NSW 20–21
  summary process 70–72

M v Director of Public Prosecutions 92
McCann and Ors v United Kingdom 126
McClintock v Jones 161
McNeil v Wisconsin 195, 196, 198, 199
Magistrates' Court
  see Local Court
Magna Carta 56, 76
Medellín v Texas 230
Mile v Police 163
Miranda v Arizona 195
Misuse of Drugs Act 1971 (UK) 84

National Security
  control orders generally 26–31
  court processes and 26–29
  terrorism 25–31
  terrorist organisations 26, 27
Non-adversarial Justice 146
  see also Problem Solving Courts
  see also Therapeutic Justice
Norman Conquest 7, 46–47
Normative Perspectives
  adversarialism 192, 200
  autonomy of law 38, 183–186,
    211, 221–225
  discourse 4, 9, 14–19, 25, 42, 63,
    120, 125, 133, 151, 166, 185,
    189, 205–210, 211–225
  doctrine 4, 9, 17, 21, 25, 188,
    192, 194, 200, 211, 214
  future of law and justice 220–225
  genealogy 3, 9, 14–17, 120,
    123–124, 189, 200–205, 218
  hermeneutics 5–6, 14–17, 218
  normative theory of the trial
    17–19
NSWLRC 93, 228, 230
NZLC 96

*O'Loughlin v Chief Constable of
    Essex* 83
ODPP 34, 63, 69, 78, 108, 109,
  124
Ohio v Roberts 179, 181, 182
Ordeal
  abolition of 57, 61–62
  generally 52, 56–57, 61–62
  mode of proof 52, 56
Organised Motorcycle Clubs
  *Crimes (Criminal Organisation
    Control) Act 2009* (NSW) 231
  *Serious and Organised Crime (Control)
    Act 2008* (SA) 30, 87, 231
  *Totani and Anor. v The State of South
    Australia* 30, 82, 87
Osman v Southwark Crown Court 83
Osman v United Kingdom 126–128

Packer, Herbert 202
Participation 4, 14, 20, 24, 34, 98,
  126, 128, 151, 211, 216, 220

Peace
  borh, in 52
  oath of fealty 52
Penalty Notice
  *Crimes Legislation Amendment
    (Penalty Notices Offences)
    Act 2002* (NSW) 72
  infringements 34, 36, 66, 67,
    71–72, 81, 151
Plea Bargaining
  see Charge Bargaining
*Police and Criminal Evidence Act
  1984* (UK)
  see Law and Order
Policing
  see also Law and Order
  arrest 82–83
  cautions 151
  charge 79–80, 83
  hue and cry 59
  law and order 82–85
  over-charging 71, 79
  prosecutors 34
Politics
  law and order 2, 18, 128
  reactionist 214
  restraining 14, 122
  sectarian 224
*Powers of Criminal Courts (Sentencing)
  Act 2000* (UK) 162
Pre-Trial Process
  see also Bail
  see also Charge Bargaining
  adhesion proceedings 142
  auxiliary prosecution 139
  discovery 143
  division of trial 41
  generally 15, 24, 25, 33, 41, 87,
    98, 99, 101, 104, 120, 131, 138,
    139, 142–143, 146, 173, 189,
    205, 219
  human rights issues 25
  ICC 138
  inquisitorial process 205, 219
  management/monitoring of
    accused 87, 146
  plea-hearing 105
  police 24
  procedural justice 15

Pre-Trial Process – *continued*
  statute and   33
  victims' lawyer   98–104
  witness statements   173
Presentment
  appeal of felony   51, 53, 73
  assize of eyre   57–59
Preventative Law
  see also Control Orders
  see also Organised Motorcycle Clubs
  A v Secretary of State for the Home Department   26, 111, 113, 118, 227
  apprehended violence orders   28, 29, 111–112
  bail   27, 28, 29, 111–112
  keeping the peace   27–29, 111–112
  recidivism   25, 29, 33, 82
  Thomas v Mowbray   28, 111, 113
  Prevention of Terrorism Act 2005 (UK)   26, 112, 117
Private Prosecution   53, 108, 124
  in civil systems   139, 141
Private Settlement   44
Problem Solving Courts
  see also Therapeutic Justice
  Community Court   2, 22, 33, 143, 144, 146, 147–151
  Domestic Violence Court   9, 22, 23
  Drug Court   9, 22, 33, 143, 144, 172, 218
  England and Wales   147–151
  interdisciplinarity   143–144, 145–147
  Lee v State Parole Authority of New South Wales   145
  Mental Health Court   22
  New York State   9, 22, 23, 143, 145, 218
  origins of   144
  processes   145–147
  role of   143–147
  Sex Offence Court   22, 23, 145
  social services and   145–146
  victim-centred approach   145–146
  Youth Court   22

Procedural Justice
  accusatorial trinity   202–203, 217
  art. 6 ECHR   31–32, 111, 117, 124, 126–133, 134–135, 172–174
  fair trial and   200–205
Proof
  ASBO   82, 91–92, 213, 222
  blood feud   40, 43–47
  civil standard   31, 36, 82, 91–92, 112, 153, 160–161, 213, 222
  control order (anti-terrorism)   28
  criminal standard   28, 204
  grand jury   67–69
  modified criminal standard   91–92
  ordeal   52–57, 60–62, 72, 227
  petit/petty jury   15, 59, 67, 75
  trial by battle   57, 60, 62, 72–74, 193
Prosecution
  see also Adhesive Prosecution
  see also Auxiliary Prosecution
  assize of eyre   53–59
  CPS   34, 78, 99–100, 149–150
  ODPP   34, 63, 69, 78, 108, 109, 124
  police   79–80
  presentment   53–54
  problem solving courts   145–147
Provocation
  abolition of   92–93, 94–95
  Crimes (Homicide) Act 2005 (Vic)   94–95
  Crimes (Provocation Repeal) Amendment Act 2009 (NZ)   93
  Criminal Code Amendment (Abolition of Defence of Provocation) Act 2003 (Tas)   93
  Green v The Queen   95
  history of   94
  R v Smith   93–94
  reform of   95
Public Hearing   173, 174
Public Prosecution   34, 35, 68–69, 78–79, 92, 109, 176–177
  nolle prosequi   78
  s9 *Director of Public Prosecution Act 1986* (NSW)   109
Public vs Private   121–125

Punishment
  see also Sentencing
  feudal law and   42–47, 51–60
  rationales of   27
  victims and   42–47
Pupino, Criminal Proceedings Against
  12, 31
Purposive Law   183–184

Quarter Sessions   59

R v Akbar   159–160
R v Babic   161
R v Berg   157–158
R v Bowen   160
R v Braham   161
R v C   161
R v Camberwell Green Youth Court
  119, 131, 135, 173, 174–175, 193,
  194
R v Cheppell   160
R v Cook   190–192
R v Daley   161
R v Field   161
R v Forsythe   161
R v Longman   83
R v Martin   136
R v McDonald   161
R (on the application of McCann and
  others) v Crown Court at
  Manchester; Clingham v Kensington
  and Chelsea Royal London Borough
  Council   91–92, 213–214
  see also ASBO
R v P   122, 154
R v Pitchfolk   159
R v Previtera   156–157
R v Sellick and Sellick   135, 137
R v Swain   190, 230
R v Thomson and Houlton   70–71
R v Tzanis   157–158
Rape
  ECHR cases   13, 128
  NSW law and procedure   96, 125,
    133–134
  offence   2, 12, 97
  victim impact statements   159
Rehabilitation   27, 110, 114, 146,
  147, 153, 154, 162

Responsive Law   184
Restorative Justice
  see Sentencing
  circle sentencing   152–154
  compensation   160–164
  forum sentencing   153–156
  restitution   101, 110, 153,
    160–164
  Sentencing Act 1995 (WA)   147
Rhetoric, Trial as   19–24
  see also Discourse
Royal Justices   54–57, 59, 60, 61, 62
Rowe and Davis v United Kingdom
  230

Sanchez-Llamas v Oregon   197
SBF v R   158–159
Secretary of State for the Home
  Department v AF (No. 3)   26,
  116–118
Secretary of State for the Home
  Department v MB and AF   26,
  110, 114, 116
Seneviratne v R   191–192
Sentencing
  see also Rehabilitation
  see also Victim Impact Statements
  circle sentencing   152–154
  contrition   154
  Crimes (Sentencing Procedure) Act
    1999 (NSW)   153, 155–157,
    229
  Criminal Law (Sentencing) Act 1988
    (SA)   162
  forum sentencing   153–156
  proportionality   152, 157
  punishment and   151–164
  restorative justice   110, 124,
    153–156
  revenge   43–45
  Sentencing Act 1995 (WA)   147
  Veen, R v (No. 1); Veen, R v (No. 2)
    152
  victim impact/personal statements
    156–160
Serious and Organised Crime (Control)
  Act 2008 (SA)   30, 87, 231
Serious Organised Crime and Police
  Act 2005 (UK)   82–83

Sex Offenders
  Fardon v Attorney-General (Qld) 10
  preventative detention 10
  trial process 29, 33, 82
Skaf v The Queen 134
SN v Sweden 23, 133
Social Systems 207–210
Sociological Power 9
Sociology of Law 122, 183–186, 209, 221
Stakeholders of Justice 2–15, 17, 19, 38, 125, 135, 138, 146–148, 211–212, 223
State, The
  see also State Power
  criminal law and 123
  defendants and 164
  duty to protect life (art. 2 ECHR) 126
  fear of state power 220
  individual rights and 109
  monopolising justice 151
  threats to 110
State Funded Counsel 20
State Power 1, 14, 17, 18, 34, 35, 87, 110, 183, 197, 205, 220
Statements
  see also Victim Impact Statement
  community impact statement 150
  discursive formation and 167–170, 187, 205, 219, 224–225
  ECHR 129–132, 173, 174–183
  evidence 31–32, 99–100, 102, 103, 108, 135–137
Stephen, Sir James Fitzjames 39
Summary Offences Act 1988 (NSW) 70
Summary Process
  see Local Court
  history of 70
  infringement and penalty notices 3, 34, 36, 66, 67, 71–72, 85
Sweden, Criminal Process in
  see also Adhesive Prosecution
  see also Auxiliary Prosecution
  adversarial process 137–142
  brottsoffer 140–141
  Code of Judicial Procedure 141
  courts and 140
  inquisitorial process 139
  målsägande 140
  målsägandebiträde 141–142
  private prosecutions in 139, 141
  stödperson 141
  victims and 140–141

Therapeutic Justice
  see also Problem Solving Courts
  England and Wales 147–151
  New York State 9, 22, 23, 143, 145, 147, 218
  problem solving courts 22–24, 143–151
  victims generally 22, 31–32, 97–110, 138–139, 145–147, 155–158
Thomas v Mowbray 28, 111, 113, 228
Totani and Anor. v The State of South Australia 30, 82, 87
Treaty on European Union
  see also Pupino, Criminal Proceedings Against
Trial
  antiquity of the trial 39–40, 42–47
  blood feud 43–47
  customary justice 42–47
  double jeopardy 66, 92–93, 95–97
  forensic process 64
  local government 51–60
  of animals 48–51
  process *see* Trial Process
  provocation 93–95
  reconstructive trial 64
  rhetoric 19–24
  transgressive 3, 33, 65, 120, 206, 211, 223
Trial Process
  see also Pre-trial Process
  appeal of felony 51, 53, 73
  committal 67–69
  compensation 164
  ECHR 129–132, 172–173
  evidence 174–183
  fair hearing 117
  grand jury 20, 33, 34, 56, 67–69, 195, 200

hearing   28, 31, 33, 34, 70–71, 104, 106, 114
independent tribunal   2, 18, 31, 34, 35
judge   2, 5, 7–8, 17, 20, 88, 191
petit/petty jury   15, 59, 67, 75
plea-hearing   105
prosecution   34
public hearing   173, 174
rape trials in NSW   96, 125, 133–134
right of appeal   10, 17, 114
sentencing   98–100, 103, 154, 157
Trials for Felony Act 1836 (Imp)   63
Truth
  adversarial process and   41, 63, 121, 171–174, 217–220
  combat effect   8, 17, 40, 122
  doctrine and   183–186
  Foucault and   4–5, 14–17, 166–171
  inquisitorial process and   201, 204
Tything   51–52
Tything Man   51

United States Constitution *see* Constitution
United States v BP Product North America   105–106

V v United Kingdom   172–173
Van Mechelen and Ors v The Netherlands   132
Veen, R v (No. 1); *Veen, R v* (No. 2)   152
Vendetta
  collective   44
  judicial intervention and   47
  restrained   43
  unrestrained   42
Vengeance *see* Customary Justice
Victim
  antiquity   42–44
  Assize of Clarendon   53–54
  Assize of Northampton   55–56
  Compensation   160–164
  ECJ   13, 31–32, 126–133, 135, 203
  ECtHR   13, 31–32, 126–133, 135, 203

feudal justice   44–47, 51–60
forum sentencing   153–156
human rights generally   31–32, 125–137
ICC   110, 124, 138, 219
problem solving courts   145–147
Pupino, Criminal Proceedings Against   12, 31
victim impact statements   98–100, 108, 156–160
victim lawyers
  see Victims' Lawyers
Victims' Advocate Pilot   98–100
Victim Impact Statements
  Australia   156–158
  benefits of   156
  England and Wales   98–100, 159–160
  homicide cases   98–100, 156–160
  s3A *Crimes Act 1900* (NSW)   157
  United States   102, 103
  victims' lawyers   98–100, 102, 103, 108
Victim Rights Act 1996 (NSW)   156
Victims' Lawyers
  Antrobus, In re   103–107
  Australia   108–109
  Crime Victims' Rights Act   101–108
  Dean, In re   105–107
  England and Wales   98–100
  In re Huff Asset Management Co.   104–107
  Kenna v US District Court   102, 107
  Maxwell v The Queen   109
  plea bargaining   100–108, 109
  R v DPP, Ex parte C   109
  United States   100–108
  United States v BP Product North America   105–106
  Victims' Advocates   98–100
  writ of mandamus   103–107
Violence
  Bloch, M.   46–47
  customary   42–47
  Elias, N.   45–46
  human existence and   46
  Jacoby, S.   43–44
  personal   42–44
  state   46–47

VLRC 95
Voice and Participation
  see Participation
  see also Agency

Watts v Indiana 199
Windisch v Austria 173, 230

Witold Litwa v Poland 215
Woolmington v DPP 28, 204
Wright v McQualter 79

*Youth Justice and Criminal Evidence
  Act 1999* (UK) 131, 135